From the Mouths of Babes

The Criminal Trial of a Sunday School Teacher

Paul Grey

LOST
COAST
PRESS

From the Mouths of Babes:
The Criminal Trial of a Sunday School Teacher
 For information, or to order additional copies of this book, please contact:

Lost Coast Press
155 Cypress Street
Fort Bragg, CA 95437
(800) 773-7782
www.cypresshouse.com

Cover design and illustration: Charles Hathaway
Mendocino Graphics

Library of Congress Cataloging-in Publication Data
Grey, Paul, 1949-
From the mouths of babes : the criminal trial of a Sunday school teacher / Paul Grey.-- 1st ed.
p. cm.
ISBN 1-882897-61-7 (pbk)
1. Grey, Paul, 1949--- Trials, litigation, etc. 2. Trials (Child sexual abuse)--Missouri--Kansas City. 3. Child witnesses. 4. Truthfulness and falsehood in children. I. Title.
KF224.G74 G74 2001 00-048158
345.73'02536--dc21

Manufactured in the U.S.A.

First edition

2 4 6 8 9 7 5 3 1

Dedication

This book is lovingly dedicated to all those who supported my wife and me throughout our ordeal. You made all the difference in the world to us. The book is dedicated also to those who have been through experiences similar to mine.

Permissions

Scripture taken from the *Holy Bible, New International Version.* Copyright © 1973, 1978, 1984 International Bible Socity. Used by permission of Zondervan Bible Publishers.

When Child Abuse Comes to Church by Bill Anderson © 1992 Bethany House Publishers. Used with permission.

Excerpts from Sunday, March 19, 1995 *Boston Globe* "Questions prompt reexamination of Fells Acres sexual abuse case" by Charles M. Sennott reprinted by permission of *Boston Globe* via Copyright Clearance Center.

Dictionary of American Biography, editor D. Malone, Reverend Samual Parris quotes used by permission of the American Council of Learned Societies.

Frontline "The Child Terror", October 27, 1998 transcript used by permission of *Frontline*/WGBH.

A Delusion of Satan: The Full Story of the Salem Witch Trials by Frances Hill use with permission of publisher, Doubleday, a division of Random House.

National Review September 6, 1993 article "Trial by Therapy" by Mark Sauer & Jim Okerblom ©1993 by National Review, Inc., 215 Lexington Avenue, New York, NY 10016. Reprinted by permission.

Reuters, May 4, 2000 story reprinted with permission, copyright ©Reuters 2001.

VOCAL/Colorado article by Frank Lee, quoted from by permission, Dr. Graham Jeambey, Victims of Child Abuse Laws.

Contents

Foreword

Paul Grey is not a professional writer. He is an engineer and a devout Christian who made a serious mistake. He volunteered to teach preschool Sunday school, and he let a two-year-old girl sit on his lap. That was his great crime. A distressed mother, apparently phobic about sex abuse, decided that Grey must have molested her daughter. Not surprisingly, she got the toddler to say so, which was enough to set the wheels of our "justice" system in motion. Grey discovered that once you are accused of sexual abuse, most people automatically assume your guilt, regardless of a lack of evidence. Most of his church "friends" turned away from him. He was arrested and tried for a terrible crime.

And so he wrote this book. His voice is at once anguished, informed, compassionate, puzzled, outraged and, above all, honest. Grey has written a firsthand account of what it feels like to go to court to face horrifying allegations. "I was still dizzy from the pace of the trial and from the phenomenal injustice to which I was being subjected," he writes. "It was dream-like."

More like nightmare-like. This book is an important, cautionary tale, because it could happen to anyone in the United States tomorrow, without warning and without justification. For the last two decades, we have been living through a largely unheralded, but gigantic, sex abuse witch-hunt. It dwarfs what happened in seventeenth-century Salem in the numbers of people affected, and it is ongoing.

Grey is one of the lucky ones. He only had to spend his life savings. He only had to move to another town and start his life anew. He only had to feel the terror of the wrongly accused. Many more innocent people now populate our prisons, convicted of sexual abuse they didn't commit. No one knows how many, but it is certainly in the thousands, probably tens of thousands.

Paul Grey did nothing wrong, other than be in the wrong place at the wrong time. Stories such as his are far too common. Since 1995, when I wrote a book about false accusations of sexual abuse, I've heard many men and women describe their similar ordeals. And it is all so unnecessary. I have often repeated what should by now be obvious: Yes, sexual abuse does occur, and yes, we should be alert for such possibilities. But we should also remember that a person is (hopefully) presumed innocent until proven guilty, and that repeated questioning of children can result in changed memories and false allegations.

— Mark Pendergrast
Author of *Victims of Memory*

Purpose

My intent is to give the reader more understanding about cases involving allegations of child sexual abuse, particularly those in America since 1980. Surely we could all attain greater discernment in this area. To this end I present my own case in detail. This is a historical narrative, including some of my thoughts about the psychology involved. My case provides some excellent examples of how such cases are sometimes mishandled. My hope is that readers will learn from these examples.

As Saint Paul said, "These things happened to them as examples and were written down as warnings for us." (I Cor. 10:11.)

(All Scriptural passages quoted herein are from the *Holy Bible*, *New International Version.)*

Flashback

Seated at the defense table in the new suit I had bought for the trial, it felt like a dream. For over ten months I had expected to wake up each day and find that the whole ordeal had been just a nightmare. During each day I expected to receive a message that the police were dismissing the case and acknowledging that they should never have pursued it in the first place. I was constantly in a state of expecting vindication. Those months seemed like a lifetime.

Now the trial was underway. I was glad of it because I knew that the uncertainties about my future would finally be resolved. I had never spoken to my attorney about court procedure. I think he assumed that I understood such matters. I didn't.

Just moments after the judge gave some instructions to the six jurors, a young girl, not quite four years old, walked cheerfully up the aisle. She was with her father, whom I had never seen before. I looked at her as she stood with her father on the witness stand. I didn't even recognize her. Even though I had on several occasions walked around the small classroom while holding her, though she had often sat on my lap, delightedly pulling at my beard while I tried to keep the students focused on the day's lesson, and though she was one of the most entertainingly cute kids I had taught during my Sunday school years, I couldn't recognize her in the courtroom. She was much taller, much less baby-like, she was talking rather than babbling, and her face had changed considerably.

In the kindest voice he could muster, the prosecutor asked, "And did your teacher ever put anything into your private area?"

Cheerfully, Elisa answered, "Just his finger."

All the notions I had entertained for months, that the child herself would finally vindicate me once given the chance, were dashed within seconds. I kept wondering, "When on Earth will this nightmare end?"

In the same singsong voice, the prosecutor was asking, "And is your teacher in the courtroom today? Do you see him here?"

Elisa looked to her left, where the six jurors and two alternate jurors were sitting, and swept her eyes over them, past the prosecutor's table, toward me. It was not a moment I would want to relive.

So, how did I ever get into a mess like this?

I. How It Started

The Phone Call that Changed Our Lives

My emphasis in this book is on allegations of sexual assault on children under five years of age. I considered titling the book *It Could Happen to You*, which the reader should bear in mind. A similar case, built upon similar "evidence," could materialize and destroy you or a loved one on any given day. This will continue until America is moved to change its investigative techniques.

On a Sunday in March 1993, I was at my usual place in church, surrounded by kids who had been under my care for half their lives. I had been teaching Sunday school in the same community for seven years, and was probably the most trusted Sunday school worker other than the Children's Church director himself. As usual, the kids were climbing all over me during the pre-class music session led by two of my adult friends. No adults had volunteered to help me that day during class time, which followed the music session, so I had to ask one of the maturest children in the church — an eleven-year-old — to be my assistant. She accepted gladly; her little sister was in the class.

To one side of my classroom, behind one of the walls, the pastor's wife was teaching the class of four-year-olds. She too had trouble enlisting adult volunteers. On the opposite side, connected to my classroom by a door, the over-thirteen class was meeting. The sanctuary was behind a wall on the third side, and the nursery was within speaking distance across the hall.

That Sunday was routine in most respects. I was tired after the services were finished, due to a two-year-old newcomer, an active boy who persistently needed attention.

Three days later, I was awakened by an early-morning phone call. It was the Children's Church director. He told me that the mother of one of my youngest kids was going to notify the police that I had molested her daughter. That child had been one of my greatest admirers; the very notion was absolutely ridiculous. After all, I was surrounded by witnesses and had years of rock-solid reputation. No one could possibly believe I would do the monstrous things alleged by this fearful mother, a newcomer to our church. Could they?

Hours later, after a workday in which I accomplished nothing, I finally got to see my pastor, the person crucial to revealing the absurdity of the allegation and restoring relations between the fearful mother and me. The meeting did not go as I had expected. The pastor insisted that the accusation would make the newspapers and had me sign some papers before asking me to leave. I absolutely could not understand what was happening. I assumed that the pastor must have been influenced by some factor I knew nothing about, because I knew he couldn't possibly turn on one of his most trusted leaders without some reason.

Modern-Day Tension in America

Child sexual abuse is an intensely emotional issue. It tears lives apart, leaving deep, lifelong scars. As America has focused on battling this problem, the number of accusations (many true and many false) has risen dramatically. Today, anyone could be accused, especially those who work with kids.

The first contemporary witch-hunt of notoriety was the McMartin daycare case in California, in which 360 children were incorrectly diagnosed as having been abused. Since then, the country has experienced a modernized form of witch-hunting.

The McCarthyism of the 1950s produced similar panic-based behavior. With that in mind, the McMartin case and others like it have often been called America's third witch-hunt.

My case involved two individuals (primarily) who injected their fearful thoughts into those who trusted them. I will discuss them later. In the 1990s, the trusted individual often was a therapist. No therapists were involved in my case.

Another common "trusted" source of information is the media. Almost all of us have experienced rage after reading or hearing a news story about a child abuser who, apparently, was freed on a technicality. But the reality may have been that the journalist and the editor of the story merely wished to make it appear that it was only a technicality that prevented justice from being served. The "spin" that gets put on a news story could be nothing more than a pandering to sensationalism, and perhaps the journalist's perception of reality may be subject to error when the story is highly emotional. I hope my story can help encourage the reader to entertain doubts concerning sensational news stories, and to read between the lines.

My own case didn't get so out of control as the high-profile national ones. Let me say at the outset that I have never done anything inappropriate with a child, nor have I ever entertained a sexual thought concerning a child. The charges against me were false, even ridiculous.

Parents who endure false accusations have their lives torn apart. Not only are they publicly labeled as monsters, but also their children are forcibly removed from them. They agonize over what their kids must go through in the foster homes where the state places them. Sadly, this happened recently to friends of mine in the same small community that conducted my own witch-hunt.

In the months before my trial, my doctor expressed his opinion about how sexual allegations are treated in the 1990s: "When an accusation of sexual assault is made, the community forgets all about your years of service and the endless list of good things you've done."

My Background

I should say a few things about myself — including a number of my quirks — to allow a better understanding of my case. Even my longtime friends may learn something new about me from this brief description. If, in the interest of full disclosure, I list more quirks than necessary, please don't let that give the false impression that I am being critical of myself. The reader needs to understand me to fully understand the points I shall make later.

I lived my childhood years in Kansas City. Born in 1949, I'm the youngest of three. Before my fifth birthday, we moved from the city to a typical, very modest, blue-collar suburb. I don't recall having any serious childhood fears. My family had enough income to meet our basic needs. As far as I knew, all the other families in our suburb were basically like us. My life was very secure. I spent my happiest times playing baseball at the neighborhood park.

I thank God regularly for having given me such good parents, though I couldn't appreciate them as much then as I do now. They spent few hours in leisurely pursuits, other than watching a little bit of TV. They were active in church and scouts. They were non-drinkers, but not militantly so. When we moved to the suburbs, we started going to a Presbyterian church. I hated to go, but it was required of me until I moved out of their house at age eighteen. One hour Sunday morning was all that we attended. My father was a deacon, and made numerous phone calls as part of his duties.

I've always had friends in the places I've lived and worked. In grade school, most of my classmates and I were in the same class, year to year. This comfortable arrangement ended when I reached seventh grade, which, academically, was my year of greatest learning.

Even after his mind began deteriorating, my father made deliveries for Meals on Wheels until he no longer could. In St. Joseph, Missouri, my grandfather used to walk to the hospital every day and visit various rooms just to spread cheer. He was so friendly that children and dogs would sometimes become frightened when he greeted them with his exuberant voice. (My accuser was suspicious of me from the very first time we met, thinking my behavior too friendly). Except for den mother duties and a brief period of Sunday school teaching, my mother's good deeds were performed at home, and I am grateful for that.

I was never sexually abused. On rare occasions I was spanked, and I deserved it when I got it. My mom was always hesitant to spank me, or even to ask my dad to do so. I used her reluctance to my advantage. I learned just how much I could get away with, and tried to stay just inside that limit. At school I also learned the limits, and had as much fun as I could within them. I didn't want to see what would happen if my transgressions got too serious. "Controlled" is the best term to describe my lifelong behavior. I got into some typical schoolboy troubles; no more and no less. Because of my non-threatening demeanor, sense of humor, and high academic aptitude, nearly all my teachers liked me. Excellent grades were not a high priority; I usually maintained a B average.

My best friends in high school were low-key juvenile delinquents. As a result of our misdeeds I had to go to juvenile court twice, for throwing rocks at a train and for damaging a couple of small trees in a residential area. The police told me that my records would be burned on my seventeenth birthday. During the witch-hunt in New England, I wondered whether the Kansas City police had actually kept their word.

On the Missouri side, where I lived, the drinking age was twenty-one. On the Kansas side, it was eighteen, so my friends and I went to Kansas regularly after we turned eighteen. On about three occasions, I got stopped for drunken driving. I was allowed to pour the beer out and go my way. Today such leniency is uncommon. I recognize that I was guilty of a very serious act; I could easily have killed someone through my thoughtless behavior.

At eighteen I registered for the draft. America's presence in Vietnam was at its peak. The probability of being sent there was very high. I had absolutely no desire to be in the military. This wasn't a matter of conscientious objection; it was just my basic desire always to have fun and never have to do anything unpleasant. The fact that others were going there did not make me want to do my fair share. I was just being selfish. To meet my mandatory obligation, I enlisted in the Air Force, which minimized the likelihood of serving in Vietnam. The price I paid was four years (people drafted into the Army had "only" a two-year obligation — if they survived).

In my twenties, long before I was married, I committed adultery on several occasions. I consider those the most reprehensible acts of my life. Adultery destroys families. Also in my twenties, I often smoked marijuana; when I started doing so I abandoned my interest in alcohol. In my thirties and up to the present, love of food has been my most serious vice.

I love dogs. It tears my heart up when I am around a suffering dog. The cat I inherited by marriage also affected me deeply. Whenever he had any kind of affliction, I could never relax completely, at home or at work, until the issue was resolved and his health restored.

During my military years, my one clear-cut goal in life was getting out. When I was released, the GI Bill paid for college. I was ecstatic as I went to my classes, freed from the hated Air Force and back in my beloved Kansas City. I was interacting with professors and friends and books instead of military people who had authority over me. That love of college didn't exist prior to my military service. I view this as a character improvement engendered by having endured hard times. I enjoyed college every year, and eventually earned a Ph.D. in physics.

I can't seem to keep up with fast-paced conversations for very long; my mind tends to get sidetracked. If I miss anything important, I read about it later, or ask questions. I excelled at college, but absorbed very little that my professors said; I learned everything from studying the books afterward. I love stupid puns; I can't explain why. Before I drive to a new place, I study the map. I pay all my bills on time. I pay little attention to space launches and I never liked *Star Trek* — highly unusual for a physicist.

I am non-argumentative. Whenever I'm with people who enjoy verbal jousting, I just let them say whatever they want, and I don't bother to respond. I assume that people can see past verbal manipulations. This is a faulty assumption, as proven by the world of politics. I suppose my nature is due to a combination of heredity and upbringing. All the math, science, and engineering in my background are subjects that generally have a right way and a wrong way to do things; argument is irrelevant. I learned that if I did things the right way, then nothing else would be required of me. I think that I expected life to be somewhat similar: if I could live my life "right," my actions and deeds would speak for themselves. Scripture agrees with this notion. Scripture is also full of instances where bad things happen to innocent people.

I met Darcie, my wife-to-be, when we were both college students in Kansas City. She's from Indiana. I love my in-laws and my family. Darcie and I got married when I was thirty-three. She is eighteen months younger than I am. I became Christian at age thirty. The early years when I was forced to attend church while living with my parents had nothing to do with accepting Jesus as my personal savior. If you're wondering whether it's unusual for a physicist to be a Christian, the answer is no.

I love to travel; the only constraints are time and money, because of which I have not yet been to Europe, Asia, or Africa. I've been all over the U.S., except for Alaska. I like to read. I don't take the newspaper, because I feel obligated to read it in depth and I don't have the time for that. I'd rather spend the time reading classics: *War and Peace*, *Moby Dick*, *David Copperfield*, etc. Much more enjoyable than the classics, and much less edifying, are *The Three Stooges*. I love watching them, along with Soupy Sales and other such infantile shows. For weekend TV, my choices are politics, baseball and football, and *Saturday*

Night Live. When the *Beavis and Butthead* series ran, I was a regular viewer (not that I should have been). I like Kurt Vonnegut novels. I'm somewhat compulsive about completing sets of things: if I know the names of twenty-four of the workers in my group, and there's a twenty-fifth whom I don't know, I feel compelled to learn that person's name even though it may be unnecessary from a work standpoint.

I like people. Learning about other cultures is my primary joy in life. I enjoy interacting with societal misfits as much as with popular people. The so-called misfits are interesting, and God (according to Scripture) views all of us as sinners. I still enjoy everything about Christmas. I love politeness, but I'm afraid that it is diminishing as time progresses, presumably due to the entire world watching American TV shows. I dislike all inconsiderate behaviors, and I see more of them as the population increases. When I'm in public places (such as when Darcie and I are mall walking), I occasionally have strongly affectionate feelings (non-sexual) toward a few people that I notice. I think I'm simply identifying with them as they go through daily life. I mentioned this to Darcie, who said that it happens to her, occasionally. It's all right with me that I have these feelings, because I know it's a good thing to love one's neighbors. I never seem to experience such affection for my fellow drivers or even their passengers.

Deficit spending was, in my opinion, one of the most immoral things Americans did in the latter part of the twentieth century. We, the voters, spent the money, leaving our children and grandchildren to pay the debt. I don't enjoy being in large groups; I'd much rather spend time with just two or three people. I love all kinds of music: salsa to opera, and everything in between. Bluegrass is my favorite, particularly the instrumentals. I still buy "oldies:" The Beatles, Cat Stevens, Abba, Gloria Estefan and hundreds more.

Politically, I am a "bleeding-heart conservative" (Republican leader Jack Kemp used that phrase). I disagree with hardcore "America first" thinking because I feel the same toward all people, regardless of what country they live in. I would rather spend my money on the neediest people in the world than on relatively needy Americans. I strongly dislike the socialistic trends in America today for that very reason. When left-wing policies lead to higher taxes (to be spent in America by the government), people like me end up with less money, which diminishes our ability to send aid to the people we wish to support (in Africa, Latin America, etc.). To me, it seems like government officials have used taxpayer money to curry favor with American voters at the expense of the world's neediest people.

I think federal taxes should be a fraction of what they are now. I think socialism rewards the lazy and punishes the hardworking. I think it removes the incentive to strive for excellence. Nonetheless, my perception is that Americans are increasingly demanding that the Federal government take on more basic caring functions that families used to handle on their own. Many Americans try to see how little they can give in taxes and how much they can get from federal policies. Such a widespread practice cannot be sustained. The federal budget is finite, but many people don't treat it as such.

I love food, especially spicy. I'm slightly less than six feet tall and weigh about 185 pounds. I'm somewhat of a cheapskate when buying things for myself. When I see a police car, I don't alter my driving habits or get nervous, because I'm not the kind of driver they're concerned about. You could think of my personality as that of a stereotypical engineer. I would never consider buying new clothing merely to update my wardrobe in accordance with popular trends. I'm completely comfortable working amidst hundreds of engineers. A few of them go into management; most forego the higher salary and accompanying stress, and remain "worker bees." I don't mind accepting responsibility when somebody has to, but I'm not tempted to do so for money or recognition. With the witch-hunt now behind me, I would describe my life as being comfortable and fun.

I think the wisest advice ever given is Proverbs 3: 5, 6. "Trust in the Lord with all your heart and lean not on your own understanding; in all your ways acknowledge Him, and He will make your paths straight." In the 1980s and '90s, America seemed intent on trying to discredit these verses. I'm convinced that the results will be disastrous.

My core religious belief is that I will go to Heaven after this life, not because of good deeds I've done, but because I have accepted God's own provision, paid for by the sacrifice of Jesus Christ. My deeds in this life will always fall far short of God's perfect standard, so I'll always be unworthy of such an arrangement. That's why it's called grace — it is unmerited favor. I choose to accept this incredible offer; it's that simple. As a result of this belief, acquired at age thirty, I am filled with gratitude. That's what controls my behavior. Children want to please their parents: why should it be different with children of God?

Establishing the Setting

How did I end up in the church where the accusation took place? When Darcie and I moved to New England from the Midwest in 1985, I wanted to visit as many churches as possible. I knew that once we settled into one, we would be too busy to get to know much about the others. We visited dozens of churches. One of them was Reverend Jake Grozny's church. Its newspaper ad contained the words "Christian Fellowship" and it looked promising, so we visited on Palm Sunday in 1985. Rev. Jake led the worship (with guitar and with voice), then Rev. Jake said some prayers, then Rev. Jake gave a sermon, then Rev. Jake told some people to pass out palm branches, then Rev. Jake said a last prayer and dismissed us. Afterward, Darcie and I never said anything negative about the church to anyone, but whenever we thought of it, the phrase "one-man show" stood out. We didn't visit Rev. Jake's church again until years later, so we don't know how his congregation's Christian life evolved during those early days. I'll return to this subject, because Rev. Jake's church is where the accusation eventually took place.

For the uninitiated reader, when I use the word "worship,"

just substitute "church music." There is a distinction, but I won't go into it here.

Eventually, the people in one of the small churches in the area captured our hearts because of their love for the Lord. We stayed in that church until it died a few years later. It had about fifteen families. It seemed that for every new family that would join, another would leave due to a job-related move, so the church never grew. The worship and Scripture teaching were very edifying, and we never had any serious complaints. We disagreed with the pastor concerning the necessity of formal membership, but that wasn't a big deal. Eventually, the voting members chose to end the struggle to keep the church alive with such small numbers.

Years later, the assistant pastor of that church and his wife were there for us to do anything possible to fight the accusation against me, even though we had had very little contact with them over the years. I'll bring them up again.

That church was the first where I taught Sunday school. I taught the ten–to-twelve-year-old group. Usually, there were four students. It worked out great; the kids and I thought the world of each other. One incident stands out as an example of this period: one of the boys had been bothered by nightmares. I told him to confidently call on the name of Jesus the next time it happened. He did, and his nightmares stopped from that time. I look forward to seeing all those students of mine in Heaven.

For Bible-believing Christians who don't happen to be Catholic, choices in New England are more limited than they are in the rest of the country. Christians tend to further limit themselves by rejecting many churches for the sole reason that their music arrangements aren't very rousing. Church searching in New England can be very frustrating for picky Christian families.

I'd like to offer some insight into how I think. My worldview is based primarily on the Bible. This doesn't mean that I am a good person; it just means I believe in the authority and accuracy of the Bible. When I consider the many sources that propose various rules for living a successful life (Ann Landers, Dale Carnegie, Deepak Chopra, *et al*), I simply conclude that the Bible is the one that is repeatedly proven true, and I trust it. If I ever come to distrust it, I'll look elsewhere. It took an initial step of faith to come to this trust, but not an act of blindness. My Scriptural references in this book represent my own logic.

A few months after our nice little church disbanded, Darcie and I were invited to a going-away party for one of the single sisters from that church. While at this party, we talked with the pastor of another local church, which this sister of ours had been attending. We had visited his church once and were impressed with what we had seen. We "fell in love" with this pastor, and knew by night's end that we wanted to support him in his ministry.

Pastor Dave's church was part of a small denomination that had a long history and a very set way of doing things. The reason we were so excited about his ministry was that he was trying to make changes in ways that we entirely agreed with. The obvious danger: who asked us to come in and change things that that denomination had done in a particular way for hundreds of years? (That question also describes the way New Englanders feel about outsiders who move there — we lived in "the land of steady habits.")

Pastor Dave had experienced a major strengthening in his own relationship with the Lord by embracing modern-day, i.e., Hosanna-type, worship. Short songs expressing our personal relationship with the Lord, with lyrics simple enough to memorize so you can close your eyes and not stare into a hymnal are a key element. Being among other worshipers who are similarly focusing on God rather than on each other works extremely well. Any technique that truly gets us to focus on our Creator is good. This modern form of worship really hit the mark with Pastor Dave. Darcie and I agree, and we recommend it highly to any Christian group that's never tried it.

Pastor Dave's "superiors" and nearly half of his small congregation didn't share his enthusiasm for change. A regional board put him (essentially) on trial. They had him submit a paper on the subject "Does God speak to man today?" That way, they could judge whether he was teaching things that were overly objectionable within the denomination. His answer to the big question was "Yes, God speaks to us today," which he didn't embellish with claims of audible voices or the like. Not swayed, the board prepared to kick him out. Rather than wait for that, the church voted to withdraw from the denomination. Those who wanted to maintain the traditional ways started a new church of their own, so there were two tiny churches in place of the small one that we started with. Of the two, the traditional church is alive to this day.

Regarding the way Pastor Dave was booted out, I disagree with that group's doctrine, but I don't deny their right to run things the way they choose. As God tells us through Saint Paul, "One man considers one day more sacred than another; another man considers every day alike. Each one should be fully convinced in his own mind." (Romans 14:5.) In this case, both groups seemed fully convinced that they had done the right thing, and neither intended to stop preaching the good news of Jesus Christ.

I also taught Sunday school during our years with Pastor Dave's church. Once again, I taught the 10–12 age group. I think one reason why children like me is that I appreciate their sense of humor. In Pastor Dave's church, the kids and I liked each other very much. For example, shortly before the accusation, one of my students said that if he were going to be like any of the adult Christians he knew, he'd want it to be me. I never heard this until after the accusation, and it really encouraged me through the agonizing months.

Our new church, after the split, was tiny, no more than ten families. After we continued meeting in this manner for several months, Pastor Dave and the other two elders decided to merge our group with another church, which belonged to a relatively new denomination whose worship music he had found so inspirational. He asked Rev. Jake about the possibility of our church merging into his. Rev. Jake wanted one condition: that those from Pastor Dave's church not criticize anything about his church for a year. That sounded fine to me. The likelihood of a group of white-collar, longtime Christians from an established denomination criticizing a group of newly saved, blue-collar Christians fresh from a life of drugs is quite high, and nobody was asking us to come in and change the way they do things.

Our numbers boosted the size of Rev. Jake's church considerably. From then on the church grew a lot. It was encouraging to see so many people from dysfunctional backgrounds expressing their commitment to the Lord. This was a big contrast with the previous denomination, where people would do a study on this or on that, then do another study, and seemingly have little contact with the rest of the world. In Rev. Jake's church, there was no shortage of people escaping from desperate circumstances. The reason I found this atmosphere so motivational was given by Jesus, who said, "Blessed are the poor in spirit, for theirs is the kingdom of heaven." (Matt. 5:3.) God is able to work with people who see their need. In contrast, comfortable people don't see their need and usually have no desire to draw closer to God. For this reason I think affliction is a tool God often uses for our spiritual benefit.

When we started attending Rev. Jake's church, one of my best friends made a reference to how terribly immature that church was. I thought she was being overly harsh just because it was so different from her own church. In hindsight, she was right.

When we first started attending our new church, I called every family in the old one to give them a pep talk about the change. Giving encouragement is something I try to do regularly. The fact that this church ended up abusing Darcie and me so badly is just one of many ironies about my case. But I suspect that witch-hunts in general are laden with irony. Recall how Richard Jewell was demonized after risking his life to save others at the Olympics in Atlanta.

Early Days at the "Scene of the Crime"

For the first few weeks in Rev. Jake's church, I felt self-conscious about the large group of us who had suddenly challenged our new church's physical capacity. My conscience dictated that I begin helping in some capacity, so all the newly reborn Christians in the church could have an opportunity to enjoy the worship, fellowship and teaching with a minimum of distracting church commitments. I decided to offer my services in some small capacity in Children's Church. The Children's Church leader, Phil, had a pastor's heart, and I have never regretted supporting him in his ministry. It was the right thing to do.

At this point, the reader may wonder if I continually sought jobs working with kids because I enjoyed it so much. The answer is no. I don't attend church for enjoyment; I'd prefer to stay home and watch football or read the paper. But sometimes I try to do what I think the Lord wants me to do. To be sure, God doesn't depend on my help or anyone else's. Think of a very young child who wants to help mom clean the house or help dad with yard work. The desire to help is pleasing to the parents, and I suspect we are pleasing to God in a similar way when we make our meager offers of servanthood. Scripture describes my motivation perfectly: "Christ's love compels us." (II Cor. 5:14.)

I understood the impact that a caring adult can have in encouraging children to trust God. Although I disliked church when I lived with my parents, I never had any negative feelings about our first pastor. When I was six, I had to attend some kind of church event in the basement at his house. All I wanted to do was get out of there. I didn't misbehave; I just hated being there. Though I can't remember why, the pastor lovingly picked me up and walked around with me for a while. I became completely at ease because I knew the boss was on my side. God's love reached me through this man. And even though I rejected everything Christian for over twenty years after he was gone from my life, a light of remembrance of that one event helped to eventually draw me in and give my life to the

Lord. That pastor's simple act was the model I had in mind as I worked with kids of all ages.

The immediate need Phil had was for an adult to help keep the kids under control during worship. While the adults and most of the Sunday school teachers were upstairs enjoying their favorite time of week (worship), the kids were all in one group downstairs, with Phil leading them in a few songs, accompanied by a man playing guitar, and one or two other brave adults. (Pardon my use of the corny word "brave," but I really respect and admire people who sacrifice themselves to work with kids). In my opinion, Phil was anointed in God's eyes for the job. After his brave performance leading the kids in worship, with a Bible story thrown in, he would continue working with them until the Sunday school teachers showed up. Then the little ones were rounded up to go off with their teacher, then the next age group, and so on until all the kids were accounted for. The two- and three-year-olds were taught by a man, who would take them to a room in the corner of the basement. I had a lot of respect for this brave guy. At the time, I couldn't imagine how he could handle the responsibility.

To be sure, it was often a real struggle trying to keep thirty or forty kids aged two to twelve under control. It's hard to teach about the love of Jesus when, at any given moment, several kids are misbehaving. Phil did a great job. Note the important fact that one of the things Phil said to me during our brief first meeting was, "Sometimes the little ones just need a lap to sit on." He was referring to the fact that the toddlers were apt to leave their seats and walk around, disrupting the older kids in the process, and was telling me how I could best help him. My role of kindhearted policeman with occasional lap duty was one I approached with some trepidation, but God took care of us and things went smoothly.

When a child asked to go to the restroom while the big group was together, a child in the five-to-twelve age bracket would just go upstairs by him- or herself, and I would keep an eye out for abuse of the privilege. Younger ones would be escorted.

Usually, girls between eight and twelve were selected to be the escorts, especially if they were from the same family as the requesting child. There weren't too many regular-attending families in the church, maybe thirty. I might have been an escort a couple of times, but I don't remember any particular instances. In such cases, the escort would wait outside the restroom door for the younger one to finish. If further assistance was needed, the task was given to one of the older girls or else someone would go into the congregation and fetch the mother or father.

When summer arrived, Sunday school format changed. We would still meet together as a group during worship, and I continued to help in that area. But after children's worship, the kids would go outside and play kickball. Some of the teachers got to take a summer vacation, because some adults other than the usual teachers would help with the kickball sessions. The two-to-three-year-olds would continue to go into the brave man's classroom for their usual class. The four-year-olds would also stay with their teacher. I think the five-to-twelve-year-olds all played kickball.

Phil had a new ministry for me: providing snacks for the kids. I would usually bring cookies and juice for this purpose. We'd give the two-to-four-year-olds their snacks first, sitting at picnic tables, then they would be ushered away by their teachers before the big kids came by after their kickball session. The final part of the morning was impromptu; there was a variance in the time when the adult service would end, and we had to watch the kids until the adults came to get them. This was challenging, because the adults would not necessarily make a beeline to get their kids afterward. They would frequently engage in conversations with each other. I regard providing the adults with this opportunity for fellowship as one of the greatest gifts that Children's Church workers give. But it was a real challenge, because there were so many older kids running around. Swing set duty may sound easy, but the responsibility of knowing where every young child is at all times is anything but.

I can't remember whether Phil or I first brought up the possibility of my teaching when summer came to an end, but I took over the ten-to-twelve-year-old class—a nine-month commitment. Things started off a little shaky, but then the older, more difficult kids chose to stay with their parents rather than continue attending the class, and my group became manageable. Once again, the kids and I thought the world of each other. One of the boys in my class had been one of the biggest terrors among the Children's Church workers for several years; now he's a stable young man who becomes more mature every year, capable of going into his own ministries. The most touching experiences in life, to me, are when I see my former students serving the Lord.

During this nine-month period, I continued helping Phil with the entire group of kids during worship, before Sunday school classes started. Had there been other volunteers to cover this area, I could have spent the time with the adults instead, which I would have preferred. But I felt a strong commitment to Children's Church, and did what I thought God wanted me to do. When the nine-month commitment ended, I served snacks again during the summer, as I had the previous year. Phil's wife, Betsy, was teaching the two-to-three-year-olds at that time. Their previous teacher, the brave man — who happens to be a lawyer — had conflicting summer commitments, and chose to make himself unavailable for the succeeding nine-month term.

By the end of our second summer at Rev. Jake's church, I had a couple of other ministries. Rev. Jake had decided to start a Sunday night service. Originally, this was built around a series of contemporary Christian concerts. There were many groups who performed there, including a few of the best-known Christian artists in the country. After the first Sunday night, it was obvious that there was no provision at all for the kids. But they attended in abundance, just as they did Sunday mornings. One regular family who attended only during the evening service had eight kids. Rev. Jake told Phil that it was his responsibility to provide for the children, so Phil dutifully spent every Sunday night working with a large group of kids of all ages while the adults enjoyed themselves at the concert upstairs. Phil received a half-time salary from the church.

Phil's wife and Rev. Jake's wife are sisters. They have a third sister who used to work there as a secretary. I liked all three of them very much.

Occasionally an adult would come downstairs from the concert and help Phil with the kids for a while, but not consistently or according to any schedule. Rev. Jake never tried to solicit any help for any aspect of Children's Church; all the responsibility was dumped on Phil without any support. When I saw how he had gotten roped in to a non-stop Sunday evening commitment, thereby missing out on the concerts — the most fun times the church had to offer — I supported him. I helped him so he wouldn't have to shoulder all the responsibilities of the large group of kids by himself. I told him that this really wasn't my chosen ministry and that I only did it because nobody else would volunteer. It really was pretty unpleasant. I had a bit of a sour attitude about missing every concert because no one else was willing to help, but it wasn't that big a deal. Serving God is good policy, and I have no regrets. Being confident that we've done the right thing is worth more than a lot of life's other pleasures; it yields peace of mind.

I remember one Sunday night when Phil specifically requested that I help him by taking the youngest kids — alone — into the room in the corner of the basement, to protect them from the dodge-ball game. I was teaching the twos and threes by then, so I knew the younger kids.

The other new ministry Darcie and I had by the end of our second summer was a Friday-night prayer group at our home. The leader was one of the maturest individuals in the church. Besides the leader, Phil usually attended, along with a number of others. This lasted for a year. I'll say more about this group later. In fact I was getting stretched thin due to all my commitments, and really would have liked to shed the Sunday evening responsibilities.

At the end of the second summer, I was completely committed to aiding Phil with his important ministry. The lack of assistance from the majority of the adults made me more rather than less determined to help. In order to volunteer in a way that would make things as easy as possible for Phil, I told him, "Just fill all the teaching positions with volunteers, and I'll take the class that nobody else volunteers for." That class ended up being the two- and three-year-olds. Phil's wife didn't want to teach it any more because their daughter was in the class. The brave man — a lawyer — was no longer available. I learned later that he was concerned that "something would happen." What happened to me was exactly what he feared. Another lady in the church said she "got a word from the Lord" that I was going to be accused of sexual molestation. She was upset that she hadn't told me this prior to the accusation. It wouldn't have mattered; I would have ignored it, because I was so well known by Phil and the parents and kids, that any accusation would be quickly recognized as false. Or so I thought.

My fear and trepidation increased as I pondered taking over this class. I did all the relevant reading I could manage, which helped tremendously. We used a book written by a lady from the Christian Reformed Church. It laid out everything for teaching twos and threes. I did my homework diligently and it paid off.

I had the luxury of a full-time adult helper. Mary was new to the church. I met her before she had been there very long (I made a point of getting to know everyone in the church that I could). Mary said she loved kids and was willing to volunteer her time for their benefit. Since there weren't enough volunteers among the other adults, we accepted her offer despite her being a newcomer. At first, both she and I were pretty intimidated concerning the commitment we had made with the twos and threes. I was forty-two at the time; Mary was roughly half that.

Probably the biggest reason why this was such a big step for me was that I don't have kids of my own. In 1980 I chose to get a vasectomy. I've never regretted that decision. Though it seemed unlikely that I would encounter a Christian woman who felt the same way, I did; Darcie has never wanted to have kids either. We've been married since 1982, and were good friends for seven years prior to that. As our friends would vigorously testify, our (now-deceased) cat provided twenty-one years for any pent-up parental outlet that may have needed expression.

Just because we didn't want to have kids of our own doesn't mean we care less about children than most adults do, and we've both had lots of exposure to them over the years. I was unaware that there is societal suspicion against childless adults — until the accusation happened. In fact, during the deliberations, one of the jurors wanted to know whether I had kids. The judge told the jury that it is illegal to use such prejudicial issues to determine innocence or guilt. Nonetheless, this societal prejudice is real.

Years of teaching Sunday school in New England didn't represent my only experience working with young people. I taught college physics for eight years; I had over 1,000 different students during that time. I loved working with them (most were engineers), and had an excellent teaching reputation. I think the secret to my success was that I identified strongly with the students, and put in the extra time to try to make things go better for them. Usually, I really enjoy doing things that help people. As of this writing, for example, I've donated blood forty-one times.

A brief story illustrates my relationship with my college students. Near mid-term a student came to see me. He told me that he had been doing poorly in class because of personal problems. His parents lived in a part of Lebanon that had been occupied by Israel during a period of high tensions. He hadn't heard from them in six months and he was sick with worry about them. That evening, I prayed at length for his situation. He performed well in class, but we didn't speak again for several months. When we did, he told me that the very evening after he'd informed me of his situation, he received a phone call from his parents and learned that they were safe and healthy. I've experienced many such "coincidences" in my life. God answers prayer. If you don't pray, I encourage you to try.

Just a month or two prior to the accusation, the church sent a letter to most of the congregation. It had a picture of Darcie and myself, and said very flattering things about us in a feature article. We were trusted — until the accusation hit.

My New Job Teaching Two- and Three-Year-Olds

It was very entertaining to work with the twos and threes; they're absolutely adorable. It would be a pleasure to work with them if someone else was responsible for their safety, and if they would behave, and if they weren't so messy and loud, and sometimes smelly. Of course, we don't have the option of taking the good without the bad. It's hard work but it's also very rewarding. The kids held a special place in my heart, just as my ten-to-twelve-year-olds had. My biggest concern was safety. I don't know much first aid, I felt responsible for the kids' wellbeing, and I know that toddlers are fragile.

Mary was my assistant for five or six months. When she left the church, Fred entered the scene. Fred was a mature young man; older than Mary was. When he started attending the church, he volunteered to help with kids in any way possible. In fact, he was embarking on a career change, and felt God's calling to commit himself to working with kids. He was extremely good with them, and as far as I was concerned, he was a gift from above. By then, I was more relaxed in my new role. Our twos and threes class was one of the most upbeat places in the church, and it didn't feel like much of a sacrifice to work with the kids rather than hang out with the adults. The largest number of kids I ever had on a Sunday was twenty-seven. Fred was with me that day; it was not a relaxed day.

I can't remember all the details of how we handled the kids' restroom breaks during the months when Mary and Fred assisted me. Regularly, I would solicit the help of an older child. This was easy since I knew all the kids in the church. The older ones tended to have a distinct preference for helping me rather than attending their regular class. Maybe some people would accuse me of exploiting child labor, but I felt that these older kids matured greatly as we gave them adult-like responsibilities. And toddlers really are fun for older kids to be around. We all liked the arrangement. So when children had restroom needs, our child assistant would generally take them, leaving me with Mary or Fred and the rest of the class. I have to confess that I should have been a bit more cautious about who escorted whom to the restroom. No thought of sexual molestation ever crossed my mind when our child helper was a girl, and, since I knew my boy assistants well, I doubt the notion ever crossed my mind concerning them either. I can see now that every church should have a policy in place to protect the children and the adults. I should have been recommending such policies to Phil, but the fact is that the necessity never dawned on me. Plus, Rev. Jake had a history of staying uninvolved with all Children's Church personnel issues, and we assumed he would not solicit helpers for us. What we needed were more volunteers.

Consider who ended up assisting the young kids on their potty breaks: usually, due to a lack of adult volunteers, a girl between ages nine and twelve. Sometimes the escort had to enter the stall and help the child wipe. Concerning potential accusations, that's extremely risky, unless everyone in the church trusts all of the assistants. On some occasions, my adult helper would escort the child, leaving the adolescent assistant to help me with the class. I now realize that this arrangement was also very risky to the escorts.

Concerning the subject of restroom breaks, what if the child assistant is a boy? There is a much greater societal fear (backed by statistics) about boys escorting young kids alone, and churches should avoid it to protect themselves. I can't even remember what I would do during the days when my assistant was a boy (over 90 percent of the time it was a girl). I probably kept the boy with me and sent the adult assistant. I remember for a fact that Fred escorted some kids on their potty breaks. One time, a mother became hysterical because she showed up after church to get her daughter, but the child had been escorted to the restroom by Fred and they had not yet returned. That brings up another truth: there is a societal fear about grown men escorting kids to the restroom. This clashes with modern American sentiment that men should take on more of the tasks traditionally handled by women, and vice versa.

My room didn't have a horizontally divided door. I had been asking Phil for one, and he had been meaning to do something about it, but before we could get things arranged the way we wanted, the accusation happened.

One of my friends told me that, when he would step into the church restroom, if a child were in there, he would step back into the hall until the child was gone, to avoid all suspicion. My witch-hunt lawyer told me that when his seven-year-old daughter brings any friends to his house, he locks himself in his library until the visiting kids are gone. From a legal standpoint, they are doing the smart thing to protect themselves from a society gone crazy.

Each year, Sunday school classes began in late August. At that time, the kids who were in my class were selected by age as follows: if they were four or older, they weren't in my class. For the children under four, if they were at least two, then they were to be in my class for the entire year. The result of this method was that at the end of the school year, there were many four-year-olds in my class.

I had only three options for trying to keep track of all the kids in my class: shut the doors, leave them open and have adult volunteers help keep watch, or put a stretch-gate in the doorway. As a matter of keeping tabs on the kids, I chose to keep the doors shut, as I had seen my predecessors do. But a lady (who enjoyed our class) visiting our church with her young daughter one day, said to me, "Our church would never allow doors to be shut the way you do here." From that day on, I began asking Phil to get the horizontally divided door installed, like on the nursery across the hall from my classroom, where the top half of the door could be kept open but the kids couldn't get out.

There were two doors to my classroom. One went to the hallway, about fifteen feet from the most heavily traveled part of the church; the other led to the room next door, which at the time of the accusation was used by the class of thirteen-to-fifteen-year-olds. In previous months it was unused. During those months, after worship was over and I had finished with the Bible story, Phil's wife, Betsy, would take the two-year-olds into the unused room, which had some toys, and I would keep the three-year-olds. Elisa, allegedly the victim, was among the two-year-olds during that period. To this day, her mother probably doesn't even know that her child wasn't always in my care during the seven months that she attended my class.

I taught the two- and three-year-olds for a total of nineteen months. Elisa was in my class for the final seven. When Betsy and I would split the kids into two groups, that was the way we really wanted the classes: separate. But Betsy was only available occasionally, and there were no other volunteers. For lack of teachers, we had to combine the two ages.

Meeting the "Victim"

The school year started at the end of August. I had completed the first year of teaching the twos and threes (twelve months' duration; we didn't take the kids outside during the summer), and I told Phil that I wouldn't mind teaching that class again. His own daughter would continue to be in it, so his wife's reason for not teaching it remained valid; plus she worked long hours and was the mother of three. Since I had the routine down, teaching the class was much quicker and easier for me the second time around. I had spent many hours developing teaching materials during the first year.

Elisa was two and a half years old when the Sunday school year began, and she started attending my class at that time. That was when I first met her. She had been at the nursery across the hall during the preceding weeks. Her mother, Joan, a Catholic who apparently wanted to try a non-Catholic church, would bring her two kids (Elisa's older brother was about five) to Sunday school, then she would attend the adult service, retrieve the two kids, and go. The father did not live with the family. The only time he came to the church was when he and his wife met privately with Phil for marriage counseling sessions.

During the seven months that Elisa attended my class, there were usually fewer than a dozen kids present. Nearly all of them knew each other, and most were four years old by the time of the accusation. These factors placed Elisa in a distinctive category: she acted like, and in fact was, the baby of the class. She didn't participate in the rousing merriment of the others. Instead, she just wanted to watch from a safe distance, on my lap if I was available. This took place in the presence of the other kids, an adult helper, and an older child helper. There were a few times (maybe four or five Sundays) when one of my two helpers was absent. I took roll during the first year because the teacher's manual suggested it. I stopped doing it the second year because I couldn't see any benefit. I didn't keep any records of which helper(s) I had on specific dates. Such records might have been a tiny bit helpful to me after the accusation.

Elisa spoke on very few occasions during her time with me, but I knew she was absorbing her environment. I've had students who never spoke a word for a solid year, and their parents told me that the child would talk about Sunday school all week long, and sing every Sunday school song at home (but would never sing even one word during my class). I knew I was getting the message across to them, and I never felt it was wasted effort. Saint Paul refers to this as laying the foundation. (I Cor. 3:10.) My goals with the kids were to convince them that God loves them and, toward that same purpose, that church is enjoyable. Providing for their safety and peace of mind was consistent with these goals.

I knew that Elisa was living without a father in her home. On one occasion when I was teaching them the weekly Bible story, I made a remark about mommies and daddies. Elisa said one of her few discernible sentences at that time: "My Daddy?"

On other occasions, she had joyfully tried to tell me about some aspect of her life. I couldn't understand any of it, and I diverted her attention to some aspect of our class activities. The only word I consistently recognized when any of my students uttered it was "potty." Many times, their body language was such that they didn't even have to speak the word. The only verbal communications I recall ever receiving from Elisa were her responses to multiple-choice questions, such as "Elisa, what color is this?" She never caused me any problems, was fun to work with, and was as cute as a toddler can be.

Second Year of Teaching Two- and Three-Year-Olds

After the first year, I decided that I should try to better inform the parents about circumstances in the classroom, and give them a chance to object. One of the main things I wanted to let them know was that the snacks the kids received usually contained sugar. So, at the beginning of my second year of teaching the toddlers, I made a sign and hung it from the class doorway, where it stayed for about three weeks. The sign asked parents to let me know if they wanted special diet arrangements to be made for their children. One of the sons of a church leader was on a strict no-sugar regimen. As an activity to reinforce the weekly Bible story, there was one week when we would choose a volunteer child, blindfold him, then feed him one of the items on the table and see if he could guess what it was. When I placed the Teddy Graham into this boy's mouth, he immediately spit it out. He was being perfectly obedient to his mother's instructions. This boy attended my class very few times because his parents went to the early service. During the weeks when I was training a lady to teach the twos and threes for that early service, I had my only experiences as a bathroom escort. The obedient boy I just mentioned is one of only two children I ever escorted into the restroom, even though I had worked with about 200 kids during my three years in that church. The boy was mature; he didn't need any restroom assistance. (And he obediently and cheerfully washed his hands without having to be asked).

When Elisa's mother saw the sign about diet and sugar, she told me not to give Elisa any sugar. I can't recall her words, but I do remember being left with the feeling that she didn't have any appreciation or understanding of how much work was involved in taking care of the kids in that class. In contrast, it was a pleasure to accommodate the wishes of the obedient boy's mother; it was obvious that she cared about her son *and* about his teachers.

It was tactically difficult to feed Elisa raisins and orange juice while her classmates were having a rousing good time with cookies and berry juice at the same table. Many adults will say that I should have just given raisins and orange juice to all the kids, but my choice was a conscious one that I never regretted. I treated the kids as I would have liked to be treated were I in their position. Sometimes the kids would make a berry-stained mess of their nice clothes, and some of them may have had some extra sugar-induced energy when their parents picked them up, but I only heard one parent grumble about my choices during the nineteen months that I taught them. The only reason I bring up this topic is to inform the reader about my earliest interaction with my eventual accuser. Have you ever extended a favor to someone, received no acknowledgment, and felt like the person took it entirely for granted? That's the kind of feeling I had about Joan. This wasn't a big deal; Sunday school teachers notoriously work without recognition (other than from God). I simply felt that Joan was unaware that I was performing a service for her. In hindsight, I suspect that she thought I was working with kids solely for purposes of sexual gratification.

Unknown to me was the fact that Joan had gone to ask Phil about me in the earliest weeks after this class started. Her question to Phil was "Can this guy be trusted? I think he pays too much attention to my daughter." Phil assured her—or so he thought—that I could indeed be trusted. I never found out about this incident until many months after the accusation.

Joan was usually late bringing Elisa to class. This could have been a calculated effort to make sure everyone was present in my class before she felt safe dropping off her daughter, but that's idle speculation on my part. Recall that the first half-hour of the Sunday service was worship time for the adults and for the multi-age group of kids downstairs. When I took over the class of two-to-three-year-olds, Phil and I decided to start a separate worship group for the twos, threes, and fours. Some brave adult volunteers made this possible. Two of the volunteers were a husband and wife from my previous church; their daughter was in my class. Kate, the wife, had taught the very same age group (two and three) in a previous church, using the same lesson book I used. There was also a man who volunteered to assist with toddlers' worship. He helped on alternate weeks; Gary and Kate took care of the remainder. These three were mature adults, and as helpful as anyone could be to a Sunday school teacher.

It was a struggle, even unsafe, having four-year-olds mixed with two-year-olds in a tightly packed room with kids moving around. Rev. Jake's wife taught the fours. Her room was next door to mine both years that I taught the little ones. The first year, she would remain with the adults during worship, then come get her four-year-olds afterward. The second year, Phil and I decided to keep the four-year-olds downstairs during worship. In that year, when Elisa attended my class, the adult worship leader(s) would be with me for the first half-hour.

One of the special aspects of teaching very young kids is that many of them have rarely been left in the care of anyone other than their parents. The teacher must be able to impart a sense of security to them. After the accusation, one of my co-workers told me that in his church there is a man who does nothing but ease young kids through this Sunday morning transition from parent to teacher. My co-worker's son would not allow anyone (even his teacher) other than this man to take him from his parents. The man would then leave the boy in class when the boy seemed ready. I identify strongly with this man. There were quite a few young kids in Rev. Jake's church whose anxieties were alleviated whenever I was present. I am honored by the trust that the children placed in me.

This aspect of my relationship with the youngsters extended to some of the older ones also, such as those I dealt with Sunday evenings. Usually, the older ones were more interested in fast-paced activities, and I had little significance to them other than as the guy whose permission they would ask if they wanted anything. But there was a boy, six years old, I think, who was about as troublesome as they get. He had been known to leave his mother's care Sunday evening and go throw rocks at cars in the parking lot. He was a victim of sexual abuse, so the story goes. When Phil was trying to teach and this particular boy was acting out in terribly distracting ways, Phil ordered him to sit on my lap. The boy did, and after getting to know me, his behavior got much better when he was with me. I made it a point to spend time with him and pray for him every Sunday night. In the midst of his disturbed thoughts, this boy knew that he could trust Phil and me. Of course, he was still a big nuisance to everyone around him, classmates included. Hopefully, he'll give his life to God some day and find peace.

The manner in which Elisa's mother dropped her off in my care was awkward. In my opinion, Joan's distrust of me was why. Other parents, who trusted me, would simply wait until their child's attention was diverted, then exit. In the early weeks, the child would typically cry very briefly when he or she realized that mom or dad had left. My adult helpers and I would then make every loving effort to win the child over with fun diversions. Children who thought they could get their parent back by crying loud and long would try to do so. When convinced that crying would not bring a parent back, they would turn their attention to the class like the rest of the pupils. I identify strongly with the kids in this area. When I was their age, I would have done anything in my power to prevent my mom from ever leaving me if I could have gotten away with it.

In my opinion, Joan's hesitance to leave Elisa in my care

allowed Elisa to conclude that she could get her mom to stay by exerting sufficient effort. Sometimes after Joan would leave the room and listen outside the door, she wouldn't hear any objection from Elisa, who had become entertained by the worship leaders, the other kids, and me; then Joan would leave for the adult service. I remember one occasion when Joan stepped outside but left the door slightly ajar. When Elisa looked up and saw her mom looking in, with the obvious threat of leaving, Elisa let out a loud cry. Joan came back in and said, "Oh, honey, do you want me to stay?" With a loud wail, Elisa answered, "Yes!" Was Joan responding to the child's concerns or to her own fears? There were other occasions when Joan left the room, listened outside the door, heard Elisa start to cry, then promptly re-entered. What Joan didn't know was that every time Elisa cried in my class (and there were few such occasions), it was when she thought Joan was within hearing range. The rest of the time she was a very contented child. I'm sure Elisa never cried for more than a minute during her seven months in my care. The weaning process must be agonizing for parents; I sympathize with them.

Joan could have stayed with us as long as she wanted; maybe she just didn't realize it and I didn't make the offer sufficiently clear. I was uncomfortable around Joan; maybe I was concerned that she might misinterpret my asking her to stay with us as flirtatious. At this late date, I just don't remember how clearly I conveyed the offer to her. It was not uncommon for parents to stay with their children, and when they did, it was a treat for me: I enlisted their assistance. In all cases, they were more than willing to help. And even though I loved the kids, my real joy in life was communicating with adults involved in my ministry. Fellowship with them while serving the kids was very enjoyable. In the weeks immediately preceding the accusation, a woman new to the church stayed with me for her son's benefit. She also had a nine-year-old daughter who was very fearful of going to her own class. I just kept the mom and both youngsters with me for a few weeks, and eventually introduced the daughter to her would-be teacher. By the time of the accusation, all three were regularly and cheerily attending the group of their peers, having gained peace of mind by exposure to me and my class.

The boy in this family left me with a special fond memory, though I only knew him for a few weeks. He wasn't physically active, but he was challenging in other ways. He would verbalize very negative things in adult form; not foul language, but pessimistic. He would try to convince me, for example, that he should abandon his construction projects because they were doomed to failure. As I've said before, I try to encourage people. I do recall feeling as if I had on a couple of occasions shown this child that his pessimism was unnecessary. The fond memory was generated the last time I ever saw this family. I went to the church to meet with Rev. Jake and three of my friends to complain about how my case had been handled. The boy's mother was saying some nice things to me as I approached the church. She directed my attention to the fact that her son was calling to me from the backseat of their car, saying, "I love you." God knows that boy is my true witness, in contrast to the false witnesses who made life so unbearable for Darcie and me.

How the Class Was Conducted

During the first year with the toddlers, I switched classrooms with Rev. Jake's wife. The new room, which was the scene of the alleged crime, was rectangular, with a six-foot-tall supply cabinet in one corner. Nothing else other than table and chairs was in the room. Everything there was at all times in clear view of every person in the room. We'd keep the table folded up during worship. After the worship leaders left, I'd have the kids help me unfold and set up the table, which they loved to do, then place the chairs. Then the kids would seat themselves. The youngest ones needed help doing so. During the remaining forty-five minutes, the kids were not forced to stay seated at all times, but they usually did so. Probably 70 percent of my pupils in that second year were girls; that made things more manageable. Bill Cosby once made an insightful remark about young girls being capable of sitting politely for a period of time, while their male counterparts could do so only if someone laced their milk with Thorazine. My lack of a rigid requirement for the kids to stay seated wasn't a major problem.

The first item on our weekly agenda was a Bible story. I would bring specially made materials to enhance the story. There were fifty-two unique Bible stories, suggested by the teacher's manual. The kids seemed fascinated with the story on most occasions. Of course, there were days when their attention was fixed elsewhere, and the story seemed a wasted effort. But I would reinforce the story during the remaining time as we performed the other activities. After the story, we'd get out the crayons. The kids would color a picture that reinforced the week's theme. On rare occasions, a child would ask to do something other than color, such as work with Play-Doh. Those requests were politely denied. Our coloring sessions went smoothly. I probably taught that class for eighty weeks, and all eighty times, my adult assistants and I lavished the kids with praise about what a great job they had done coloring their pictures. More often than not, the older child helper would enjoy a coloring session of her own during this period.

Once the coloring session was over, the kids got a snack. This was another reason why the older kids were so willing to help with the toddlers; they were never left out of snack privileges. Each week I would ask if any of the toddlers wanted to help by passing out napkins or cups. There was never a shortage of eager volunteers, and, as the months passed, I tried to make sure each child got an opportunity to help. Seldom could I get a volunteer to say a pre-snack prayer, so I would say one, along the lines of: "Jesus, thank you for the milk and cookies; Amen." Then things would get unusually quiet as the kids had their snack. This brief interval gave me a moment to collect my thoughts, speak a few more words to reinforce the day's lesson, and regain my energy for the remaining class time. My description might make it sound as though teaching this class was easy, but it wasn't. A few days before the accusation, a brave man, who worked every Sunday in the nursery across the hall with his wife, and had heard the noise from my class for nineteen months, remarked, "I don't see how Paul Grey can stand it working with the twos and threes." The answer is, God gave me the necessary patience. In my pre-Christian days, I wouldn't have been able to bear it.

Once we got the snack remnants cleaned up, we would have some type of construction activity. It would frequently involve construction paper and glue sticks, but the kids made many other things, such as macaroni necklaces. The construction activity would also reinforce the weekly lesson. On the very last day I ever taught, for example, the lesson was from Genesis, about when God created animals. The Bible story before coloring time involved the kids trying to mimic various animals. For the construction activity, they made turtles. Construction paper legs, head, and tail were fastened to a paper plate, which they colored green.

Each year, Phil would order a set of colored five-by-seven-inch cards that depicted the story of the week, with a short narrative summary on back. Each child would take one card home to keep. When our construction activity got underway, we never knew when the parents might start showing up. I tried to place in each parent's hand the child's construction project, the lesson card, and the crayon artwork. This trio of common-theme items provided parents an excellent opportunity to reinforce the child's lesson during the following week, teaching according to their parental preferences. To make it possible to send the children home with their own things, my helpers and I would write the kids' names on their work before they walked away from it. When possible, we'd staple the three items together to minimize the chance of things getting misplaced.

The total time I spent with the kids each Sunday was about seventy-five minutes. Other adults — worship leaders — were with me for the first twenty to thirty.

The Mother's Police Statement

Nearly all the names I use in this book are fictitious. I do this to protect identities. I use real names when I mention some professionals in the field. My reason for protecting my own identity is simple: no one in our new community thinks that Darcie and I might be child molesters, but if they heard that I had once been accused, some who don't know me would assume guilt. We don't want to sacrifice the peace of mind we enjoy in our community.

Other than the alteration of names and addresses, the following is the mother's statement to the police, verbatim, with no omissions:

> My daughter Elisa and I attend (Rev. Jake's) church on (Anystreet in Smithville). While attending church services Elisa attends the Sunday school. I have been suspicious of her teacher (Paul Grey) from the first time I met him about 7 months ago because he paid so much attention to Elisa. He would continually comment about how pretty she is. I thought this abnormal. He would also put a chair next to him and have her sit next to him or he would put her on his lap automatically. On 03/21/93, when I arrived to pick Elisa up from Sunday school, I saw Paul Grey about to sit her on his lap. But when he saw me he stopped and put her down. He then handed me her papers with his right hand and appeared to be covering up his genital area with his left arm. It then appeared to me he had an erection and I tried to see if this was true but he kept trying to cover himself with his left arm. While driving home after we left church I asked Elisa if he always put her on his lap? She said yes. I then asked if he put other kids on his lap? She said no. I then asked her does he move around with her on his lap? She said he wiggles. She then said wiggle, wiggle, wiggle, and laughed. This morning when she woke up I asked her does she remember when I asked her about her teacher (Paul Grey). She said yes. Then I asked her if he touches her anywhere? She said yes and patted her genital

> area. I then asked her if he has her touch him? She said no. I then asked does it hurt when she gets touched by him. She said yes, he hurts my booboo. For the past three months when I would wipe her genital area she would say be careful I have a booboo, or don't wipe my booboo. I have noticed redness in her genital area but I thought that it was from her potty training and she had been wiping herself the wrong way in her genital area. Elisa is 3 yrs old. She was born 02/22/90. I also had asked how he touched her? She said with his finger, and pushed hard against her genital area and stated, "ooh." I then asked her if she likes when he touches her? She said, "no, it hurts."

I'll discuss this statement later in some detail.

Welcome to Wonderland

As I prepare to discuss life after the accusation, I feel compelled to quote at length from Frank Lee, in a *VOCAL/Colorado* article he authored. (VOCAL stands for Victims Of Child Abuse Laws). I have never met or corresponded with Mr. Lee. I cannot improve on his words, which are right on the money.

> According to Lewis Carroll, a little girl once fell into a deep, deep hole and before her experience ended she found her every value, her very judgment — even her sanity — questioned, twisted, and perverted.
>
> Being falsely accused of sexually abusing a child is nearly identical to Alice's bizarre adventure. When you look back upon it, you will label it — without exception — the *most* insulting, the *most* humiliating, the *most* devastating experience of your entire life!
>
> No matter who you are or what your past experience, I guarantee that you will not escape the attack of this dragon without deep scars on your emotions and your psyche. You *can*, however, take steps to minimize the destruction to your life and integrity.

Falling, Falling, Falling The first thing you will probably experience is total fear, confusion and bewilderment. Disorientation. Disbelief. You'll be shocked and overwhelmed. You'll probably ask a thousand times, "How can this be happening?" "How could it happen to *me*?"

Your blood will turn cold each time the phone or doorbell rings, or an unidentified automobile pulls into your driveway. Panic will overtake you when a stranger approaches.

And self-pity will engulf you. In your heart and in your mind, you'll go over and over and over again the things your friends, neighbors, acquaintances, co-workers—perhaps even your spouse and children — have forgotten, that you are a good provider, that you have cared deeply for others, and worked and sacrificed for their welfare!

Why? Why? Why? Next you will question yourself, your wife, your friends — even your God. "Why me? Why are they doing this? What have I ever done to them?

Into the Maelstrom Though your life has just been forced into the most confusing maze ever devised by diabolical minds, your every step will be monitored, (mis)interpreted, and reported.

When you become enraged at the injustice (and the more it becomes real to you, the more you *will* become furious), you will be labeled "defensive." If you deny guilt, the social workers and "therapists" will inform you that since all child molesters deny guilt, denying guilt proves guilt; however, if you do as they ask, and question your own heart and motives, rather than being satisfied with your sincerity they'll shout in triumph over the total destruction of your confidence, "*Gotcha!*"

Join the Club Let me begin by assuring you that you are not alone. Like you, thousands in the past decade have experienced the feelings of their minds becoming whirlpools. Estimates place the percentage of false allegations anywhere between 65% and

92% of all reports made. Though you certainly feel like it in those first critical hours, you are not alone!

Who Are They? Perhaps only you know your accuser and why he/she has made the false allegation. Many are vindictive spouses, eager to hurt, punish for lost love, and so on. Often, babysitters, neighbors, "professionals" or even friends or relatives make a report out of jealousy, ignorance, unsubstantiated suspicion — or even spite for some non-related event.

The "Crusaders" But as for those who pose as "investigators" of the charges, there is more certainty. Some are air-headed idealists who have, in the midst of a pandemic hysteria, convinced themselves that every touch, every caress, every caring gesture by a male is sexual and therefore constitutes abuse.

Many are man-hating feminists who either were or imagine themselves to have been abused by a male in the past and have projected their feelings about *one* perpetrator upon an entire gender.

Keep in mind that just like the Spanish Inquisition, you face a stacked deck: accusation by one who, if he/she recants, will be guilty of perjury; investigation by police who are rewarded only for arrests that result in conviction; prosecution by district or county attorneys who are promoted or win re-election by their percentage of guilty verdicts; evaluation by "expert witnesses" who will risk neither their reputations nor their future fees by disappointing the prosecutors who hire and pay them; judgment by juries that have been brainwashed into thinking that every man is a (potential or actual) abuser; trial by judges who are re-elected by appearing hard on offenders.

Even your defense attorney will receive the same payment whether you are convicted or not and *may* even consider your conviction a bonus. *There is nothing to be gained in your acquittal by any of these persons except you!*

The Steamroller Once the process is launched it is virtually impossible to halt. After a psychologist has declared that your accuser suffers from post-traumatic stress syndrome, to learn that no sexual abuse exists would convict him/her of (a) lying or (b) causing the very stress he/she "discovered."

After a district attorney has invested time, energy and reputation into convincing a grand jury of your guilt, more would be willing to fabricate evidence to substantiate that stand than could ever find the courage to admit error.

The Constitution Doesn't Apply to You In high school civics class, you learned that you are presumed innocent until proven guilty — beyond a reasonable doubt. You were also told that you have the right to face your accuser and have him/her questioned by competent counsel, and that hearsay evidence cannot be used against you.

Know this: None of the above applies in your case. Hiding behind "the innocence of childhood," it is very likely that your accuser will give "testimony" taught him/her by professional counselors or prosecutors by way of videotape and never be questioned, or that cross-examination will be with kid gloves due to fear of prejudicing a jury.

Survival Checklist

- If a child is not your own, avoid any unnecessary contact.
- Volunteer nothing. What you consider innocent statements, photos, love notes, etc., can and will be used against you in ways you never dreamed possible.
- No matter how good the offer sounds, *never* waive *any* rights or plead *nolo contendere*; in your case that translates to "guilty" and some day you'll pay a heavy price for your compromise (prison time or probation, heavy fine, community service, mandatory and highly abusive therapy, having to admit guilt which will aid in future convictions, separation from your family, *inability to have your case reopened if and when the truth should be found, etc.).*

- Prepare for the biggest shock of your life. Complete strangers will come to your aid while beloved and trusted friends, close associates, and even relatives will betray and abandon you. Be prepared to be called all manner of names that you've never heard before.
- Recognize from the start that your life will never be the same, even if you are exonerated. You will never again feel really free to express love for children.

Nicaragua

Another part of the story needs mention here, to further illustrate my standing in the church when the accusation occurred. The man who led the Friday-evening prayer group at our house was in charge of HOLA, an organization that supported an orphanage in Nicaragua. When we started attending Rev. Jake's church, Darcie and I chose to keep a distance from the Nicaraguan ministry. In college, I had taken fifteen credit hours of Russian, and I wanted to put it to use if I got involved in any type of foreign outreach. Although Central America was not in my plans, eventually we felt that God wanted us to take on a Nicaraguan commitment. We did, with the expectation of a lifelong responsibility.

Our monthly pledge was linked to a specific boy at the orphanage: Javier. Within a month or two of our taking on this commitment, the HOLA leader introduced, for prayer, plans for an upcoming trip to the orphanage. Within weeks, I was on the list of adults who would be making the trip. I wrote to tell Javier I would be visiting. During this time, I diligently studied Spanish, which I had not done for twenty-five years.

Seven adults from our church went, including Mary (my classroom assistant), and the HOLA leader. Mary's brother, a non-Christian from another city, also went. Two women from another sponsoring church in Oregon joined us in Miami.

One of my friends, whom I had known before our switch to Rev. Jake's church, was scared to death about going. She had tried to back out, but the tickets were non-refundable. She went. We spent lots of time encouraging her, and she grew to love it there.

On Sunday morning, a few hours after our arrival, we were ushered to two buses, where the kids awaited us for the half-hour trip to church. I asked a few people where I could find Javier. They pointed toward the back of the bus. When I joined Javier, it was a complete surprise to him to see me. He didn't speak a word of English. He told me that he had written me four times. I had received only the first letter. My letter telling him of my upcoming visit never reached him; typical of the inefficiencies in Nicaragua. The information sheet Darcie and I had received about him was in error. He was sixteen years old, not fourteen. One of the things I told him on the trip was that during the next five days I wouldn't be spending all my time with him, but that he could know with confidence that he was my special one above all the others. My intent was to spend time with all the kids at the orphanage, so none of them would be neglected. Javier understood. The children there cherish their relations with their sponsoring families, and the vast majority of sponsors were not present — on that trip or any other.

The orphanage did not have a large group of very young kids. Instead, it was a rural community that was linked to the mother church in the big city of Managua. Fewer than twenty children under the age of thirteen lived there. There were more than twenty teenagers, and also quite a few adults. There was only one orphan under the age of six; Mary was infatuated with her. The community also encompassed a farm attempting several types of crops.

The children's director there was a reverent young man who worked for IBM before he left the U.S. to wholly give himself to this ministry. One of the ten visiting Americans gave him a present someone had sent: a briefcase, stocked with underwear. (Jim was in the practice of giving away everything he owned, and had no underwear as a result.) One of the things he told us in preparation for our five days there was, "Please don't neglect the adults completely; the kids aren't the only ones who need your encouragement." I took his words to heart as much as any of us did. Five of the visitors, including Mary and her brother, were a nonstop whirlwind of activity among the kids. I felt like spending more of my time with the less conspicuous adults and teenagers, taking advantage of my Spanish. It was the best time I've ever had in my life. I deeply regret that these Nicaraguan friends have been taken from me.

By the time we left Nicaragua, Javier and eleven other teenagers had asked me to correspond with them. I did this for the next seventeen months, until the accusation occurred. I wrote each of them a different letter several times a year. A friend who was raised in Puerto Rico helped me by correcting my written Spanish. I added an adult Nicaraguan couple to my correspondence list in the final months. Darcie and I were on the verge of becoming lifetime sponsors for these godly adult workers. I typically spent four or five hours a week writing letters to (and reading letters from) all my Nicaraguan friends. In some cases, my letters were the only ones the teenagers ever got; their sponsors never wrote.

Just before I was introduced to one of the teenage girls at the orphanage, I was told that she had been sobbing for a long time before meeting us, because her sponsor, one of Rev. Jake's most avid followers, had several months earlier ceased all communication with her. This happened after the poor child had bared her soul, telling her sponsor the awful details of her history. Months later, I learned why the sponsor chose to cut the girl off so abruptly: "I just couldn't handle it." I choose to reveal this story because I believe it really does describe how some of Rev. Jake's followers conduct themselves when scandalous allegations are afloat: they choose to run from the scene, to avoid discomfort. The vast majority of Christians I have known are unlike the poor examples discussed herein.

We didn't just hang out at the orphanage all week. One night we visited the hospital in Managua. What I recall most vividly was a room with eight adult patients in it. Each was on a bed barely wide enough for one person. There were cockroaches on the walls, and no chairs for visitors. Since most people down there don't have cars or transportation home other than their legs, the visitors would typically choose to stay at the hospital for extended periods. That means they'd either have to stand or get into the very narrow bed with the patient.

Of the eight in that room, two accepted Jesus that night; a third seemed well on the way when someone came and made us leave to join the others in the waiting bus. One of the two who chose to receive Jesus had a patch over one eye. The other eye looked at us with clear recognition. After we spoke awhile, he asked his wife to hand him a transparent bag, inside which was a shattered bullet that the doctors had removed from deep beneath the now-bandaged eye. I know that my friend from Rev. Jake's church who was in that room with our Nicaraguan host and me will never forget the moment when the patient gave his life to Christ in spectacular verbal fashion. My friend was so overwhelmed that he had to leave the room for a while.

Please note the fact that after the trip to Nicaragua, I had more contact with the people at the orphanage than anyone else from our church had. Rev. Jake knew of little more than a few programmatic aspects of the orphanage. That was also his relation with Sunday school.

Another Police Statement

I interacted with the vast majority of adults in Rev. Jake's church, chatting with them every chance I got. During the seventeen months preceding the accusation, when friends asked me what I was up to, I would regularly mention to them that HOLA was my primary ministry, more than Children's Church. Darcie had taken on collecting monthly checks from the dozens of HOLA sponsors and doing all the associated accounting. When she took on that role, she corrected a chaotic situation, as the leader of HOLA acknowledged. Our work also involved getting out a monthly newsletter and reminder to every sponsor.

There were sponsors from Alaska, Mississippi, New England, Oregon, and many other states.

During the Sunday evening service, just a few hours after the last time I ever taught, I met for a while with Mary and our friend, Linda (who had been so terrified about going to Nicaragua). We spent some time praying for Linda, who was experiencing serious short-term depression. Mary hadn't been attending Rev. Jake's church for a year, but she was contemplating going to Nicaragua for a missionary visit of several months. After we prayed for Linda, and in Linda's presence, I mentioned to Mary that I identified with her in that her two ministries were children and Nicaragua, just like my own. Taking into account my full-time job with the military lab, plus other church commitments, these two ministries really took up all my spare time, so I identified with my HOLA co-workers and with my fellow Sunday school teachers very strongly.

Here, verbatim, is what Mary wrote about me at the police station a few days later:

> I was an assistant in the 2-3 year old Sunday school group at (Rev. Jake's) church in (Smithville) for approx. nine months from August of '91 until May of 1992, under Paul Grey. Paul always seemed nice, but was very quiet so I don't know him well. However, I will never forget the first time I met him at the church, I saw Paul go up to a retarded thirteen-year-old boy in the sanctuary and ask if he could pray with him. The boy left the room with Paul for about three minutes, then I saw his mother go and get him. I had a bad feeling about that at the time, but didn't think of it again until now.
>
> In October of 1991, I traveled to Nicaragua with Paul and some other people to the orphanage we sponsor there. We check up on the place and try to build relationships with the children. Paul sponsored a boy there, and my brother, John Doe, mentioned that Paul went off with that boy while in Nicaragua. Paul's wife was not on the trip.
>
> Paul seems comfortable with the children and I have

> seen him be affectionate with them. I happened to be at church the Sunday before I heard about these allegations, and Paul asked me to take a little girl to the bathroom. There were about eight little children in his class, and when I got back, he had a little dark-haired girl on his lap. She was new to the class and I can't remember her name, but Paul told me what her name was and said she was a very special little girl.
>
> There were always two people in the classroom with the little ones, except for when someone was on a bathroom trip. I never saw Paul kiss a child on the mouth or do anything inappropriate.

Mom's Call to the Police

Early on a Wednesday in March 1993, Darcie and I were awakened by a phone call. It was Phil, on the verge of tears. He told me Joan was making an accusation about sexual molestation perpetrated on Elisa. I didn't even realize I was the accused (I thought it must have been the child's father) until he spelled it out for me. Earlier, Phil had received a call from Joan, whose single purpose was to get my name, which she didn't even know, so she could relay it to the police. She was not *asking* Phil for his opinion of me, as she had months earlier. Phil and his wife then prayed for me, and for Joan and Elisa, for the remainder of the night. Phil called Rev. Jake and asked him what should be done. Rev. Jake quickly formulated a strategy. He told Phil to have me come over to his house that evening, "and we'll just listen to what's going on."

Joan called the police after she got my name from Phil. A state inspector eventually visited Joan's house, and asked questions about the allegation as Elisa sat on Joan's lap.

Emergency Room Exam

Joan went to her job that morning, but was emotionally incapable of her duties. She ended up taking Elisa to the Emergency Room to be examined. The nurse who took notes of their visit noted that Elisa had "Just wet pants." The five things noted by the examining physician were: "Soft; no tenderness. Vulva normal. Erythema around interior (last word very short but indecipherable). Hymen appears to be intact. No discharge noted." (*Erythema* means "redness.")

The story became rampant in Rev. Jake's church that the exam had concluded that sexual molestation *may* have occurred. The local newspaper later reported that the results of the medical exam were consistent with sexual assault. I don't know if they even saw the actual report.

If readers can picture themselves going to work after having received a phone call like the one I got from Phil that morning, then perhaps they can understand a bit of what it was like. Being identified as an accused child molester was far worse than anything I could ever imagine. Knowing full well that I had been serving God more faithfully than at any other time, I was convinced that He wouldn't let such a crazy destruction of my life happen. When I got to the office, I told the two men in the cubicle next to mine what had happened; they are both kindred spirits who are very mature and who love kids. They were quite sympathetic. When my office mate of six years arrived, she, bless her heart, spent most of the day, despite her pressing duties, trying to reassure me. Her own kids were about two and four; encouraged by my daily example, she and her husband had taken initiative to provide Sunday school services for toddlers at their Catholic church. Every Monday, she'd ask about my teaching experiences the preceding day. She was in full agreement with me that such a crazy accusation would quickly fall apart.

Rev. Jake Gets Involved

After work, just hours after the accusation, I went to Rev. Jake's house, as he had requested. At his initiative, I spoke with him not only that evening, but on several other occasions.

At the time, Rev. Jake had two elders, Phil, and Elder #2; he had several months earlier stripped a third one of his elder status after the man became very popular while teaching on Sunday evenings. Rev. Jake also had another avid follower whom he wished to designate as an elder. (Most outsiders would describe this man as being Rev. Jake's bodyguard.) So, the meeting at Rev. Jake's house involved myself, Rev. Jake, who led the entire meeting, the other two elders, and the elder-to-be. Phil was asked to begin things by relating Joan's story. He told us that Elisa had awakened, "screaming," from a nightmare, then had proceeded to tell Joan "things that a child can't possibly know about." Phil acted extremely upset, which surprised me. The police, according to what Rev. Jake told me two weeks later, never showed any interest in talking to Phil; they always insisted on talking to Rev. Jake. Incidentally, Phil knew me about a hundred times better than Rev. Jake did.

Before Rev. Jake abruptly ended the meeting, asking me to leave, he tried to get me to sign a few things. He also had given a clipboard to each of his three "elders" and told them to write down things I said at the meeting. Rev. Jake wrote copiously. The other three men wrote little, if anything.

Rev. Jake went to the police the next day. I didn't see his written statement until two months later, and had no reason to suspect that he would have done anything to harm me. Thus, I was unaware that he wrote, among other things, "We told Paul of the accusation against him without details. He flat out denied it. Paul stated, 'Obviously you're talking about grabbing her crotch.' Then he stated, 'What else could it be?' He also mentioned at this time, 'When you pick up a child, your long fingers would touch the breast area.' Looking back now, I feel these comments might be significant."

Immediately after Rev. Jake went to the police and wrote his statement, the police decided to arrest me. I didn't know that they had made such a decision, or that Rev. Jake had written anything negative. I was still convinced that the accusation would be seen for what it really was, and the case would be dropped. I was utterly convinced of this for the next two agonizing months. During this time, Rev. Jake would call me "to see how things were going." I still thought I was talking with a friend, someone from my own church family, *not* my accuser. I was confused about how he argued with everything I said concerning my case. He implied, time after time, that the police had all sorts of concrete evidence against me, but that he as a pastor was not allowed to share it with me.

The other three men at the meeting were made to vow to keep silent about circumstances involving the accusation, thereby leaving Rev. Jake as sole spokesperson. My case was narrated to our friends according to Rev. Jake's interpretation.

I considered Phil one of my best friends. After all, I had dedicated the majority of my "free" time to helping him with the kids for three years, and clearly had helped him more than anyone else. He was my junior by more than ten years. In contrast, Rev. Jake never once set foot in the Children's Church activities. Aside from listening to his Sunday morning sermons, I had little contact with him; when I did, it was usually brief. This was calculated on my part: pastors are usually pretty swamped by people with needs, and I wanted to help by keeping Rev. Jake's time free for the important aspects of his ministry. Most assuredly, I felt no inclination to try to impress him in any way. Christians I've known in the past have had good discernment, and I merely assumed that Rev. Jake was one of them. I had ignored a couple of warning signs indicating otherwise, but I didn't want to be "overly judgmental."

Prior to the accusation, I often prayed for the adults at that church. Of all the adults I had spoken with more than five times, I probably spent personal time, praying for their special needs, for about 90 percent. But I knew that my personal prayer time, alone before the Lord, wasn't what it should be; my motivation was low. I mentioned this once to Rev. Jake to see if he had any suggestions. He suggested that I use the time when I drove to work, using some prominent landmark along the way to remind me of what I was supposed to be doing. I took his suggestion, and it worked like a charm. (Chalk up one good point for Rev. Jake.) Each day as I drove to work, I began my routine by praying for Rev. Jake and his family. This wasn't a new thing in my life; Scripture exhorts us to pray for church leaders. (I Thes. 5:25.) Anyway, for well over a year, I spent a few minutes each day praying for Rev. Jake. Of course he didn't know about it, nor did anyone else, another of the many ironies of my case.

Rev. Jake is seven years my junior. The majority of occasions when I spoke with him were times when, before or after work, or after Sunday morning services, I stopped by to use the office copier for HOLA work or Sunday school work. There was never any unpleasantness during these encounters. Rev. Jake didn't know all the adults in the church. He didn't know Joan, though she had been attending there for over a year, and he had no interaction with the kids. He knew the children of his long-time followers, and that was about it. Since I knew virtually all the kids and all the adults, I knew more people who currently attended the church than Rev. Jake did.

When a church consists of only a few dozen families, interaction among them over a three-year period tends to encompass their lives. Typically, the adults who are heavily involved in ministries spend most of their free time on those volunteer activities. The remainder of their "free" time is taken up by the things all families must do: shopping, housework, phone calls, letters, etc. Special church events occupy additional time. So, for these volunteers, church is basically their whole life. I've become quite close to many Christians over the years within less than a month of getting to know them. Three years in such a setting seems like forever. For the church leaders, family-like trust within the group is even higher. I took pains to encourage rather than criticize the leadership. At the risk of sounding immodest, my role in that church was one of servanthood, which Jesus identified as the best indicator of proper behavior. (Matt. 20:26.) In contrast, Rev. Jake thought my behavior was "odd," as will be seen when I discuss his courtroom testimony.

One More Statement to the Police

After I left our initial meeting, Elder #2, according to Rev. Jake, said, "I don't think he did it." But a few days after Elder #2 spoke these words, his wife wrote a police statement about me. Their daughter, Dottie, had been in my class for nineteen months. I think she only missed one Sunday. That means I logged more time with that child than almost any other I have ever been around. Phil's daughter probably had more time with me than Dottie, because of her attendance Sunday evenings. This shows one of the illogical things about my being treated with such suspicion: the daughters of both elders in that church, including Rev. Jake's own niece, had been in that class with me every day of the nineteen months I taught it.

Elder #2 and his wife had never been involved with Children's Church during my three years there. The final day I ever taught, when Elder #2's wife dropped off Dottie, I thought I would share with her an indicator of how Dottie was important to me. I told the mother that I chose DOTTIE to be my computer password at work. She was touched to hear it, and rightly so.

Yet, a few days later, something possessed this woman to write to the police a statement making me look bad:

> "My family and I have been members of (Rev. Jake's) church in (Smithville) for approx. eight years.
>
> We first met Paul Grey when he came into our group with another church. Our daughter Dorothy "Dottie" was in Paul Grey's Sunday school group for the past two years. Dottie turned four in January.
>
> My husband is an elder in the church. When I heard of the accusations against Paul Grey, I immediately thought

of my daughter's reluctance to go to Sunday school for the last couple of months. She would throw a fit when I'd try to leave her there — which I did — and I'd almost have to pull her off of me. I attributed this to the fact that my husband and I had been on a trip for two weeks, but I realize that it had started before we left.

After the accusation was made, I asked Dottie about "bad touches." At first she said "no," but then she told me that a little boy (younger than she) who had been visiting us had given her a bad touch in the bathtub.

I never witnessed anything inappropriate at Sunday school, but I feel Paul Grey is a strange man.

Now that I think about it, he said something that I thought was odd. He told me that he used Dottie's name in his computer program at work.

Dottie has not been upset at going to Sunday school since Paul Grey left.

My older daughter Brittany is 11. During the past year, off and on, she has been a helper in Paul Grey's class. We have talked about this in the house, and Brittany told me that Paul Grey held Elisa on his lap all the time. She also told me that before Elisa was there, he used to hold a little girl named Jasmine like that."

Dottie's mother was on the right track when she said she had previously believed that Dottie's unusual behavior coincided with the parents' trip to Chile. I remember the occasion during that period when Dottie was extremely upset. Her mother, as she dropped Dottie off in class, told me it was just a phase she was going through. Dottie was a climber, a real action figure. She never showed a desire to sit on my lap as many other kids did. She just wanted to engage in activities. On the rare occasions when Brittany assisted me, she would have Dottie get on her lap during worship time, and Dottie usually didn't object (sometimes she did). On the day that Dottie was so upset, I held her on my lap for about ten minutes, while she sobbed and sobbed. This was heartbreaking to me, considering that I had spent so much time with that child over the years, and this is the only occasion I ever recall holding her on my lap. But I felt she would eventually come out of her depression. Meanwhile, Gary and Kate were about eight feet away, face to face with Dottie and me. I saw the positive sign start to come when Gary and Kate launched into the song that begins, "If I were a butterfly, I'd thank you, Lord, for giving me wings." The kids would gesture with their hands to emulate the creatures in the song. I could see that Dottie was at least thinking about making a butterfly with her hands. Also, she was all cried out. Within another minute or two, she hopped off my lap and was fine for the rest of the hour. I'm sure that Dottie had been upset for a long time about her parents leaving her, and that's what her mother had noticed.

Concerning Brittany's statement, "before Elisa was there, he used to hold a little girl named Jasmine like that," Jasmine's mother wrote a letter in my behalf as the trial approached. I saw Jasmine one summer day, many months after the trial had ended, at a family get-together. She remembered when she used to attend my class. With a big smile, she gave this summary: "That was fun." I recall another child, Chrissy, who spent a lot more time on my lap than Elisa did. She was in the class of four-year-olds taught by Rev. Jake's wife when the accusation occurred; so was Jamine. I saw Chrissy at her parents' house about a year after the trial. She said that she didn't even remember me. She sure did like me, however.

Summary of the State's Case

Four people wrote statements for the police. The statements, the medical exam results that I quoted in their entirety, and the inspector's very brief interview with the child, comprised the entire police case against me. There was nothing else.

The warrant for my arrest was just the state inspector's review of the written statements, the medical exam, and the interview. The warrant ended with the following paragraphs:

> That Rev. Jake Grozny stated that the church has always addressed the issue of safety, for the adults, the children, and to avoid the appearance of evil. However, although the procedure has been to always have someone else in the classroom, he can state that in the past two months, this system has not been carried out correctly by Paul Grey, and it's possible that he had the opportunity to be alone with a child.
>
> That based on the aforementioned facts and circumstances this detective believes that probable cause does exist to charge Paul Grey . . . with Sexual Assault in the 1st degree, and Injury or Risk of Injury to Children.

A Case of Real Child Abuse

Meanwhile, to try to bolster the case, the witch-hunters used a child. In their zealotry, they asked Dottie's older sister, Brittany, to testify against me. The prosecutor simply wanted her to say, on the witness stand, that I held Elisa on my lap "all the time," just as her mother had written in her statement. The most despicable part is that Brittany had been sexually molested at home by a member of Rev. Jake's church just weeks prior to the accusation against me. The police knew about this. The state inspector had broken down in tears when she was at Brittany and Dottie's house interviewing them about my case.

Rev. Jake had told me that there was a case of sexual molestation in his church not long before the accusation against me was made (the case I just mentioned). He tried to persuade me that he knew from experience that even the most seemingly stable individuals might be guilty of this great crime. The man in this case was someone I didn't know, and, as I've said, I knew just about everyone in that church. Brittany's parents made the mistake of letting this unmarried young man baby-sit their three daughters in their home. When Brittany disclosed what had happened, Rev. Jake believed the man rather than believing her, so I'm told. Rev. Jake told me several times how the man denied the charge, then confessed, and cried, and Rev. Jake cried, and then they went to the police station. Anyway, the guilty young man was truly an unknown in the church, whereas I was among the most known and trusted.

The Days Following the Accusation

The most incredibly uncanny aspect of our lives after the accusation was the resounding silence of our telephone. Can you imagine having your child die, and nobody bothering to call you to express sympathy? That's what it was like. Within two weeks, everyone in the church knew of the accusation, but no one called. This was absolutely devastating to us. It was as if each of our good friends let us know that they really didn't care about us enough to be sullied by our personal problems. Can you imagine just two of your best friends telling you this within a week? In our case, it was dozens of our favorite people. They might as well have sent us a letter, signed by all, saying, "We never thought much of you anyway." Even years after the incident, I'm stunned at their lack of consideration.

Just one week after the last time I taught Sunday school, Rev. Jake made an announcement to the church — from the pulpit — about the accusation. He didn't mention my name. One witness remembers him saying, "He's not going to get away with this." The congregation must have been greatly shocked, and wondering who this monster could be. Rev. Jake, remember, had made the other elders vow to keep silent on the matter.

At the meeting at Rev. Jake's house the evening following the accusation, Rev. Jake asked me what "we" should do about it. I tried to give him a response that I thought would be acceptable to everyone, so nobody would harbor any fears. First I said I would stop teaching Sunday school until the accusation was resolved. Then I realized that as long as I went to that church, kids would be approaching me and jumping onto my lap. Also, I didn't want Joan to stop attending because of me. So I explained to Rev. Jake and the others that, to make sure no parents would be uncomfortable, Darcie and I would just attend another church while the situation was settled. Rev. Jake relayed my offer to the congregation as follows: "It looks like a wolf has gotten in among our sheep. Since the accusation, this man and his wife have left our church." His implication was clear: the child molester and his wife were trying to escape justice.

A week or two after the meeting at Rev. Jake's house, when he spoke with Darcie and me, we tried to clear up the "misunderstanding" that had occurred, since, after we called our friends, they expressed surprise that we had "left the church." At that meeting I said to him, "OK, let's reverse the situation; how can we get back in?" He didn't respond. I asked a second and a third time. Finally, on the fourth time, he mumbled, "Well, I'd have to talk it over with the leadership." It was dawning on me where the real problem was. Darcie had spotted it much earlier; I had chosen, temporarily, to stay in denial. I finally recognized the deception: inasmuch as Rev. Jake *is* the leadership in his church, he doesn't have to get agreement from anybody to do anything.

It was ironic that the accusation happened just before Easter. The reality of our utter abandonment by our church family had sunk in by Palm Sunday. The previous year, 1992, I had taken coffee cans in for the Palm Sunday class. We made them red and decorated them; then the kids played their red "drums" while I sang a short song about the triumphal entry of Jesus into Jerusalem. After the accusation, I had the 1993 coffee cans, which I had been collecting all year. I called Phil and asked him to stop by and pick them up so the replacement teacher would have materials to work with. When Phil stopped by to get the cans, I also gave him some photos of the kids. Foolishly, I believed that the police just needed a little evidence to make them see that I didn't have a fascination with any one child, as Brittany's words implied. (I still didn't know about Rev. Jake's written statement to the police). So, I gave Phil two rolls of photos, including the negatives, to give to the police, so it would be clear to them that I was revealing everything. During my nineteen months of teaching the toddlers, I brought my camera to church on two occasions. My goal was to give the parents pictures of their children attending their first year of Sunday school. I felt it was something the families would be glad to have as the years passed. I also took the photos in to work, where they got rave reviews from my co-workers.

There was only one photo of Elisa among all those pictures. In it, she was obviously very happy, digging into the basket of crayons and smiling. I never saw those photographs again. When I had a friend ask Phil about them after the trial, he said he didn't remember any. The police also said they had never seen them.

The Sunday following Palm Sunday is Easter. On that day, the church already had all the teaching materials I had created. We had a big Easter poster that I'd made in 1992, which included a large paper "rock." When you pushed the rock to the side, a hole with a plastic container underneath was revealed, where we temporarily placed the body of Jesus. Dottie was pretty concerned when I had told this story the previous year. Her clear voice asked me, "Why did they put him in the hole?" It's a good question.

The weeks passed and our telephone remained silent. Truly abandoned by our own church family, we couldn't ignore the Scriptural comparison with the disciples' abandonment of Jesus after he was taken into custody, eventually to be crucified. I didn't ponder this similarity very deeply because I don't consider myself worthy of comparison with Jesus in any way. Still, we could have reflected on the similarities; Romans 6:4 gives us Scriptural justification.

Another reprehensible example: Recall that hearsay evidence may not be introduced in a criminal case. In a fax that Rev. Jake sent to the prosecutor's office, he told the prosecutor, "Joan also asked another mother in the classroom what questions to ask her daughter, and the second mother now believes that Paul Grey also molested her daughter." This "second mother" never materialized.

Rev. Jake's proclamation to the police about a second accusing mother represented our biggest fear: that hysteria would produce more allegations. I think the police wished to avoid getting wrapped up in anything like the Satanic Ritual Abuse cases. For one thing, they didn't have the resources; for another, those cases were all being discredited. But the fact is that, with our own pastor telling the police there was at least one more suspected victim of mine, the probability was sky-high that another accuser would appear. Thank God it didn't happen. It was months after the accusation when I learned that Rev. Jake had done this. The state is required to turn over everything to the defense; this fax was given to us months after the statements, the warrant, and the medical exam, but Rev. Jake had sent it not long after the accusation. Nothing in the fax was used against me at trial.

Rev. Jake told not only the police that my list of victims was apparently more than just one child, but he also told this to my friends. One of them said to Rev. Jake on the phone, "Why is everyone so upset about some mother nobody even knows making a crazy claim about her kid?" Rev. Jake authoritatively told him, "it wasn't just one child." This should further clarify why our phone was so incredibly silent following the accusation.

One of our very best friends remained supportive of us, but this support took a nosedive when she got a phone call from Rev. Jake. He literally told her to back off because (he said) he knew what he was doing. He used every bit of spiritual "authority" he could muster, and a number of distortions, to accomplish his goals. And he succeeded.

The feeling Darcie and I had during those bleak months is best described by a scene from a horror movie. Picture a man and wife realizing that aliens are overtaking the people of Earth. Everywhere they turn, the good people of earth are turning into glassy-eyed, murderous creatures with whom communication is impossible, though their appearance hasn't changed. Finally the man and wife run for safety, aliens in pursuit. They run to a safe haven with a few of their most trusted friends.

The aliens give chase, but the little group makes it to safety. As they get inside and lock the massive doors, safe at last, their most trusted friends proceed to reveal their own glassy eyes and break down the door so the aliens can come get the couple.

Although it was devastating, eventually it became clear that the only place where people really treated us like child molesters was Rev. Jake's church. Months after the accusation, we found out why. Even though that group was heavily pressured into treating us like villains, not everyone swallowed it. But the ones who believed in my innocence obediently kept silent.

Supportive Co-Workers

My co-workers at the military lab were of tremendous service to me, including many co-workers from other companies. Every day for those ten and a half months between the accusation and the trial, I would talk with them about what was going on in my life. Each day they supported me for lengthy periods of time. I had discussed every aspect of my case with co-workers on many occasions by the time the trial arrived, and they made it apparent to me that the entire world hadn't gone crazy, merely a certain group of people. I spoke with everyone I knew about the case. Between fifty and a hundred friends sympathized with me at work. I can think of only a couple who seemed to avoid the topic of my tribulations. One was a good friend, and I'm certain that he knew I was innocent. I'm sure the other one did also; I still see him occasionally on business, and he obviously likes me. My co-workers provided me with the best possible environment for psychological survival during the witch-hunt. May God bless them now and forever.

Darcie's plight was much worse than mine was. The overwhelming grief engendered by the witch-hunt nearly killed her. In Pastor Dave's church (prior to Rev. Jake's), she had been on the worship team (she has a degree in flute performance). She had to pull out of her worship team commitments one day because she had suddenly and violently come down with what turned out to be chronic fatigue syndrome. She was afflicted with it for over seven years. It has now gotten much, much better in many measurable ways since we moved away from New England. Her health was at its very worst during the year that we were terrorized by the witch-hunt.

As a result of her lack of energy, she couldn't attend very many events, so she didn't know people at the church to the extent that I did. That's why she had the ministry of running the finances for HOLA. She had been praying for some way she could serve the Lord within her physical limitations, and this was one of the possibilities that was presented, by way of personal request from the woman who had done it previously. That woman was one of Darcie's favorite people in the church. She spent her days at church, so she was in constant contact with Rev. Jake. Several days after the accusation, the young lady told Darcie, on the phone, that there was no reason why Darcie couldn't come to their church and be supported. After all, the lady pointed out, *Darcie* wasn't the perpetrator — her husband was. She quoted the mantra of the day, which we heard more than one good friend say: "I don't really know Paul that well. I don't know what kind of movies he watches, or what magazines he reads." (I had *no* time for movies or magazines in those days). She proceeded to say that she knew a thing or two about spiritual discernment, knew about my case, had spoken with the mother, and used spiritual discernment to determine that Joan was being honest. Her words were "All I can think about is that poor mother and what she must be going through." Those words represent a common element in witch-hunt psychology. We gathered up all the financial information, ongoing correspondence, and materials that were part of the HOLA ministry, delivered them to the woman, and Darcie told her she didn't wish to work with people who thought her husband a child molester. That particular suspicion really does tend to strain a relationship.

All this took place in a county that had a psychiatric hospital; Darcie was a therapist there. The number of co-workers who supported her in daily conversations was smaller than in my case.

It's not that her co-workers were so different from mine; it was due to a number of factors. Darcie and I looked at the world somewhat differently; she assumed everyone who heard about the accusation would think I was guilty (based on our inner circle having turned into "aliens," her logic was perfectly sound), whereas I had a blind optimism that made me feel otherwise. Ignorance is bliss, some say. I had no hesitancy about telling people my story. I recall an engineer who stopped by my office for some reason; I don't even remember if I was the one he had come to see. The only time I ever met this man, he was choked with tears by the time we ended our conversation. He said very supportive things to me after I had related my circumstances. In contrast, Darcie didn't share our story with many people. My co-workers knew me, but Darcie's co-workers didn't, which made them more likely to assume guilt. So, she didn't bring it up very often. I suspect that a hospital setting is a terrible place for trying to keep something like this private. There were times when an animated group would hush when Darcie walked into their presence. Her closest co-workers were lifesavers. May God bless Renee and the others, who were a model we should all try to follow.

There were two basic categories of patients with whom Darcie worked at the psychiatric hospital: those with personality disorders (con men), who were there as an alternative to prison, and those with extreme psychoses, with whom little communication was possible. Darcie was very concerned that some of the con men would read or hear about my case in the local news and torment her with loud, public verbal abuse. The likelihood of this was very high with certain patients who did such things habitually, but it didn't happen. In sum, Darcie had a little bit of support from her workplace, but going there every day was truly agonizing for her. Think of the most broken-hearted day of your life and then imagine every day being like that for nearly a year. That's what Darcie went through.

Nonstop support came from all the people we knew from our pre-New England days. Kansas City had more supporters than anywhere else. Darcie's long-ago best friend, dating back to their junior high school days in Indiana, asked us for our Christmas correspondence list. She then sent a letter to families on the list, telling of our tragedy and inviting them to contribute to our legal costs. She and her husband were constantly in contact with us from that time on, interceding for us in every way possible and collecting information they thought might be helpful toward our defense. Prior to the accusation, we saw this couple only every five years or so. They are the best example of the Good Samaritan that I can think of. In Luke 10:30–34, Jesus says, "A man was going down from Jerusalem to Jericho, when he fell into the hands of robbers. They stripped him of his clothes, beat him and went away, leaving him half-dead. A priest happened to be going down the same road, and when he saw the man, he passed by on the other side. So too, a Levite, when he came to the place and saw him, passed by on the other side. But a Samaritan, as he traveled, came where the man was; and when he saw him, he took pity on him. He went to him and bandaged his wounds, pouring on oil and wine. Then he took the man on his own donkey, and took him to an inn and took care of him." In the parable, the priest and Levite turned their heads because they didn't want to be bothered, even though the victim was one of their own. Rev. Jake's church epitomized such behavior. When a friend of mine went to a small group of Rev. Jake's followers a month after the accusation, and brought up the atrocity of my case, he was hushed with the words "We don't talk about *that*." Back to Jim & Michele, who helped us so admirably: may God bless these Good Samaritan friends now and forever. They set the standard we should all try to follow.

There was one person who did talk about *that*. In a letter he sent out "To Leaders, Workers, and Advisors in the Church," Rev. Jake stated, "We've heard all sides of the story and feel as though we can convey the positions of each side effectively. With this in mind I would like to offer you or anyone you know who is interested or has a need to know an 'open door policy.'

That is, I'll give you as much time as you might need as often as you need it to talk about this issue." In this same letter, he said "I also would like to take the opportunity to thank you and everyone for the maturity that has been demonstrated in this situation to date."

In the days following the accusation, I continued denying that Rev. Jake was trying to make me look guilty. My good friend at work, knowing that I was disinclined to say anything bad about the people in my church, had already given her forthright assessment: "I think Rev. Jake's a jerk." Darcie was also pointing out the reality that Rev. Jake was trying to destroy me. Finally, when Darcie had one of her phone conversations with Phil, he said to her, "Paul's credibility has been going downhill lately." That was so contradictory to the young man I had served for three years that I knew things had changed, and that my leaders had abandoned me. It was perhaps my darkest moment, knowing that my church family had turned against me, but it helped me realize that I should get a lawyer, a need I had until then refused to acknowledge. Finally, I was at least beginning to know where I stood. And I knew that Rev. Jake was the source of the problems. This was a giant step out of the "Welcome to Wonderland" confusion.

One day, the police came to my place of employment. The head of Security showed up at my office and asked me to follow him. He wouldn't tell me what he wanted, but I knew what the subject matter was likely to be. After leading me to a room where two state policemen waited, he left. The state inspector for my case was one of these two. Their intent was to get me to say things my lawyer wouldn't allow me to say had she been with me. That's why they chose to show up unannounced. I called my lawyer. She had just left for court. I hated to tell the police that I didn't want to talk to them. In fact I was absolutely dying to tell what happened, and get some truth into the case. The police told me that this would doubtless be my only chance to tell them my side of the story before it went to the judge. I spoke with the inspector for about half an hour, as her male companion rudely glared at me. In the warrant for my arrest, the inspector said that I had "declined to be interviewed." (She wasn't being truthful). This half-hour chat with the police apparently didn't harm me. However, the reader should be warned: if this happens to you or your loved ones, say nothing at all to the police unless your lawyer is with you.

Polygraph Exam

Using the *Yellow Pages*, I called "Lawyer Referral Service." A woman there told me I should choose an attorney from my own part of the state, because such lawyers have the advantage of knowing the judges. The lawyer who had taught the two- and three-year-olds before me suggested one to me. It was unsettling to meet with the woman he recommended; she said that her approach would be "to go after the father," which meant she would try to make the prosecution prove that the child's words couldn't have been about her father and had to have been about me. Darcie and I didn't want a court date — we wanted the case to get thrown out immediately. The lawyer called the inspector a few times. Even though the inspector seemed to be a very nice person, my lawyer started doubting the truth of just about everything the inspector told her during their conversations. And her skepticism was absolutely justified.

My lawyer told me the police wanted me to take a polygraph exam. In their consistent deception, they told my lawyer that if I "took the poly and passed, they would drop the case." That was a blatant lie. It grieves me that the police, whom in general I would love to support, practice this type of deception so routinely. She was skeptical about the police keeping their word. I had heard the standard admonition that one has nothing to gain and everything to lose by taking a lie detector test, but I still firmly believed that the truth was so blatant in my situation that the police would see their mistake and drop the case. And they were saying the words that struck at the core of my desires: just take the test (and pass it) and you can go free. I still didn't know about all the damaging things Rev. Jake had said to them about me. My lawyer contacted a private polygraph service and suggested I go there first, rather than giving the police complete control over the situation. She was absolutely right in suggesting this.

For those who have lived life without police interaction, I relate a story about the tactics they sometimes use. One night, at age fourteen, I was with my best friend, Gil. We were at the Baptist church a block from his house, up on the fire escape smoking cigarettes, which we would not have been able to do at home. A police car pulled into the parking lot. We ducked so we wouldn't be seen, but they saw us. They called us down, separated us, and questioned us about what we were doing. We were in fact innocent of any thought of wrongdoing, unless you count smoking at fourteen. They kept us separated. Then, after some time had passed, they told me, "Your buddy tells us you were planning to break into the church and get some stuff." They told Gil the same story. I wasn't raised to defy authority, and could not even consider calling the police liars, but the fact is, they were lying. This "police tactic" is fairly common. Nobody would like to believe that the police are blameless individuals more than I would, but it just isn't so. That's why you can't let them control the polygraph process.

Another good friend told me that he had been arrested, years before I ever met him, as a prime murder suspect (he had lived with his uncle, who was the murder victim). The police gave him a polygraph test, and then told him he had better get on his knees and start praying, because the test proved he was lying. Then they left him alone in the room. As a sadly amusing side note, he did get on his knees and pray, perhaps for the first time in his life. He didn't realize that the police were watching him through trick mirrors. It turns out that they were merely lying to him about failing the test; he had actually passed it. Eventually, they got the real murderer, but the fact remains, they were terribly dishonest with my friend.

And they might have treated me in the same manner, if they could have gotten by with it.

Despite the fact that I suffered some police abuses, and my belief that such abuses are not uncommon, I am generally a supporter of the police. They are the only power that keeps our society from complete chaos. Many of them put their very lives in danger every day, even though they typically have young children of their own. They are terribly underpaid. In most cases, I believe that government is too big. The only area of government for which I am in favor of increased spending is the police. That's how highly I value them.

I went to the private polygraph office and took the exam. The man who administered it had an extensive law enforcement background, and an impeccable reputation with the state police. I had never been around a polygraph before, and, being familiar with the design of electronic devices, I was dubious about whether it could really detect when I was telling the truth. I can't remember all ten questions he asked. The first was "Is your name Paul Grey?" One of them was "Did you ever put your finger in Elisa's vagina?" Another was "Did you ever put anything in Elisa's vagina?" Another was "Did you ever have any sexual contact with Elisa?"

A really interesting question was "Aside from the ones you tell me about beforehand and I write down, can you think of any lies you've told in the last six months?" Being a Ph.D. working for the world's biggest bureaucracy, there are myriad rules that I believe weren't really intended for people like myself, but I am nonetheless legally obligated to obey every one. I thought of an instance where I was at a building where shipping was handled, and, to support the project I worked on, I needed to send some data tapes to another city. According to the rules, I should have gotten my project leader to sign some paperwork before I took the tapes to the shipping building. In other words, I needed official authorization to spend $25 in shipping costs. When I learned that I needed his signature, which I was 100 percent certain that he would have been glad to give, I signed it myself, thereby saving about twenty minutes on a busy project. This deed of mine was obviously not truthful, and I knew it. I told the polygraph man about this incident and one or two other similar ones. Then I couldn't think of any more. At that point, I answered the polygraph question.

His other interesting question was, "Aside from the instances that you describe to me beforehand and I write down, have you ever committed an unusual sex act?" Having lived a born-again Christian lifestyle for many years prior, I knew the answer was "no" relative to today's standards. But I had some doubt about whether I was supposed to define the question according to today's standards, and I also knew that I was supposed to include my pre-Christian escapades. I answered "no." When he finished all ten questions, he immediately said, "Let's go back to this one question." We had some dialogue, and I told him that I had committed adultery several times during my twenties. After I confessed these transgressions, I couldn't think of anything else that might have been lingering in my mind. We started the machine again and I answered the question, this time with very favorable results. Since that experience, I am a believer in polygraphs. That doesn't mean they work for everyone. You have to realize I was desperate for the truth to come out. A guilty person would presumably produce a different-looking set of data.

We concluded the exam with his pointing to a column of letters on the wall. One of them had a circle around it. I was instructed to say "No" every time the man asked me, "Is there a circle around this letter?" That means I would be lying on one occasion, for calibration purposes. After the whole process was over, the man went off to analyze the results. When he returned, he said, "I have no problem whatsoever with these results." The polygraph exam convinced the expert that I was telling the truth. He put this in writing; my lawyer gave his analysis to the police. We also turned over the polygraph itself, in case they wanted to second-guess his analysis of the data.

According to Phil, who may not have been a firsthand source, the police acted as if "they were shocked" that I had gone to a private polygraph service rather than to state police headquarters. Nonetheless, the only story about me that circulated throughout the church was that I had failed the polygraph test, having had problems with some question about unusual sex acts. Acceptance of this outright lie included all my best friends, though I had told them the truth just as I have presented it in the preceding paragraphs.

The people who didn't support me were all confined to one location: Rev. Jake's church. It is terribly destructive when Christians do things that embarrass the church; it hinders unbelievers from taking a chance on giving their lives to Christ. There were ten other churches in that county that had groups that prayed for me in those months leading up to, and including, the trial. Most of my co-workers were Catholic; the only embarrassing behavior among Christians was limited to one church.

The New Lawyer

The police broke their promise to drop the case after I passed the polygraph exam, claiming that the "unusual sex act" question justified their actions. They were merely lying. Co-workers were telling me I should spare no expense in getting the best lawyer possible. My attempts to find out who was the best in town got nowhere: every law firm claimed to have the best. None of my friends knew anything about criminal attorneys. Finally, a lawyer at a large firm referred me to an independent attorney, Julian Martino, as being "the best." So I switched to Mr. Martino, who'd had fourteen years' experience as a prosecutor before becoming a trial lawyer. He was helpful when I spoke with him the first time. Joan moved out of town about that time; nobody in Rev. Jake's church ever got to know her, except for a visit she made to a women's Bible study where she related her version of the accusation.

When Darcie and I went to meet Mr. Martino, he said, "The first thing I'd do" (were he to take my case) "is get the history of the mother; find out if she has mental problems." He never did. I spent several months typing information about my case for him, which was highly unusual; most of his clients were guilty, and merely needed him to cover all the technicalities that could possibly get them off. He referred to me as, "probably the most credible client I've ever had." We had a number of court dates, such as my formal entry of a "not guilty" plea.

Since Mr. Martino usually worked with guilty clients, he was no stranger to plea-bargaining. The way he described the situation to me was, "It's easy for others to tell you to stick to what's right, but it's your life that's on the line, not theirs. I've heard that jail door shut one time too many on clients who could have avoided it by taking a plea bargain."

I had the option of doing what's right by refusing to plea-bargain. I had already been burned badly by doing what was right; after the accusation, I spoke openly with Rev. Jake and with the police, assuming that my innocence made it so that I did not have to be guarded about anything I said or did. All my openness did was encourage them to try harder to get me. Having learned the hard way that my pursuers cared nothing about my innocence, I had to consider the alternative: plea-bargaining. I was facing a thirty-year term in a maximum-security prison, which I doubt that I could have survived. It wasn't an easy choice.

The first plea-bargaining offer I received was two years in a local minimum-security institution. That certainly wasn't what I had in mind, and there was no way I would consider it. A few months later, as the trial approached and it became increasingly obvious that the state had no case against me, the prosecutor's boss eventually demanded that he offer me a no-jail-time bargain. Against his will, the prosecutor had to make this offer, at which time my lawyer told me that although he rarely advised one way or the other, he strongly urged me to take the offer. And he had a perfectly valid point: a jury of strangers would have a substantial probability of falsely convicting me, based on emotions and distortions. This was always true in the '80s and '90s in cases of child sexual abuse. I refused the offer of no jail time, which, by the way, was never taken away. In the final weeks, and throughout the trial and the deliberations, I could have accepted it at any time.

I was tempted to have a trial by judge rather than by jury, because I was convinced that a professional would be able to get past the emotions and see the truth better than a jury selected at random from the community. My lawyer described the jury pool as follows: "They pull these people out of line at a 7–11 store." He was adamantly opposed to a trial by judge. He said, "That's just too much responsibility to place into the hands of one man." And he intimately knew the courtroom mentality of the judges he was talking about. I still think I would have been better off choosing a trial by a judge, but I followed Mr. Martino's advice.

I tried to get all pertinent information to Mr. Martino so he could prepare for the trial. My notes contained several pages of facts that were favorable to me, and a small portion of one page containing the unfavorable stuff. The three unfavorable things I listed were perpetuated by Rev. Jake. Here they are, verbatim from the notes I sent Mr. Martino:

1. The child handles the (anatomically correct) doll and names me as having done that;
2. Two Christian psychologists, one whose reputation is supposedly top-notch, agree that the child has been molested, based on her doll-handling;
3. I had guessed that fondling of the genital area was the only logical assumption concerning the accusation, but Rev. Jake says that such abuse occurs only in a minority of cases.

If the reader wonders why on earth I even speculated about the likely nature of the accusation, it was in direct response to Rev. Jake's question, "What do you think the accusation could be about?" I certainly wouldn't have responded so openly had I been talking to the police, but this was my own pastor of three years, and I was unquestionably one of the most trusted people in the church. Surely my very own pastor wouldn't try to trick me, I thought, when Rev. Jake posed this question.

The three nonsensical items noted above illustrate an important aspect of my case: Rev. Jake spread misinformation that caused many people — myself included — to take a pessimistic view of my case. How on earth could I have known that all these things told to me by my own pastor, posing as my friend, were complete distortions? It was months later when I found out that the first two things were not in my file at all. Rev. Jake was merely painting a distorted picture. Item 3 is a classic example of Rev. Jake's arguing, categorically, with everything I said. There really was only one possibility of molestation anyone could have envisioned in that setting with all the kids present.

It gets worse. When Rev. Jake argued that only a minority of child sex abuse cases involve fondling of the genital area, I tried to spell out for him how illogical that was, pointing out how ridiculous it would be for anyone to think an adult was trying to fondle little breasts. But recall what he wrote to the police: "(Paul Grey) also mentioned at this time, 'When you pick up a child, your long fingers would touch the breast area.' Looking back now, I feel these comments might be significant." Rev. Jake didn't mention to the police why I had said such a thing. Do you think it was merely because he had forgotten?

When he was arguing with Darcie and me, Rev. Jake said, "I'm about 95 percent sure that child was molested; no, I'm 100 percent sure." Yet the reader knows a lot more than Rev. Jake knew. The abandonment of Darcie and me by our church shows how persuasive he was if his listener didn't know his record of deception. He also told us that the "prophecy group" in his church had pretty much indicated that they believed in my guilt. Then he said, "No, I'd better not say that." He used to tell me that none of the people in the church were worrying about the case, as I assumed they were. Based on the absence of phone calls and letters of encouragement, that's one area where he may have been right.

Rev. Jake seemed to express everything about my case in the form of an accusation. Referring to the meeting at his house, he said, "It just blew us away how calm you were; it just blew us away." He acted as if that constituted proof of my guilt. I once saw an abuse case on TV where a father reported his child's tragic accident, and the man ended up being tried for the child's murder. The only "proof" of his guilt was that his words to the 911 operator were supposedly much too calm for a father under those circumstances. The man was trained to handle emergencies. It was the world around him that acted irrationally, not the man himself.

A few months before the accusation, as class ended and I was complimenting Joan about what a sweetheart Elisa was, she left me speechless by responding, "Well, we don't treat them according to the way they look." She said it with what seemed a cold smile on her face, and I said something like, "Of course not." Actually, I treated *all* the kids as I would have wanted to be treated were I in their position. But it left me with a strange feeling: did this newcomer think she was teaching me, the trusted Sunday school teacher, how to treat children impartially? She made that statement at the busiest time of the day, and I didn't think I could say anything that would make her see things my way, so I just chalked it up as another example of the ingratitude Sunday school teachers commonly receive. The thought of her making a false accusation to the police never crossed my mind. After the accusation, when I told Rev. Jake about her statement, he said, "I don't think what she said is strange; I don't think it's strange at all." It took me a few weeks to realize that he would simply argue with anything that anyone had to say in my defense. Until I came to that realization, I was very confused. I couldn't figure out why he told me, a week after the accusation, that when my trial got underway, "Your friends will testify against you." As I will show later, no friends testified against me at the trial: just Joan and Rev. Jake.

Months later, after Rev. Jake must, I believe, have known that the charges were untrue, I went to one of my numerous court appointments. There my lawyer told me, "Your pastor is in the prosecutor's office, and he says you made a hand gesture at the meeting, and he says you wanted to plead guilty to the charges, but your wife wouldn't let you." My lawyer and I were shocked. We made no response. We knew by then that there was nothing to be gained by any form of communication with Rev. Jake.

Can I Get a Witness?

My lawyer told me that I could have only three different people testify as character witnesses in my defense. I don't know if this was a law, or merely my lawyer's recommendation of the best overall strategy. One of my chosen witnesses was my assistant pastor from two churches earlier. My pastor from my previous church also volunteered to testify for me, but he is so soft-spoken that I felt that someone else could more forcefully represent my case. It's worth noting that Pastor Dave was ready to testify in my behalf even after others in the church had tried to make him suspicious of me. My office mate was one of the other two character witnesses. I thought her testimony would make it clear to the jurors that there are women who know me and trust me. Fred, my assistant for several months, had such great things to say about me that my lawyer thought the jurors might be likely to tune him out; he was disqualified for being too much of an advocate. My wife was available to testify, but I felt that if any juror thought I was a child-molesting liar, that juror would also discount anything that Darcie said in my behalf. A few other women co-workers volunteered to testify for me. I planned for one of them to do so until, just before the trial, my lawyer told me that all my character witnesses were required to have seen me interacting with children. I had talked with my friend Stephanie many times about kids (and about most other interesting topics in life), but she was disqualified when I learned the rules at the last moment.

Seeking a woman who had seen me with kids and would testify in my behalf, I called my friend Kate. She and her husband, Gary, had been in the room with me, leading the music, and had also been in the previous church with me. Only one thing about asking her assistance made me uncomfortable: I hadn't heard from them in many months. This was one of those "Welcome to Wonderland" experiences Darcie and I had been undergoing since the arrest. I knew that Gary and Kate knew how ridiculous the charges were — after all, they were with me and they even knew how much Elisa liked me — but they didn't contact us during our months of agonized waiting. Anyway, I called Kate, who graciously volunteered to testify.

My lawyer told me that the character witnesses could be questioned only within a very narrow range: Had they formed an opinion about me, and what was their opinion regarding whether I might be likely to molest kids? If they knew such-and-such, would it change their opinion? If the answer to the last question was "yes," then that witness provides no benefit to the case.

There was a man in the church who had been an elder in our previous church, and was the father of four. His three-year-old daughter, upon hearing that some people had said bad things about Paul Grey, immediately burst into tears and said, "No! I like him. Can we go see them?" That child, whom I knew from the day she was born, never spoke a single word during her entire year in my class. Her parents were acutely aware that Sunday school was, by far, their child's favorite time of week. Her father had a master's degree in physics from Princeton, and worked at the same place I did. When you combine all these factors, you come up with someone who knew beyond doubt that the accusation against me was false; one of my most ardent supporters, a man in my inner circle of friends, who understood me as well as anyone. But when I asked him to testify for me, he said he was willing, then had second thoughts and said, "Although I've never seen any questionable behavior in you, I do have some questions in my own mind about you, *based on some things that Rev. Jake has told me*."

When this man said, "Rev. Jake says you never really came right out and denied the charge," I immediately told him that was an outright lie, which it is. Yet my friend stopped being so supportive of me around that time.

That man represents a reality that dominated my relations with Rev. Jake's congregation: if people were going to spend any time with me, they were going to hear me talk a lot about Rev. Jake's mistreatment of my case. But it's not possible to sustain such mutually contradictory relationships, so these people felt heavy self-inflicted pressure to stop communicating with me. The only other man in that church who worked at the lab where I did best illustrates this. He was extremely supportive, and both his kids had been in my two- and three-year-old class. But he left a note at my desk one day telling me that despite knowing all the things I said were right, he really wanted to keep attending Rev. Jake's church. Christians can understand this sentiment; it is very painful to leave a church where your family has established roots. This man's note also told me, very gently, that the problem was my anger. I've never heard from him since that time.

One of the results of our ordeal is that I acquired a great love of the book of Job. In the opinion of most scholars, this book was the first Scripture ever written, even before Genesis. Its main point comes up immediately and clearly: Satan requests permission to make Job miserable, and God allows it. Job gets a nonstop barrage of arguments from his friends, who insist that his misery is the result of his wrongdoing, and that the only problem is his unwillingness to confess it. But he was absolutely innocent—"blameless" in God's own words. It's not the tremendous suffering of Job that I identify with, but the aspect of being falsely accused, even by one's own supporters. It is significant to me that the very first Scripture God ever gave us was about how we sometimes get attacked through no fault of our own, and undergo a season of undeserved suffering. Eventually, Job emerges victorious.

I strongly considered having my niece (on Darcie's side) testify for me, since she has spent lots of unsupervised time with me since I first met her at age three, in 1981. Joan thought I wanted to molest Elisa "because I paid so much attention to her." Had my sister-in-law been similarly fearful, she would have shot me long ago; my affection for Elisa was nothing compared with my love for my niece. I also considered having my second godson testify, since I lived upstairs from him for a few years beginning when he was a year old. I also considered my brother's son, whom I have known and loved since the day he was born, but the limit of three witnesses, plus the long distances involved were prohibitive.

This brings a legal point to mind. Even if my niece, godson, nephew, and 2,000 other people told how properly I had behaved with them during their childhood years, it's legally viewed as irrelevant: the accusation did not involve them.

Salvador was one of the boys in my class the first year. He got me confused with Saint Paul when I told stories of Paul's escapades from the book of Acts. I was Salvador's hero: in his mind, I had escaped from Damascus in a big basket, escaped on horseback in the middle of the night, etc. It took his mom a while to figure out what he was talking about. Salvador called me at home a few times, once to tell me, ecstatically, that he had "hit mommy in the butt with a 'nowball.'" Once he just left a message on the answering machine. It said, "I love you, and Jesus loves you. God bless you."

Salvador's mom called me two or three weeks after the accusation. She'd had an exceptionally vivid dream about me the preceding night. In it, I was so incredibly alone, so abandoned, that, after she awoke, she felt she had to call me. I was pleased that God was apparently speaking to my friends about me. I told her what was going on. She was not aware of the accusation until I told her. I encouraged her to tell Elder #2 about her dream and phone call. She did. That was the last I ever heard of her, or of Salvador. Salvador's opinion of me made no difference to the police; they never heard it.

The Nightmare that Started It All

Recall the first description I ever heard about Elisa's "initial disclosure" of the allegation. At Rev. Jake's house, Phil was asked to relate Joan's middle-of-the-night phone call. He said that Joan had told him that Elisa had awakened, screaming, from a nightmare. When I heard this, my heart was broken for Elisa; I cared for her a lot. Within a month, I learned from a friend that Elisa had not had a nightmare at all; it was Joan who had the nightmare. I thought my prayers had been answered: the truth had finally come out; the police were sure to drop the case. Furthermore, I was relieved by the knowledge that Elisa had not suffered any abuse.

Joan was not inspired to make the allegation against me by just any random nightmare. Specifically, she dreamed that I had abducted Elisa from Sunday school. This was surely a notion she had seriously entertained during the preceding months. Her exact words, when she was asked in the trial what her nightmare was about, were: "That I went to pick up my daughter from the Sunday school class and that she was gone, and her teacher was also gone."

I doubt there could be more terrifying feelings on Earth than those of a mother who has lost her children to an evil person. Joan was in this very state of mind when she awoke Elisa, who had been sleeping next to her, and began questioning her, starting with, "Does your teacher ever touch you?" Very shortly after waking from this nightmare, Joan called the police.

Bracing for the Long Battle

When I found out that Joan had lied in her initial story to the police, I was positive the case would be dropped. When it wasn't, I decided to write down all the facts about her nightmare. Here are some of the notes I sent to Mr. Martino: "I mentioned it to Rev. Jake, and he said it was untrue. So I asked Phil, in a separate phone conversation, to verify that I was correct. He did. I mentioned it several times thereafter to Rev. Jake, but he never acknowledged it. (His response was: 'I don't know that for a fact.') He only accepts input that matches his own agenda."

Remember, by the time I wrote this note, Rev. Jake had heard Phil's account, following the accusation, of what Joan had told Phil about Elisa's having awakened, screaming, from a nightmare. And Joan had by then talked with Rev. Jake on the phone, telling him she had awakened from her own nightmare about me abducting Elisa, just before she made the accusation. Now, how was it possible for Rev. Jake to be telling me that my assertion that Joan had lied to the police was untrue? As you see in my note to Mr. Martino, "He only accepts input that matches his own agenda." Even though the truth about Rev. Jake was terribly difficult for me to accept, life got a little easier once I learned the truth: Rev. Jake was out to destroy me, and was using deception to do it.

A friend of mine asked a few families in Rev. Jake's church to write letters of support about me to my lawyer. Four families did. One man he contacted declined to write such a letter. This man later told me that the reason was because his oldest child had been molested at age two by a baby sitter. Two of my favorite women in the church had been sexually molested as kids, and did not support me at all. Recall Mary's police statement: "I will never forget the first time I met him at the church, I saw Paul go up to a retarded thirteen-year-old boy in the sanctuary and ask if he could pray with him. The boy left the room with Paul for about three minutes, then I saw his mother go and get him. I had a bad feeling about that at the time." Well, that mother was one of those two molested women.

As Darcie would testify, I spent a great deal of my time in the early days agonizing over what those poor elders must be going through as they tried to protect their teacher from the societal attack that had been launched. I also felt terrible about the pain and suffering my friends in the church must have felt as they witnessed the witch-hunt perpetrated on their trusted friend. I still think it would have been that way had Rev. Jake behaved like a normal pastor. But the reality is that I was terribly wrong.

Scriptures I had never particularly noticed came to have vivid meaning. Many of David's psalms, written when he was in hiding to keep from being murdered, express Darcie's and my situation perfectly. Psalm 55: "If an enemy were insulting me, I could endure it; if a foe were raising himself against me, I could hide from him. But it is you, a man like myself, my companion, my close friend, with whom I once enjoyed sweet fellowship as we walked with the throng at the house of God."

In Psalm 35: "Ruthless witnesses come forward; they question me on things I know nothing about. They repay me evil for good and leave my soul forlorn. Yet when they were ill I put on sackcloth and humbled myself with fasting. When my prayers returned to me unanswered, I went about mourning as though for my friend or brother. I bowed my head in grief as though weeping for my mother. But when I stumbled, they gathered in glee; attackers gathered against me when I was unaware. They slandered me without ceasing. Like the ungodly they maliciously mocked; they gnashed their teeth at me.... They do not speak peaceably, but devise false accusations against those who live quietly in the land."

Psalm 109, too, had vivid meaning for Darcie and me in the weeks preceding the trial: "O God, whom I praise, do not remain silent, for wicked and deceitful men have opened their mouths against me; they have spoken against me with lying tongues. With words of hatred they surround me; they attack me without cause. In return for my friendship they accuse me, but I am a man of prayer. They repay me evil for good, and hatred for my friendship." Maybe the reader can see why, over the years, I have looked to the Bible for guidance.

My original notions, that Joan would talk to me and see the truth and the whole thing would be dismissed as "poor communications," were misguided. The very worst part of the accusation was the possibility of being identified in the news as an accused child molester. The evening following the accusation, Rev. Jake told me that the story would undoubtedly be in the newspapers. I thought he just didn't understand how ridiculous the allegation was. Could it be that he knew something that I didn't, which would make newspaper coverage of the story a certainty?

The first newspaper account merely quoted from the warrant, saying that I was charged with first-degree sexual assault and risk of injury to a minor. A capsulated police log is not as damaging as a headline.

After one of my (numerous) court dates, the long-dreaded article came out. It cited Rev. Jake's written statement to the police. The article said that after Rev. Jake confronted me about the allegation, I said to him, "Obviously you're talking about grabbing her crotch." A couple of ensuing articles stated that Joan told police that Elisa complained of pain for several months, and that she finally revealed to Joan that I had touched her vagina. It went on to say that other witnesses had seen me paying an unusual amount of attention to the "victim." I cannot use the actual newspaper quotes without naming the newspaper, and thereby revealing the location where all this occurred. As you can imagine, our lives in the community were destroyed. It was obvious that after the trial we would have to move to another part of the country.

After the newspaper articles came out, I was concerned that some crazed zealot might come to the house — the articles had given our address — and do something violent. The article containing Rev. Jake's quote prompted a woman in a neighboring state to write a letter to the editor.

The lady said she was greatly disturbed when she read that I had sexually abused my three-year-old Sunday school pupil for about seven months. She went on to quote some of the misinformation she had learned from the "victim" literature of the day, claiming that "statistics" show how victims block out their childhood after they become adults, to avoid reliving the trauma that they had experienced as a child. She also said that "statistics" show that one of every four girls will experience sexual assault by the time she reaches her eighth birthday. She commended the "bravery" of Elisa, which will prevent Elisa from becoming a victim like others. (Does she mean bravery for disclosing the abuse? For taking me to court? I'm not sure.) She lamented that I brought a halt to Elisa's childhood, and exhorted my community to become more enlightened about the prevalence of child abuse.

Another woman, who worked for a child protection agency, responded very differently to the same article. I spoke with her on the phone once; she told me that when she read the article, she could tell that the accusation was false.

One month before my trial, another letter (which was not about my case) to the editor was published. The author said it is unconstitutional to bring a charge against someone based on nothing but hearsay, but that an increasing number of such cases were occurring. He said that such cases inflict great pain and stress on the children involved, because those children know that something very wrong is being done in their names. He said there were no laws against false accusation in our state, and that this encourages people to use children as a tool for inflicting damage with impunity. He said we all need to protect children, and give them the opportunity to tell their own story, rather than allowing somebody else to speak for them.

Not long thereafter, a woman responded with a letter of rebuke to the man's letter I just cited. She said that the man's organization was obviously ignorant of how the legal system works concerning child abuse cases. She said that the child is first interviewed by the police, then by a social worker, then by a child expert, and, if necessary, by a prosecutor. She said that our county has a team that includes all these professionals, and that this team reaches its conclusions based on a responsible evaluation. She claimed that less than 2 percent of all accusations are false, and that the man should have been aware of "these studies." She said that investigations of child abuse are very thorough. She claimed that eight thousand American children are raped each week, and blamed the man's ignorance for causing the problem to keep getting worse.

These two letters were not about my case, but show how life was progressing in the community and, I think, accurately reflect the debates that were going on throughout America.

The prosecution's game plan was straightforward. In the prosecutor's own words, "If that child gets on the witness stand and points to that man and says 'he put his finger in my private', that is the entire case."

The burden of proving the state of my mental condition was placed on me. I set up an appointment with the president of the state association for the treatment of sex offenders. I went there expecting him to put me through a series of tests to see if he would conclude that I had any pedophiliac traits. Instead, he said his testing should be in accordance with my attorney's game plan, for which he had received no guidance. He wanted me to see a psychiatrist on the other side of the state first, then test according to that psychiatrist's recommendations. A major problem with this was that the trial was due to start within a month, and there wasn't time. Meanwhile, Mr. Martino had been in contact with a lady who was a child expert, for the same purpose: getting these tests done so we would have the results in court. She kept asking him to send the entire file, not just the little bit he had sent. The problem was, that *was* the entire file — the state's entire case. She refused to be involved with a case that had so little information. My case was so unsubstantiated that we couldn't even get an expert witness to participate. We were called to court to begin the trial, and, when Mr. Martino said we hadn't had our psych evaluation done yet, the judge said he'd grant us one delay; we would go to trial next time he called us, ready or not.

I don't know how Mr. Martino came upon the idea of employing child abuse expert Dr. Shalom. He's probably not the person defense lawyers typically go to, because, in the words of one defense attorney, Dr. Shalom was "nothing but a front for DCYS," meaning his reputation was one of consistently testifying against the adult defendants in child abuse cases. We were glad he agreed to review my case. To get a thorough review done in the allotted time, Dr. Shalom got assistance from two of his Ph.D. colleagues. One, Mark Solomon, is a specialist in child and family psychology, including abuse and neglect matters; the other is a child developmental psychologist. In writing, Dr. Shalom made it clear to Mr. Martino that they were not committed to testifying on my behalf, but only to performing the best possible review so they could assess the evidence against me. And he made it clear that he rarely concludes that evidence against a client is unreliable and/or contaminated.

The tests and interviews were extensive. There were so many questions about all aspects of sexuality that it got to be embarrassing. It was an unpleasant process, but I was glad of the opportunity. Dr. Shalom, too, was frustrated by the state's scant file on my case. That's why he enlisted the assistance of his child developmental psychologist colleague, Dr. Marcus White, with whom I met for several hours. Dr. White asked for a parallel class history of the two youngest kids in my class. He asked me about all sorts of things I had never considered, the same questions being applied to Elisa and to Julia, the child Mary took to the restroom on my last teaching day (daughter of Linda, who'd been so fearful about going to Nicaragua). One of our best friends in the church, Linda was extremely supportive through the first few months after the accusation. After that, we never heard from her.

Even though they were of similar age, the personalities of the two children Dr. White asked me about were very different. Elisa wanted to hang out with me and watch the other kids from a safe distance, while Julia wanted to mingle with the other kids. The time I spent with Dr. White pointed out something I had never even thought about: Julia was a very bright child, who could display her quick wit in devious ways. One time, a man dropped his child off in my class, and began to close the door. Seeing this, Julia quickly put her hand in the vicinity of the hinge, then shrieked when he closed it. When he opened it, horrified, she laughed at him for falling for her trick. Julia was so aggressive that it seemed like I had a class full of four-year-olds, with one two-year-old, Elisa. Elisa was right on the verge of starting to play with the others when the accusation occurred.

The result of the many hours I spent with the three psychologists, and their analysis of the numerous tests I took, was that all three concluded that the source of the accusation against me was nothing but a fearful mother. Mr. Martino was thrilled: Dr. Shalom would be my key witness, and we thought he would be fantastic. Dr. Shalom said, in a letter he wrote me, "My reading of the state's documentation indicated that there never was a case against you." Of the psychological examinations, he wrote, "Neither I nor Dr. Solomon found any evidence of pedophilia."

Recall that Rev. Jake told me that two Christian child experts, one of supposedly high acclaim, had examined Elisa, and concluded that she had been abused. Is it possible that Rev. Jake also tried to persuade the police with this story? If so, would his persuasion have impacted their decision to pursue the case? Did he manipulate the police into letting him, in effect, run the investigation and provide the conclusions? During the trial, despite Rev. Jake's misinformation concerning these alleged experts, there was no mention of any such experts having examined Elisa.

In trial, the prosecutor was forthright about why he had initially assumed my guilt, when he asked, "What axe could (Rev. Jake) possibly have had to grind against Paul Grey?" It's a question based on sound logic. The answer was much too difficult for the defense to be able to explain to the jury.

II. The Trial

Jury Selection

The trial began, of course, with jury selection. My lawyer and I were allowed only a few opportunities to reject potential jurors simply because we had a bad feeling about them (rather than a legal reason for the rejection). Trials can most assuredly be won or lost by a good or bad job of jury selection. (O. J. Simpson's criminal trial jury will probably be cited for many years as an example of this.) I had absolutely no means of getting a jury favorable to me. The process of sitting at the defendant's table under the bright lights, having a group of people in my community come in and look at me, and then hearing them receive announcements about me being accused of molesting a three-year-old, was a nightmare come true.

I recognized one of the prospective jurors, a young woman who worked at a video store near our home. I don't think she recognized me. She disqualified herself by saying she would not be able to vote "not guilty" if she thought I was guilty despite a lack of evidence. Coincidentally, one of her co-workers at the video store was a friend of ours, who had been married to one of the most criminal-minded men ever to attend Rev. Jake's church. Darcie and I had spent time and effort on that couple. He was concerned about his likelihood of someday becoming physically abusive to their infant daughter; he knew himself. It was a family with minimal likelihood of following the straight and narrow path. They were divorced before she began work at the video store. The wife liked me a lot; I was living proof to her that not all men are abusive. I don't think I ever saw her after her co-worker appeared at my trial.

The judge began the jury selection process by explaining that according to law, I was not guilty of anything, and that I had not necessarily done anything to merit being there. Yet when my lawyer asked each potential juror if I had done anything wrong, the most common response was, "Of course he did; he wouldn't be here otherwise. He obviously did *something*." Usually, the judge allowed such potential jurors to be removed without using up our allotted quota. One man who had also given this same response sat patiently through all the questioning. When asked if he could vote "not guilty" if there was no evidence, he said no. The judge should have dismissed him then, but didn't. Now that the man knew the correct answer, he was asked the question again. He again answered truthfully, rather than giving the "correct" answer, and finally the judge rejected him. Bless that juror for his honesty.

The worst juror for such a case is one who cannot overcome his or her emotions, but knows the correct answers to the screening questions. That person might not even wish to be on the jury, but how can you realistically expect anyone to say they can be rational about so reprehensible a charge as child molestation? We rejected one man whom I thought would have been fine. Mr. Martino was concerned about his past link with a police-related organization. As far as I was concerned, jury selection was in God's hands.

We ended up with a jury of three men and three women. Two of the women appeared to be in their twenties. One had a math background, which I erroneously thought might cause her to identify with me. She said she had some exposure to kids through a nephew or niece. She answered the question correctly regarding being able to vote "not guilty" if she really thought I was guilty despite insufficient evidence to prove it beyond reasonable doubt. I'm pretty sure she was the one "problem juror" at the end of the trial. She never looked at me the entire week. The two alternate jurors, who attended the entire trial but were not used, were both young women.

Roe Stayton, a Colorado attorney who has defended many child abuse cases, once told me that he likes to choose jurors who give the "wrong" answer, who say they'd vote to convict if they thought the defendant was guilty despite a lack of convincing evidence. It shows they're honest, in his opinion. Mr. Martino didn't see it that way. Jury selection occurred on Friday and Monday. Tuesday morning, the trial started with Elisa the first witness.

Courtroom Testimony

The state had appointed an attorney to watch after Elisa's interests. This lady was supposed to stand with Elisa on the witness stand. The prosecution asked for, and was granted, permission to modify the procedure by having Elisa's father take the stand with her. In granting permission without objection, Mr. Martino wished to avoid every appearance of being tough on the child or her mother.

The Child

It was uncanny to see Elisa come cheerfully walking up the aisle with her father, whom I had never seen. The previous time I had seen Elisa, she was thirty-seven months old. Now she was about to turn four, and she seemed a different child altogether. I don't know when her father had resumed living with the family. All I know is that Elisa was very cheerful.

Both lawyers had to question Elisa from their seats, theoretically to prevent the defense attorney from intimidating the child. During the prosecutor's questioning, Mr. Martino was seated next to me; just the two of us at the defense table, under bright lights in the center of the room. The prosecutor's table was adjacent to ours. The state inspector and prosecutor were the only ones who used this table. Elisa faced the prosecutor. I was about five feet from the center of her vision. In order of observability, the top three candidates in the room were the prosecutor, the state inspector, and myself, in that order. Nobody was allowed to come or go while Elisa was giving testimony.

*Here is Elisa's unedited testimony, beginning with the prosecutio*n:

Q – Good afternoon, Elisa.
A – I know.
Q – Remember, I want you to talk in a big girl voice so we can all hear you, OK?
A – I will.
Q – Can you tell us what your full name is, please?
A – (Elisa responds with full name).
Q – And do you remember what my first name is?
A – (Gives correct answer).
Q – OK, and could you tell us how old you are, please?
A – Three.
Q – You're three years old?
A – Yeah.
Q – And when's your birthday?
A – In February.
Q – In February. And how old will you be on your next birthday in February?
A – Four.
Q – OK. And who lives with you, Elisa?
A – My brother and my mom and my dad.
Q – OK. And do you have any pets?
A – No. But a cat comes to our house.
Q – And do you know your ABC's? Can you do your ABC's?
A – A,b,c,d,e,f,g,h,i,j,k,l,m,n,o,p,q,r,s,w,x,y and z.
Q – OK. And can you count to five?
A – One, two, three, four, five.
Q – Elisa, do you know what happens if you tell a lie?
A – You'll get in trouble.

Q – OK. So you know it's important to tell the truth?
A – Right.
Q – OK. And do you remember a time when you went to church with your mommy?
A – Yeah.
Q – OK. And did you have a teacher at your church?
A – Yep.
Q – OK. And did your teacher ever touch you in your private?
A – Yes.
Q – OK. And could you stand up with your daddy, and come down and show us what you mean by your private, please?
A – Make me do that again, right?
Q – Could you show us where your private is, please?
A – Right here. (Indicating)
[OK. Your honor, might the record reflect she's pointing to her vaginal area?]
Judge: [The record should so reflect].
Q – And did your teacher ever put anything into your private area?
A – Just his finger.
Q – Thank you. Would you have a seat again, please? Now, Elisa, did you get a boo-boo from his putting his finger in your private? You have to speak up. I can't hear you.
A – Yes.
Q – OK. And did your teacher do this at church?
A – Yes.
Q – OK. And did you tell anybody about this? Did you tell your mommy?
A – Yeah.
Q – And did you tell the police?
A – Yeah.
Q – Did you tell the people at the hospital?
A – Yeah.

Q – And is your teacher in the courtroom today? Do you see him here?
A – No.
Q – Can you look around and tell me if you see him here?
A – No.
Q – OK. Now, Elisa, what you just told us, is that the truth?
A – Yes.
[One moment, please, Your Honor. Thank you, Elisa. I don't have any other questions for you. Thank you.]

Cross-Examination by Mr. Martino:
Q – Elisa, my name is (gives name). I've got a few questions for you, OK?
A – Oh.
[Judge: You see who's talking to you?]
[Elisa: Yes.]
Q – Elisa, do you remember Sunday school?
A – Yeah.
Q – Do you remember your teacher?
A – Yeah.
Q – What do you remember about your teacher, Elisa?
A – I don't know.
Q – At Sunday school, Elisa, who took you to the bathroom?
A – My teacher.
Q – Your teachers?
A – Yeah.
Q – When you went to the bathroom, did the teachers help you wipe?
A – Yes.
Q – Elisa, do you remember the first time you told your mother about the story you just told us?
A – Yeah.
Q – Was your mother worried at the time you told her?
A – No.

[Mr. Martino: I have no other questions.]
[Prosecutor: Nothing further, your honor.]
[Judge: Who's that with you?]
[Elisa: My dad.]
[Judge: Well, you and your dad can go now, OK?]
[Prosecutor: Thank you, Elisa.]
[Judge: Thank you.]

The preceding testimony was actually a historical event. The courthouse where it took place has the longest uninterrupted usage as a courthouse in the country, and Elisa was the youngest witness ever to testify in the history of that courthouse.

I told you how strange it felt to see Elisa appear so suddenly after all the months of our "Welcome to Wonderland" experience. But the blood-curdling moments were when she looked at me when asked to point out her teacher. She looked right at me at least twice. I sat motionless, neither smiling nor scowling, and she chose to keep her gaze a little more to her left, toward the slightly smiling jurors. I think she might have recognized me if I would have given her a big smile; we'll never know. But the fact is she didn't recognize me. Oddly enough, I probably wouldn't have recognized her in a crowd either; she really had changed a lot. My unsmiling, shaven, dressed-up appearance, sitting in a courtroom, might have struck her as being very different from our Sunday school setting. My attorney had a beard. He and I have no resemblance to each other.

The Child's Mother

Immediately after Elisa's testimony, Joan took the stand. I couldn't believe how quickly the courtroom events were happening. It was a huge contrast to all the months I had spent waiting for the truth to come out. Now the pace was so fast that it made me somewhat dizzy, and I remember it as if it were a dream. I'll cite all topics in Joan's testimony that I haven't mentioned elsewhere. Joan referred to the service at Rev. Jake's church as "mass," demonstrating how much an outsider she was. Only a handful of women in the church had ever met her. She estimated that she had missed about five Sundays during the seven-month period. Also, she said they had attended services there for seven months prior to the time when Elisa started attending my class. One brief exchange:

Q – (Prosecutor) Did she ever refer to anyone else by the term of teacher?
A – No, she never has.

[My question to the reader: How does Joan know Elisa's name for my assistants? Elisa had just told Mr. Martino that her teachers had helped her wipe when they took her to the restroom].

Q – (Prosecutor) Now how did Elisa react to going to Mr. Grey's room? How did she act?
A – She would cry.
Q – Had she done that before?
A – No.
Q – Now, did you leave the services early that day?
A – Yes, I did.
Q – About how early?
A – I would say about ten minutes early.
Q – And why did you leave early?
A – For some reason I was restless.
Q – OK. And where did you go when you left the service?
A – I went back and looked into Elisa's room.
Q – And when you got to that room, what did you initially see?
A – I saw Mr. Grey getting ready to put my daughter on his lap. And it appeared to me that he had an erection.
Q – OK. And how close were you to Mr. Grey when you made these observations?
A – About two to three feet away.
Q – And how did Mr. Grey react when you came into the room?
A – It was very quick. He was starting to put my daughter on his lap, and then he never actually put her on his

lap. He was reaching to pick her up and put her — and then he put her down. And he had a piece of paper in his other hand, which he covered his genitals with. So I wasn't able to get a second look, as I was trying to.

Q – OK. And what did you do at that point?

A – I took my daughter and I left.

Q – Did you say anything to Mr. Grey?

A – No.

Q – Why not?

A – Because I wasn't absolutely sure of what I had seen. I was trying to see it a second time, and I was in shock as well.

Q – Did you talk to anyone from the church about what you had seen on that day?

A – Not at that point.

Q – Why not?

A – Because I wanted to make sure, before I said anything.

I have omitted a few of the less germane exchanges in these portions of Joan's testimony; court cases are necessarily filled with them. A bit further along, she described the dream later in the week in which I had abducted Elisa, and stated that at 3:00 A.M., after waking up from this nightmare, that was why she started questioning Elisa. The police came to her house within an hour, and stayed for a couple of hours. Joan said she thinks she was in shock as she went to her job at 7:30. At this point, as she relived the experience, she started crying on the witness stand. The last part of her questioning by the prosecutor:

Q – Did you ever speak in front of Elisa about the allegations she had made to the doctors or the nurses?

A – I didn't really have to. She started talking about it as soon as she walked into the room.

Q – And how was Elisa acting at the hospital?

A – She was very verbal.

Cross-Examination by Mr. Martino:

As he questioned Joan, my lawyer stood far back, in the jury box, to be doubly sure he did not present an appearance that could be construed as intimidating.

Mr. Martino:

Q – Isn't it true you first reported to the police that Elisa woke up and had the nightmare?

A – I don't think so.

Q – So it's your testimony that you didn't report to the police that it was Elisa who woke up with a nightmare?

A – I don't really remember. I know I told the police about the dream that I had, though.

Q – But you don't remember whether you told the police it was Elisa who woke up with a nightmare?

A – She might have woken up with a, you know —

Q – That's not the question. I'm saying, do you remember whether or not you first told the police it was Elisa who woke up with a nightmare?

A – I think I may have, yes.

Q – So that story has changed now. It was you who woke up with the nightmare?

A – I did wake up with a nightmare.

Q – Yeah. I'm saying the story has changed now. It wasn't Elisa that woke up with the nightmare? It was you that woke up with the nightmare; is that correct?

A – No.

Q – OK. Well, why don't you correct me now, OK?

A – I had the dream that I spoke of just a few minutes ago. And if I told the police that my daughter awoke, maybe she did have a dream at that point. I explained to the court that she murmured. She was sleeping beside me. As far as whether she had a nightmare or not, I really couldn't tell you, because I don't know.

Q – OK. But it's your testimony right now that you never

reported to the police that it was Elisa who woke up with a nightmare?

A – I don't remember if I told the police that Elisa woke up with a nightmare. But I am telling you that I did have the dream that I just spoke about.

Q – Did you ever tell Paul Grey that you preferred him not to put Elisa on his lap?

A – Yes, I did.

Q – OK. And when was that, roughly?

A – I don't know.

Q – Did you think that Elisa had a name for Mr. Grey's Sunday school assistants?

A – No.

Q – Did you ever consider attending the 9 o'clock service so Elisa would have a woman teacher?

A – I didn't even know there was a woman teacher in the nine o'clock service.

Q – Did you ever consider staying in Paul Grey's class to make sure Elisa was safe?

A – No.

Q – Did you ever consider telling Paul Grey that you were suspicious of his activities toward Elisa?

A – I didn't want to accuse anyone of anything until I knew for sure.

Q – After March 24th, 1993, did anybody in the church suggest to you that you should speak to Paul Grey?

A – No.

Emergency Room Nurse

The next witness was a registered nurse who had spoken with Elisa during the Emergency Room visit. She said she has seen "Maybe a half-dozen or so" children for allegations of sexual abuse. Her description of Elisa was: "She was fine. I thought she was an alert and active child."

Recall the medical exam, which had a short, illegible word concerning erythema. The nurse clarifies the missing information:

"Around the outside of the vagina the vulva area was reddened." Yet, in my last session with Elisa, my assistant was always within eight feet of me. Has any child ever been sexually assaulted under such circumstances? Or was the erythema supposed to have been a remnant of sexual assault during our previous Sunday school encounter, seventeen days prior to Elisa's emergency room exam?

Examining Physician

The next witness was the doctor.

Some excerpts of his testimony:

Q – (Prosecutor) And what did your examination reveal as far as the hymen or anything else in her vaginal area?

A – The external examination revealed the presence of redness around the external opening. Then we just retracted the vaginal entrance and saw the hymen appeared to be intact. There was no discharge. There was no bleeding. At this time we did take some cultures to check for any sexually transmitted diseases.

Q – And what were the results of those tests?

A – They were negative.

Q – And did you prescribe any medication or further course of treatment as a result of your examination?

A – No, I did not.

Q – And why was that, doctor?

A – Because there was no evidence of any infection or — there was no need to put the patient on any medications based on the examination.

Q – Were you able to come to any kind of opinion regarding the cause of the redness to the vaginal area?

A – One could explain that based on so many things. It could be related to her diaper training, potty training. It could be any kind of infection. It could be — you know, we do see those even in children who are brought in, otherwise without any sexual allegations.

Q – Could a finger have caused that redness?
A – It's possible.
One of Mr. Martino's Questions:
Q – So we really don't know where the redness came from; is that correct?
A – Yeah.

State Inspector

The following day, the state inspector was the first witness. She said she had "attended several courses on child sexual abuse" during her years with the state police. An excerpt:

Q – (Prosecutor) Where was this interview conducted?
A – It was in the kitchen of their home, and she was sitting on her mother's lap at the time.
Q – And what was Elisa's demeanor like? How was she acting?
A – Elisa was acting like any normal three-year-old.

Everything else in the state inspector's testimony is covered elsewhere in this book.

Children's Church Director

Before I begin citing the testimony of Phil and Betsy, I want to say that I really loved these two; that love never went away as they were forced to take the witness stand. Their honesty is not to be questioned. Phil had a pastor's heart and the child-like innocence God demands of his chosen ones: "I tell you the truth, anyone who will not receive the kingdom of God like a little child will never enter it." (Mark 10:15.)

Betsy probably felt more torment over my ordeal than anyone else in the church, because she knew the truth, and the truth was not discussed in the church for all those months. She, too, was subjected to the "Welcome to Wonderland" experience, because she knew everything about the situation in intimate detail, yet Rev. Jake continued acting as if my conviction was a certainty. Like her husband, Betsy cares very deeply about what is right and wrong, but nobody paid any attention to her opinions concerning my case. Beyond Phil's blind obedience to Rev. Jake, I do not blame Betsy and him for the destruction of our lives. Betsy told us, when she and Phil paid us a visit, that she was willing to testify that she had seen Elisa eagerly climb up on my lap. This contradicts the picture Joan painted in her testimony that Elisa would cry when she had to go to my class. The fact is Betsy was actually there and Joan wasn't.

Phil graduated from a Bible college. Betsy went there also; that's where they met. He had told Joan, when she approached him about me long ago, that I was one of his most trusted workers. He also told Darcie, before the trial, that I never would have been chosen to teach the two- and three-year-olds if I wasn't considered highly trustworthy. Counting the hours logged from Sunday morning worship for the first year and a half, plus Sunday evenings, I had probably spent at least 100 hours with Phil in a roomful of kids. Note his response to the following question:

Q – (Mr. Martino) Did you ever see Paul Grey go into a rest room with a child?

A – I never saw Paul Grey go into a bathroom, no, with a child.

Please recall that Phil knew me much better than Rev. Jake did. Later, I will show Rev. Jake's response to the same question posed to Phil. It illustrates the vivid contrast between the two men. There are many pages of the transcript of Phil's testimony. It was completely honest and categorically favorable to me.

Wife of the Children's Church Director

Betsy's testimony, likewise, was completely favorable to me, and entirely honest. Here are some excerpts of interest:

Q – (Prosecutor) Did you ever hear Mr. Grey make any comments about Elisa?

A – Yes.

Q – What were they?

A – He thought she was a beautiful little girl.

Q – And did you ever see Mr. Grey put Elisa on his lap?
A – Yes.
Q – How many times did you see that?
A – I really don't know. Maybe once or twice. Not every time.
Q – (Mr. Martino) Did the alleged victim constantly demonstrate trust toward Paul Grey?
A – Yes.
Q – Did you ever see Elisa cry for an extended period of time after her mother had left the class?
A – I think she cried once, but I don't think it was for a real long time.
Q – Do you recall any time when Paul was in his classroom with children and there was no helper present?
A – No.
Q – Did you ever see Paul go to the rest room with any child?
A – No.
Q – Did you ever see Elisa herself try to get on Paul's lap?
A – I think so. I think one time I saw her do that. But it's very hard to like say that clear. But I do remember her climbing up on people.

The prosecutor asked a good question for cross-examination:
Q – (Prosecutor) When you were his helper or when he had a helper, if the helper took a child to the bathroom, would Mr. Grey be alone in the room with the children?
A – Yes.

I refer to this as a "good" question for the prosecution because, technically, they are supposed to prove that a defendant in such cases had opportunity and motive. Criminal lawyers might identify this as one of the key questions in the trial.

Elder #2

Next came Dottie and Brittany's father, one of Rev. Jake's elders. This was not a happy time for him. My accusation, by virtue of mishandling, caused tremendous pain in his family. When asked by the prosecutor what I said at the meeting at Rev. Jake's house shortly after the accusation, he responded:

A – To the best of my recollection he said that he thought he should be removed from the Sunday school and also from the church, which was what we thought should be done anyway for the protection of the church.

Mr. Martino had no questions.

My Ten-Year-Old Assistant

Next was Brittany, my young helper on the last day I taught. The second question is the big one that had caused the prosecutor to solicit her testimony:

Q – (Prosecutor) Did you ever see Paul Grey put Elisa on his lap?

A – Yeah.

Q – How often?

A – All the time.

Q – And how long would you be gone when you took children to the bathroom?

A – A few minutes.

Q – And did Paul ever put any other children on his lap like he did with Elisa?

A – Only like one other girl a long time ago.

Q – (Mr. Martino) Do you recall the last time you helped Mr. Grey teach his class?

A – No.

She went on to say she was ten years old when she was my helper. The last question cited above was one that I suggested to Mr. Martino (as I did with many questions). I wanted Brittany to testify that Elisa was not on my lap during story time, or coloring, or snack time, or making turtles. In short, she wasn't on my lap except within the first twenty to thirty minutes, when other adults (and Brittany) were present. As you can see, my goal wasn't accomplished. Brittany claimed she didn't remember the last Sunday school session. But she did recall the three words "all the time," for which the prosecution prepared her, which had been written by her mother in the police statement ten months earlier. Her lack of memory worked against me, which is one of the reasons our country believes in the necessity of a "speedy trial."

My First Adult Assistant

Next came Mary. At the prosecutor's instruction, she had to leave the east coast of Nicaragua to come to the trial, which is very difficult to arrange. I've already covered Mary's impact on the case. Nothing new came out in trial. Seeing Mary on the witness stand was relatively pleasant for me, unlike seeing my adversaries, Joan and Rev. Jake. Just one excerpt:

Q – (Mr. Martino) Did the class seem like a happy class?
A – Yeah, for two-year-olds.

Reverend Jake

Finally, it was time for my real accuser to take the stand. Shortly before the trial, he had elicited sympathy from some of his followers with the notion that "It's really hard to testify against a brother." Note how, in his testimony, he seems to try to make me look bad at every opportunity:

Q – (Prosecutor) Could you tell us a little bit about your educational background?
A – Yes. I have a degree in Counseling and Administration, and I also attended Bible School.
Q – And could you tell us, during the period of 8/1/92 to 3/21/93, what was the church policy regarding adult supervision of children in these rooms?
A – It varies a little bit depending on, you know, how old the children are. But with younger children the policy is to have at least two people in the room.

Q – And is (Paul Grey's) appearance today different from what it was during the period of 9/1/92 to 3/21/93?
A – I'd say very much so, yes.
Q – And do you remember which age group he was involved with?
A – I do now.
Q – And what was discussed by the group with Paul, and what were his responses?
A – There were a lot of responses. Pretty basically our reason for being together, my reason for us being together, was I just wanted to hear what was going on.
Q – What was said to Paul as best as you can recall, and what did he answer?
A – Well, I asked him did he know why we were here, and he said. "Yes." And he made, you know, some sort of introductory comments. And then we began to ask some, just ask some direct questions. I was just searching for information trying to find out what was, you know, what was going on and what we needed to do in this. I asked him if anybody had told him what was going on or what had happened, what the accusation was. He said, "No." But he said, "But it would be grabbing the girl's crotch. What else could it be?"
Q – Was that unsolicited? Was that statement unsolicited?
A – Well, I asked him, you know, did he know what the accusation was. And that's what he said. And I asked him again, I said, "Nobody told you that?" And he said, "No." I was a little confused.
Q – The specifics as to the allegations, that's my question. What was his response?
A – We did talk specifically about the allegations. And I asked him that question again, the same question again at one point that was significant to me. You know, "Did anybody ever tell you what this was

about?" This was in a group setting, and he said, "It's about touching her crotch." And did a thing with the finger. (Indicating).

Q – Excuse me. You're making a demonstration with your hand.

A – That's what he did.

[Prosecutor: Your Honor, might the record reflect?]

[Judge: The witness has gestured with his hand extended, palm up, and wiggled the fingers or retracted the fingers.]

Cross-Examination by Mr. Martino:

Q – OK, (Mr. Grozny), when you came into contact with Paul, to your knowledge, had he spoken with (Phil)?

A – I imagine he must have, because he showed up at my house so —

Q – And (Phil) was in possession of the allegations here, is that correct?

A – I can't tell you what he was in possession of. I really— to this day I really don't know what he knew. I really don't know the answer to that.

Q – Do you know whether or not he knew there was a complaint?

A – Correct.

Q – OK. He knew there was a complaint. Do you know whether or not he knew the nature of the complaint?

A – I don't think he knew the nature of the complaint, to my knowledge.

Q – OK. So when he comes to you then —

A – Who?

Q – Mr. Grey. When he first comes into your presence, as far as he knows you could be talking about the windows on the church needing repair, or the side-walks needing fixing, or the driveway needing repair?

A – No, he knew what he was coming for.

Q – Well, but you don't know that?

A – OK. You're right. You're correct.

Q – But he knew he was coming regarding a complaint of sexual abuse?

A – Oh, I don't know if he knew that it was sexual abuse. I can't tell you that. I don't know the answer to that. You'd have to ask him if he knew that. I don't know what he knew. I didn't have a conversation with him. I don't know.

Q – So he didn't know what the nature of the complaint was?

A – I don't know.

Q – I mean, the nature of the complaint then could have been that he failed to care for the children by not supplying them with proper school supplies or singing the proper songs? Could that have been the nature of the complaint?

A – That could have been. To my knowledge I have no idea what he knew. I have no idea what was told to him or what he knew. He could have thought he was coming in 'cause kids weren't singing the right songs.

Q – Do you ever recall a particular time when Paul Grey was in the room with any kids and there was no adult present?

A – Yes, I was told of an event like that.

Q – I'm not asking you whether you were told of an event like that.

A – Did I ever see an event like that?

Q – Yes.

A – No, I never saw an event like that. But I'm in a different place when the kids are doing what they're doing.

Q – OK. Did you ever see Paul Grey go to a rest room with a child?

A – No, but he told me he was taking a child to the rest room, which is prohibited. I flipped out. That was another thing in that meeting. He told me he was taking —

Q – Prior to the accusation, did you ever have any suspicion of Paul Grey's actions with any of the children?
A – I think I did, yes.
Q – And what caused your suspicion?
A – I don't know if at the time it was suspicion. I was teaching at a Sunday night — and Paul came in and he was — and I didn't know he was in the building. And he came in and he sat down, looked around and laughed. And later I found out that he was with the kids that night, and it just struck me as odd. I just, I just — at that point I continued to kind of hold that in my mind that there was something strange about that. It didn't make sense to me. And so from that point on I kind of had a tickler in my mind.
Q – Did Paul Grey do a good job keeping you informed of everything you wanted and needed to know about the Sunday school class?
A – He didn't keep me informed about anything. It's not in my chain of command.
Q – To your knowledge, was Paul Grey constantly gentle with the children?
A – I have no knowledge of that. I have no way of knowing the answer to that.
Q – Do you recall (Joan) telling you that (Elisa) had awoken with a nightmare?
A – No, she never told me anything like that.
Q – I want to show you something. Do you recognize this document?
A – Yes, I do.
Q – Is that your signature there?
A – That is certainly my signature, and I did in fact write that.
Q – OK, Isn't it true that you sent a fax indicating that (Joan) had initially told you one story where the child had awoke with a nightmare regarding Mr. Grey, and then later changed that story to say it was she who

awoke with a nightmare?
A – That wasn't told to me. And the fax doesn't reflect that that was told to me.
Q – Didn't you indicate in this letter you sent, this fax you sent, this caused you great concern about the changing stories?
A – I heard two different stories, but not from, not from the originating party.
Q – But you do say in your fax that this has caused you — it says, "Something really significant troubles me quite a bit about this, and it's the fact that the mother has made two different stories she's telling about the discovery."
A – That's what I had heard.
Q – That's your language, isn't it?
A – That's what I had heard. Yes, and that was troubling that I had heard that. But that was not told to me.
Q – At that meeting, did you ask Mr. Grey whether or not he did it?
A – I may have asked him if he did it.
Q – Do you recall him responding, "No"?
A – I'm confused about that. I've reviewed my notes over and over again, and it's not in my notes.
Q – It's not in your notes?
A – No.
Q – And you don't have any independent recollection?
A – I don't have real good recollection. There are a few things that I focused in on that, on that meeting that I recalled very well. And I've refreshed my memory by reading over my notes. And that's not a question that I either included in my notes or have a very clear recollection about.
Q – I'd like to show you this document, and see if you recognize it.
A – I do, in fact I recognize this, yes.
Q – Is that your signature on that?

A – Yes, that is my signature.
Q – In the third paragraph, it says, "We told Paul Grey of the accusation against him without details, and he flat out denied it."
A – Yeah. This is sequentially — you'd have to read the thing, because he did come in sort of doing that. But things change a little bit as it goes on.
[Judge: Do you claim an inconsistency with the statement?]
[Mr. Martino: Yes, I do, Your Honor.]
[Judge: Full exhibit.]

(Whereupon the above referred-to statement was received into evidence and marked Defendant's exhibit "2.")

Mr. Martino had not asked Rev. Jake all the questions he intended to (questions I had written). But he interrupted his questioning to ask the judge for permission to consult with me. When Mr. Martino came to the defense table, with Rev. Jake still on the stand, he was pale, as if in shock. He said, "We have *got* to get this guy off the stand." I consented. The reason was Rev. Jake's using every opportunity to make me look bad. I had told Mr. Martino for months that Rev. Jake was out to get me, but he just didn't realize how true it was. Mr. Martino ended the questioning at that point. He had never encountered anyone like Rev. Jake.

After the jury was dismissed from the courtroom and the state rested its case, Mr. Martino filed a motion for acquittal based on the fact that Elisa had failed to identify me. The prosecutor then argued against the motion, starting with the following:

> Your Honor heard testimony of the child. She referenced her teacher. You heard testimony from several of the witnesses that the only person she ever referred to as teacher was Mr. Grey. Your Honor has also heard testimony that Mr. Grey has significantly changed his appearance since the child last saw him. He had a beard. Rev. Grozny indicated he's changed his hair. And again, we're dealing with a child of very tender years. (etc.)

Mr. Martino responded:

> Your Honor, if I may? Referring to the transcript. I'm looking at page five on my cross-examination, which was a rather brief one. But it says, Question: "At Sunday school, Elisa, who took you to the bathroom?" She says, "My teacher." And I said, "Your teachers?" and she said, "Yeah." "When you went to the bathroom did the teachers help you wipe?" "Yes." So we're talking about an amorphous group of teachers, Your Honor. And, once again, there's no identification of Mr. Grey. She sat right in that chair for a period of time. He sat right here. He was one of her teachers. And on two inquiries from (the prosecution) she was unable to make an identification on either occasion. So (the prosecutor) would like to take the focus away from the alleged victim here, and have the jury stand in her shoes with respect to some elusive identification issue. I mean, if they're going to do that they can identify somebody in this audience as being the perpetrator of this crime.

The judge chose to deny our motion. Mr. Martino then asked for, and was granted, an exception.

Child Sex Abuse Expert Witness

In cases like this, the prosecution is technically supposed to prove that a defendant had opportunity and motive to commit the crime. Failure to do so can result in the judge dismissing the case. The reason I paid to undergo a thorough psychological examination was to demonstrate that I had no motivation to do sexual things to young children.

The prosecutor fought Dr. Shalom's right to testify. When the trial started, the judge had not yet ruled on whether Dr. Shalom would be allowed to do so. With the jury out of the room, Dr. Shalom was brought in. Before the judge, Mr. Martino began the questioning. Dr. Shalom said he had testified in court hundreds of times regarding allegations of child sexual abuse. Mr. Martino had him describe the standard protocol he uses when he evaluates such a complaint. Dr. Shalom epitomizes the way our society should handle such complaints. For educational purposes, I cite some excerpts from his testimony:

> The protocol requires that I take a look at how the complaint originated. That is, in whose mind did this complaint originate? Who spoke the first words about it, and then what the report chain consisted of from person to person. Then to examine the sequence of events from a language point of view to see what configuration of words was used by each party along the way, and to what extent there was any evidence of one person passing language or ideas onto another person, as opposed to people independently finding their own words to express themselves. And then looking at whatever interview process took place in order to determine whether the process of interviewing conformed with the standards of the profession for the proper methods to be used when speaking to, especially, a very young and a pre-school child. And also to any concerned members of that child's family about a child's sexual abuse, or for that matter, a physical or an emotional abuse issue.
>
> And here, very simply what we look for is to see whether there is any evidence of tainting or contamination of the child either through the emotional state of the people who conducted the questioning, and evidence of tainting or contamination of the child because of any bias that had made itself evident in the attitudes of the people who conducted the questioning, whether the questioning itself contained any significant examples of leading questions, whether there were any social factors that were of a corrosive kind that could operate upon the narration of the child. The ultimate objective of this analysis is to determine the independence of the narration that a child gives about his or her own experience, and the extent to which that narration can be seen as a reasonable representation of the child's true experience or the degree to which it is

likely to have been or clearly was contaminated by the attitudes and views of those who spoke to the child and questioned her. Whether they were doing this either intentionally in order to perhaps coach the child in a particular direction, or if they did it unintentionally but with the same effect because of the attitudes they carried, or their anxiety and their worries.

Q – What conclusions did you reach?

A – The conclusions that I reached are clear-cut. And they are that this child was subjected to a very high level of corrosive social pressure by her mother, and to a lesser extent, but also to significant pressure by those who subsequently interviewed her, providing to the child the first ideas and then providing again repeated ideas to the child about what others thought either had happened to her or might have happened to her before the child had an opportunity to express herself.

I also concluded that there, at least, and I'm only speaking about what I saw, I don't know what might have been done that was not documented. The documentation in this case is fragmentary at best. It's a poor documentation. It only gives a limited insight into the actual events that took place surrounding the questioning of this child. But from the limited information that is available through this documentation, it is very clear that the child did not receive a full and proper interview from those who were called upon to question her based on the information that those people already had about the pressures to which the child had been subjected.

And that brings me to another criterion that we use strongly in our evaluation of child sexual abuse complaints, which is: in order to check the likely accuracy of a complaint that's brought to our attention we make an effort to develop, if the data allows for it, an alternate hypothesis about what could have led to this concern. At least one, if

> not more than one. And then to check it out to see whether it has any explanatory value in a given case. Since our experience is that sometimes things are just not the way they may appear to be, and that the gravity of these issues requires a conscientious attempt to make sure that we're not making a mistake. And I saw no evidence of any alternative hypothesis building, any attempt to collect background data about that mother and child interaction, which is perhaps — which is a very dramatic interaction that the mother and child had when the mother woke up with a bad dream, and brought her own bad dream and her own thoughts about it to an apparently peacefully-sleeping child. I saw no attempt in the documentation to pursue the significance of that report; and to find out whether that very, very dramatic event had been what had caused the child to think that an improper action had occurred.

Dr. Shalom then presented a couple of professional articles for exhibit, in hopes that the jury would be able to read them and become educated about the role of suggestibility in such allegations. One was a review article by Ceci and Bruck. At that point in the trial, Mr. Martino turned to me and whispered, "I don't like that look on the judge's face." Sure enough, the judge said, "Well, wait a minute. Where are we going with this?" Mr. Martino replied that it was to have Dr. Shalom discuss the flawed nature of the investigation in front of the jury. The prosecutor then argued, as follows:

> Your Honor, the state would object to — this is a clear usurpation of the jury's function by a hired gun, and he's invading the province of the jury. The state would renew its Motion *in limine*, cite the court specifically to *Court v. Mr. X*. Precisely the same kind of situation. The defense tries to bring in a hired gun, reads some documents and attempts to present a formal opinion as to the believability or non-believability of witnesses. Clearly inappropriate. Clearly the court should prohibit this type of testimony, Your Honor. He's clearly invading the province of the jury.

Judge: Well, let me ask you this. Did he have the complete record?

Mr. Martino: He had all the records that were disclosed to me by the attorney.

Judge: Even the statement of the mother really wasn't the mother's statement. Yes, she signed it. But my recollection is that (the state inspector) really wrote the statement, and it was her condensation, or whatever it was, of whatever the mother was telling her. You know, that's second-hand in a way.

The judge was absolutely wrong in these last statements. Joan wrote the statement. It was signed and witnessed by another policeman, not the state inspector the judge had referred to. The judge ruled, based on the fact that Mr. Martino had cross-examination rights when Joan and the Emergency Room nurse were on the stand, that Dr. Shalom's opinion should not be introduced in front of the jury. It was a wrong ruling, and terribly unfair.

There was a second aspect of Dr. Shalom's testimony: my psychological profile. Excerpts from the exchange:

Mr. Martino: I think the second aspect dealt with whether Dr. Grey fit the profile of a pedophile; is that correct, Dr. Shalom?

Dr. Shalom: That's correct.

Judge: Now what's he really going to say about Dr. Grey?

Mr. Martino: That — and Doctor you can correct me if I'm wrong, but you have said you conducted various tests which indicate that Dr. Grey does not fit the profile of a pedophile.

Judge: Who's ever accused him of being a pedophile?

Mr. Martino: Well, that's —

Judge: This is one incident. This is one incident. What's a pedophile? Maybe I don't know what a pedophile is. But a pedophile, as I understood it, is a person who's inclined to do these things compulsively and does it a lot. Who's accused him of being a pedophile, or that it's ever happened other than on March 21?

At that time, my friend Jim, who had come to New England

from Texas to support me, started making highly relevant verbal remarks from the audience, seeing my rights being trampled as I faced a thirty-year prison term. The prosecutor asked for and received an admonishment of the audience. The judge's last statement, that there was no accusation other than on March 21, was entirely incorrect. Back in the early court appearances, Mr. Martino filed a motion of specificity. He lost the battle; the charge against me was allowed to simply refer to "diverse dates." That means my alibi had to account for every minute I was in the classroom over a seven-month period. And, regardless of the judge's personal definition of pedophile, the fact is that Dr. Shalom was there to testify about my sexual psychological profile, which showed no deviancy at all. It was another wrong decision by the judge. The jury never even knew about Dr. Shalom. Our key witness was not allowed to testify. That evening, according to Mr. Martino, all the defense attorneys in town discussed nothing but the judge's incredibly bad rulings.

The reader may suspect that the judge and I viewed each other in adversarial terms. That's not the case. I always had the optimistic assumption that he knew I had been falsely accused. I have never felt any dislike for him. The two bad rulings I just mentioned caused a temporary low point in my opinion of him, however.

My Previous Assistant Pastor (First Character Witness)

The jury returned to the courtroom, and my assistant pastor from two churches ago took the stand. He had been waiting in the hall all this time because no witness was allowed to hear the testimony of any other witness. This man, my friend, had gone with me to help shop for appropriate courtroom attire. He also went to the expense of getting a new suit for himself, on a separate trip, to make himself as presentable as possible to the judge and jury. He and his wife had visited us several times during the agonizing pre-trial months. They never failed to pray for us. Those were the actions that we expected — but never received — from many families in Rev. Jake's church. This man's wife came to the trial every day, and spent hours praying for me while silently seated in the audience; "spiritual warfare," as it is called. These two truly exemplify what Christians should be. The reason why I chose the word "exemplify" is that, as a result of this man's testimony, the sub-headline in the newspaper story the next day quoted his testimony that I "exemplified" Christian behavior. This man is a true brother in Christ.

A brief excerpt from his testimony:

> Paul was always very active in serving the church. He's a man that always wanted to help other people. Our church had a number of children, and Paul also taught them in our church; and they all loved him.

When I read this brother's testimony today, it makes me sad for all the people who choose to follow Rev. Jake and miss out on true Christian examples like this man and his wife. May God forever bless their family.

My Own Testimony

I testified next. I was still dizzy from the pace of the trial and from the phenomenal injustice to which I was being subjected. It really was dream-like. I vaguely recall that the option of not testifying was available, but I never gave that notion a second thought. Some excerpts:

Q – (Mr. Martino) Was there any policy at the school regarding having an adult helper in the class at all times?

A – There may have been a spoken policy at some point, but never in my three years at (Rev. Jake's church) did anybody tell me that I must have an adult with me at all times.

Q – You had other children sit on your lap also?

A – Absolutely. Of the seventy-five kids or so I've worked with over the last three years, of the two and three-year-olds, I don't know, forty — thirty, forty, or fifty of them have been on my lap at one time or another.

Always of their choosing. I never ask them to get up there.

Q– How did Elisa react socially with the other children in the class?

A – Well, because she was one of the youngest she fell within the guidelines of a teacher's adage. I had a manual for two and three-year-olds — for Sunday school teachers of two and three-year-olds. One of the first things that it said is: two-year-olds play *near* each other, three-year-olds play *with* each other. I observed that to be the case on many occasions. In Elisa's case, she was a two-year-old for the first six months that she was in my class, and then I saw her a couple of times after her third birthday. She had not yet developed to the stage where she wanted to mingle with the other kids. So she just, she just hung out and watched them, standing, or sitting in a chair, or when the adult musicians were in the same room with us, she would be on my lap at that point. Once the adults were out of the room there were not many times at all that she was ever on my lap.

Q – Did she ever exhibit to you any anxieties, fears, or sadness?

A – No. There was one time that I recall when she made it clear to her mother that she wanted her to stay for a while in that class. Now, this was not near the end of my teaching career. It was not close to March 21st, 1993. It was several months previous to that. Maybe December of '92, or so. I remember this one occasion when she just let out a hefty yell when Joan was trying to leave. So Joan came back in and said, "Oh, do you want me to stay with you?" And I said, "By all means. Sit with us for a while." Eventually it was OK, though. It just took longer than usual that day.

Q – Now, when did you first become aware of the allegations in this case?

A – On Wednesday morning, March 24th at six in the morning, Darcie and I were awakened with a phone call from Phil. At that point, he told me that Joan was going to call the police to accuse me of molesting her daughter, Elisa.

Q – Was that the extent of your conversation with Phil?

A – No. I told him, "Don't worry, Phil." He was very upset about the whole thing. And I told him, "Don't worry. It will be seen clearly for what it is, and it will disappear."

Q – Now, did any one of those (men) lead, sort of lead the group in making inquiries of you?

A – Rev. Jake Grozny, the pastor, is the one who is in control. He was in command of the meeting.

The pastor said to me, "Do you have any idea how this accusation could have come about?" Well, this is seven at night, and I had first learned of the allegation six o'clock that very morning. For thirteen hours I had been tormented with the reality that I was being accused of child sexual molestation, and that reality was not going away. It was not a dream. My mind, which is trained to take blips of data, and they all look the same, I'm supposed to figure out the big picture. What could have caused this thing to happen? I pondered and pondered for thirteen solid hours, with a trained professional mind, and discussed it with Darcie, also. We came to the same conclusion. Our conclusion was, this lady, based upon the little bit of interaction I'd had with her in the past, has a fear of men, and she must have assumed that I touched her daughter. In the circumstances of the classroom, there is no other possibility. I don't care to be graphic about this, but if you think of the other possibilities involving other parts of my body, there is no possibility. In Joan's own testimony she said she opened the door and I was literally two feet away from her. There's just no other possibility whatsoever than to assume this woman had to assume that I touched her daughter improperly.

The hand gestures that the (two) men made today, Phil had

his palm upward. Jake Grozny was much more graphic. His mind was doing a lot more with it.

Q – What's your relationship been like with Jake Grozny?

A – They have a drastic shortage of volunteers, particularly in Children's Church ministry. Children's Church is the most difficult aspect of a church to get people to volunteer. You take a terrible beating as a teacher. There are no rewards, and it is top priority in God's eyes as far as I'm concerned. So to be as helpful as I can to the church, I feel like I should support Jake Grozny. I should support Phil. And the best means I have available is to volunteer for the things that they might like me to do.

[The prosecutor then questioned me.]

Q – (Prosecutor) Do you recall when there were times when you would refer to her as being awesome (cute)? Yes or no?

A – Once.

Q – Did you ever say, she was just adorable? Yes or no?

A – Not that I recall.

Q – But you might have? Yes or no?

A – Possibly.

Q – Did you ever say, she was so cute? Yes or no?

A – Yes.

Q – On more than one occasion?

A – Yes.

Cross-examination by Mr. Martino:

Q – Dr. Grey, how did Elisa refer to you?

A – She didn't. I never heard her refer to me at all.

Q – Did she use any form of address?

A – No. The mother just dropped her off and she stayed.

Q – Did you refer to other children in the class as cute or beautiful?

A – Yes.

Q – Was that something that was uncommon for you to do?

A – No. I almost feel like it's a duty of a Sunday school teacher of 2 and 3 year-olds to do things like that. I'm working for the kids and for the parents.

Cross-examination by the Prosecutor:

Q – Was the term teacher ever used in your classroom?
A – No.
Q – By no one?
A – No.

As the reader can clearly see, I was subjected to a trial for suspected child molestation, the "evidence" being that I had described the kids as "cute," etc. Picture yourself under similar circumstances (you have presumably made similar remarks, probably many times). Is there a different standard for men, concerning the implications of such remarks?

At that time, the only remaining witnesses were my two other character witnesses. My office mate had been in England that week, working hard, I'm sure. I had called her while she was there to let her know how the schedule was proceeding. If those two additional witnesses had been at the trial when my testimony ended, they would have testified that day.

Contradictory to my testimony about church policy, Rev. Jake had said in his written statement to the police that the church had a policy that every teacher (of young children) must have an adult helper plus an additional child helper. Some of the other teachers were upset when they were informed — for the first time ever — of the existence of such rules after the accusation. The ten-to-twelve-year-old class I taught is an example. For a year we met in a room with the door closed. Nobody ever said anything about this violating any rule until after the accusation. Joan probably could have sued Rev. Jake's church out of existence, but he convinced her that the only "bad guy" who was guilty of breaking church rules was me.

The prosecutor wanted me to say that, on the last teaching day, Brittany might possibly have taken one or more kids to the restroom, thereby leaving me "alone" with the kids. I had thought about that possibility a lot. During all those months preceding the trial, I couldn't even remember Elisa on that last day. Not until Joan's testimony did I realize that Joan had picked her up ten minutes early. I did recall Mary taking one child, Julia, to the restroom, and Kate taking three others. Of the two boys, one never had to go during Sunday school, and the other was in diapers. So I knew that none of the pupils needed to go during the last forty-five minutes. I couldn't remember Elisa. But, if Brittany had taken anyone that day, it would have been Elisa, so I was positive that I was never in the room with Elisa without other helpers present. But I've found that I can say very few things with 100 percent certainty, so, when the prosecutor badgered me for a yes-or-no response to his question, I kept telling him I was "97 percent sure," that I was never "alone" with the kids that last day. In his closing arguments, he made a big deal of my not saying 100 percent.

The next day, Mr. Martino led off by referring to a motion he had filed earlier, to admit the results of my polygraph examination. The prosecution, before the trial began, had filed a brief in opposition to this motion. The judge denied our motion. This was no surprise. Mr. Martino asked for, and was granted, another exception. The jury did not know of this exchange.

My Office Mate (Character Witness #2)

My office mate of five years took the stand. She was a young professional, and I would like to believe that she moved the two young women jurors in my favor. She was eager to vindicate me, having spent many days during a ten-and-a-half-month period talking with me about the whole ordeal and grieving over the entire unfair sequence of events. The most memorable part of her very short testimony:

Q – (Mr. Martino) Have you ever heard any ill comments about Mr. Grey?

A – Never, never. That's why this whole thing is just —

She was interrupted momentarily, then she uttered her last word, "ridiculous."

The prosecutor asked that that response be stricken. His request was granted, and the jury was instructed not to consider her last comment in any way. The prosecutor asked her if, in all the hours I had talked about my class with her, I had ever mentioned the name Elisa. She said no. Actually, she did hear the names of a number of kids over the years, but not Elisa. May God bless my friend Colleen and her family, now and always. She's a model of human decency and professionalism.

Another Adult Assistant (Character Witness #3)

The last witness was Kate, who had been with us in our previous church. I visited her in the hospital when her firstborn arrived. That child, a girl, had attended my class for nineteen months, except for several Sundays when she went to the early service. Some excerpts:

Q – Specifically, what did you do?
A – Well, during the time that I did music with my husband, Mr. Grey was also in the room helping during that time before, you know, his class actually started.
Q – When you say he was helping, helping doing what?
A – He was in just making sure the kids were doing OK, and making sure they were getting to their seats. You know, that age, sometimes they were initially shy to come in. And he would, you know, encourage them to come in and get settled; that's all. Sing with them.
Q – Ever hear any criticism of (Mr. Grey) prior to this incident?
A – No.
Q – Ever hear any praise of him prior to this incident?
A – Yes.
Q – What was the nature of the praise?
A – I always heard good things. I can't think of a specific incident, but he was always involved. He always did a lot of work in the church. He was always willing to get in there and do whatever he had to do.

Closing Arguments: Prosecutor

Immediately after Kate's testimony, the prosecutor began his summary. If the reader wonders about Darcie, she did not have to testify. My wife had become a broken woman due to the trauma. She was barely able to sit in the courtroom for a few minutes to hear testimony. The grief was too overwhelming. The prosecution certainly didn't want her to testify, so she could only have been a character witness. We didn't have her testify because we didn't think her testimony was likely to be any more beneficial than that of the other character witnesses, and I didn't want her subjected to unnecessary stress. If any readers doubt whether Darcie was truly 100 percent confident of my innocence, please know that she too has written a book about our ordeal. (It has not yet been published.)

Jurors were instructed to make their decisions based on what the witnesses had testified, not what the lawyers said in their closing arguments. Some excerpts from the prosecutor's argument:

> She sat right there in front of you, ladies and gentlemen, without hesitance when I asked her what happened to her. She didn't look around at anybody. She didn't look at me to be directed. She answered the question. Forcefully. Immediately. She testified that her teacher at her church put his finger in her private. The state would submit that's the case right there, ladies and gentlemen.
>
> Remember, Reverend Grozny said his hair is different. Again, we have a three-year-old coming in. We're asking her to identify someone whose beard has been shaved off, whose hair is different, who she hasn't seen in almost a year. So I would submit that when Mr. Martino talks to you about the identification issue, that's a red herring. That's what it is. Treat it as such. Recall that she referred to the defendant as her teacher. Teacher, someone with power and authority over her.
>
> You heard even from Mr. Martino, the defendant's last

witness (Kate): Joan didn't go around that church bad-mouthing the defendant. She had no axe to grind. Joan, again, indicated that — by the end of her testimony with tears in her eyes, she indicated she had a bad feeling about the defendant from the start, that she approached (Phil) about it, that he assuaged her concerns.

Again, Joan testified about how the defendant referred to her daughter as awesome cute. Just adorable. So cute. Those weren't terms she made up. When I cross-examined the defendant yesterday he acknowledged making those remarks.

(Again, Joan confirmed) how Elisa would cry when she would have to be brought into the defendant's classroom. Joan says she has a bad feeling. She leaves early. The defendant acknowledged on cross-examination that Joan came early that day. You heard her testimony about what she observed. From two to three feet away she observed that she believed the defendant to have an erection. He covers himself as he's about to place her daughter on his lap. And, again, if Joan had an axe to grind, at that point she could have created a scene.

And, again, with all due respect to Mr. Martino, I suspect he's going to make a (big) deal about the issue of the dream that was testified to. And, again, the state would submit that that's going to be a red herring, and treat it as such. (The doctor) said the redness could have been caused by a finger. Again, I'm sure Mr. Martino is going to say it could have been any number of reasons. But, again, when you reach that decision as to how you want to weigh (the doctor's) testimony, make sure you fit that piece of this puzzle in with all the other testimony.

(Betsy) testified she heard him make comments about how Elisa was beautiful. She saw him have Elisa on his lap at least once or twice. Again, what axe to grind does (Betsy) have? None.

(Elder #2) recalls, unsolicited, that someone touched —

he couldn't remember the exact words; someone touched the girl's genitals. The unsolicited comment of this defendant. What axe does he have to grind? None.

And ladies and gentlemen, the next witness, the state would submit, is a very key witness. Brittany, eleven years old. What does she say? She said, Elisa was on the defendant's lap all the time. All the time. Again, what axe to grind does this little girl have? She was in that classroom. Who saw better than her? And, again, she confirmed that she'd be out of the classroom when she'd have to take another child to the bathroom.

Closing Arguments: Defense

Since this book is primarily intended to let the reader know about how witch-hunts are conducted, only a few of Mr. Martino's closing remarks are given:

Not even an attempt by (the prosecutor) to get the time of the year. I mean, in a criminal allegation you want to know the time you're dealing with. You want to know at least what year they're talking about. There wasn't even a hint or even an attempt by (the prosecutor) to focus on the time of the alleged offense.

And then the State's Attorney asks if she could identify the teacher. For a second time she says, "No." No time reference to tie in. No identification to tie in. Nothing. For all she could have done — I mean, she could have looked back at that audience and said somebody in the audience was the culprit.

I'm not criticizing Elisa. God bless her. I don't know what words to use in here. You can't use beautiful, cute. Let's say likable little girl, OK?

(Recall) Doctor Grey's testimony. First time I ever put a client on the witness stand without sitting down with him or her for hours. He sat down there, and took that stand and testified for some thirty minutes without having sat

> with me and discussed his testimony for two minutes. You're going to judge his demeanor. You're going to judge his truthfulness.
>
> I don't get a second argument. The reason I only get one argument is because the state has a heavy, heavy burden. We didn't have to put any evidence on. That was not our obligation. The state has the burden to prove the defendant guilty beyond a reasonable doubt. And each and every one of you promised me that after you heard this case and after you've heard our arguments, heard the judge's charge on the law, that if you believed — even if you believed, well, maybe he did something wrong, but I am not convinced beyond a reasonable doubt, all reasonable doubt — I will vote for a not guilty finding. You promised me that. I believed your promise.

In the prosecutor's second round of closing arguments, his remarks included:

> Paul Grey is on trial, not Joan. By all the testimony Joan has attempted to be prudent and fair regarding her concerns throughout. She has absolutely no axe to grind other than being a mother who's concerned about her daughter.
>
> The state would submit the pieces of this puzzle fit perfectly on the first count of sexual assault and on the second count of risk of injury. The state would submit that the evidence is there for you to find compelling, beyond a reasonable doubt and return convictions on both counts and would ask that you do so.

The judge instructed the jury. The judge explained that the first charge, sexual assault in the first degree, could be defined by vaginal penetration, however slight, with a finger. The second charge was called risk of injury to a minor. Police in that New England state would routinely make both charges, in hopes that, if their sexual assault case failed, they could at least get a conviction on something. As is evident, the broad range of possibilities under this second statute makes a conviction much more likely, though penalties are much less severe.

The statute:

> Any person who willfully or unlawfully causes or permits any child under the age of 16 years to be placed in such a situation that its life or limb is in danger, or its health is likely to be injured, or its morals likely to be impaired, or does any act likely to impair the health or morals of any such child, shall be guilty of this offense.

"Morals," the judge told the jury, "means good morals, living, acting and thinking in accordance with those principles and precepts which are commonly accepted among us as right and decent." He also told them that the first of the two types of ways a person can be guilty under this statute is "Willfulness or unlawfulness in causing or permitting the child to be placed in a situation where his life or limb is in danger, or his health is likely to be injured, or his morals are likely to be impaired." "The second type or class of conduct which the statute regulates is the doing of any act likely to impair the health or morals of a child. Under this type or part, the defendant need not have specifically intended to impair the health or morals of a child. It is the act itself which determines whether or not there has been a violation of the statute."

I haven't speculated much about what went through the jurors' minds concerning this second charge. The wording sounds to me like, if the jury thought it was immoral for a child to sit on the lap of a man who wasn't a family member, the act itself made me guilty of this statute whether I thought it was appropriate behavior or not.

Jury Deliberations

My brother left the next morning, to begin his 1,500-mile drive back home to Kansas City. It is an embarrassment that he, who did not attend any church, did exactly the right thing, while my own Christian "family" deserted me, not even driving fifteen miles to the trial. Other than Kate and Gary on the day of Kate's testimony, only one other person from Rev.

Jake's church came to support me. When, after his wife had kicked him out, this man was going through a difficult time in his life, I would go upstairs on Sunday evening and find him. We went many times to my Sunday school room, where we could talk and pray in privacy. He was in crisis, and I'm glad to have been able to support him. When this man heard Rev. Jake testify about my suspicious behavior of coming into the sanctuary and looking around and then laughing, he knew it was likely himself I had been looking for. Each day of the trial and deliberations, my lawyer would sign a note for this man so that his new employer would know that his time off was to attend a criminal trial. My relationship with this man was typical of my relations with most people in that church. The big difference is that Rev. Jake failed to turn him against me, as he did my other friends.

When the trial ended, the most stressful period of our lives began. The jury deliberated Thursday afternoon. When they returned to the courtroom, where my supporters and I had been silently, ceaselessly praying, it was only to announce that they had not come to the required unanimous agreement. We had been hoping for an acquittal that day, and the notion of returning seventeen hours later for another day of agonized waiting was very difficult.

My friend Steve was at the trial every day, supporting me through prayer ("spiritual warfare") and verbal encouragement. He would work very late each night at his demanding job, so that he could attend. Steve had been one of our friends in a previous church, where we didn't know him for very long. He then moved away for a few years, during which we never saw him. When he moved back into town, I saw him only a handful of times. Steve demonstrated what Christian fellowship is all about. Our friend Ruth was also there throughout the trial. Her salient comment: "I've been around a lot of spiritual warfare, but this was something else." The fact is it's hard to keep praying when things get to a certain level of seeming hopelessness. Ruth and Michele also performed the most heart-wrenching task of all: staying with Darcie during her bleakest hours, while I was in court. May God bless them richly now and forever. They exemplify how we should all strive to behave.

Friday, I looked forward to the acquittal. The judge had told the defendant in the case just before mine that if he were found guilty (of the same crime I had been charged with, but with two alleged victims rather than one), the judge would impose the maximum sentence, which was sixty years. At that point, the man gave up and took a plea-bargain sentence of several years. Although one of the two victims then retracted her allegation, that didn't help him. So I was waiting to see whether the "Welcome to Wonderland" experience would continue and I would be sentenced to thirty years in a maximum-security prison or if I would be acquitted. Numerous innocent defendants have been convicted at trials like mine. Considering Joan's and Rev. Jake's misguided testimony — and the judge's refusal to allow my key witness to testify — the verdict could easily have gone against me. It happens quite regularly, and it could happen to you. Remember, even at that point I could have plea-bargained and been freed with no jail time.

I'm not sure if the following happened on Friday; it probably did. The jury asked the judge if they could be informed whether I had any children of my own, and asked if they could see what I looked like with a beard. To me, those questions were indicative of a juror or jurors who entertained suspicions of guilt. The judge said no to both questions. Concerning my beard, I wore a short, thin beard during my Sunday school teaching years only because I hate to shave. Usually, when I shave it off or re-grow it, most of my friends don't even notice. It's not the type of beard that significantly alters my appearance, as the prosecution had argued. Of course, the proper way to present myself at trial was clean-shaven rather than bearded, just as I wore a suit rather than jeans and tennis shoes.

There was one mishap concerning my attire. My friend and I had gone shopping for my suit, shirts, ties, belt, and socks for the trial. I'd never bought such expensive clothing before. I put on the new wardrobe and went to the first day of the trial. By the end of the day, I discovered that I had somehow mistakenly put on a pair of Darcie's socks. I have no idea how I was even able to get them on; her feet are half the size of mine.

My friends and I prayed long and hard in the courtroom that Friday. How many ways can you ask God to make the truth come out? We started this process at 10:00 A.M. I was told that a very loud male voice had been heard from within the jury deliberation room. Finally, at five o'clock, the jury came in and announced that they had not yet reached agreement. That was just about the most discouraging moment of all, to me. Some might think of this announcement as assuring at least three more days of not being imprisoned. To us it was nothing but agony. That weekend, Darcie was more broken than ever. Neither of us is afraid of dying; we certainly would have preferred death to enduring that weekend.

Before the accusation, one of the things we used to regularly pray about was to be used by God effectively. Darcie's symptoms of chronic fatigue were very limiting. Only a few days before the accusation, she had made a heartfelt appeal to God to be used in some powerful capacity. You've heard the saying "Be careful what you ask for, because you just might get it." Her notion was probably along the lines of martyrdom in a jungle somewhere. It shows how far we are from comprehending our Creator. Anyway, her prayer was answered: God used us in a very powerful capacity. What's been so frustrating since the trial is that no one seems to have benefited from our ordeal, which is why I felt compelled to write this book. I believe we're still waiting for the benefit to be accomplished. Maybe we won't live to see it, but I believe it will eventually happen.

When I stopped by my place of employment Monday morning, all my co-workers were eager to hear about what was going on and were unanimously very supportive. Then I went to another day of deliberations at the courthouse, beginning at 10:00 A.M. Some time in the afternoon, my lawyer, who had been within earshot of the deliberation room, said to me, "It has now gotten shrill back there." I never really suspected that the jury could possibly come to unanimous agreement to convict me, so I was just praying that they would see past the emotions and judge according to the truth. But then, I had prayed for ten and a half months for the truth to be revealed about all those who had perpetrated the case, and my prayers hadn't been answered.

Later in the afternoon, the jury asked the judge for some instructions. They said they were unanimous on one of the two counts but not on the other. They asked whether the other count could be divided in two, since it had two parts, and if they could vote separately on the two counts. At that point, I was certain that I would be acquitted of the 1st degree sexual assault charge, though no one had specifically named the charges during the jury's question. The judge told them that they could not split the charge. I also learned additional information from the jury's question: They said that on the two-part charge, the vote was 6-0 for one part, and 5-1 for the other.

At that point I assumed there was one juror who was swayed by emotion and wanted to make the classic witch-hunt choice: convict despite a lack of evidence because, with all the commotion, I must have done *something* improper. I expected a full acquittal, and the waiting became less stressful. We didn't have to wait long.

Having reached their verdict; the jury returned to the courtroom. The judge asked me to stand and face them. I frequently have problems with dizziness when I stand up. During the trial, to keep my balance I had to put my hand on the back of the chair whenever I stood. In addition to listening to the verdict, I was focused on staying on my feet. The forewoman read the verdict: "not guilty" of sexual assault. The judge asked about the "Risk of Injury" charge. Her response was, "Unable to reach a verdict."

That was a terrible disappointment. Officially, it was a hung jury, which means that if the state chose to pursue it, the case would have to be tried again. There was a major problem with that: we were out of money. Each day in court, including the three days of deliberations, cost us about $800 and cost the taxpayers thousands. When our friend Michele sent her letter to our friends across the country, they responded with financial donations and a basketful of cards and letters of support.

With several thousand dollars from our friends, and our own savings, we had just managed to make it through the trial without incurring further debt. The trial and related expenses had cost us our life savings: about $25,000. Darcie was, surprisingly, very upbeat at that point. For the first time in ten and a half months, she had seen concrete evidence that not everybody thought I was a child molester. She was ready to take on the prosecutor at that point, in a new trial. It was wonderful to see a ray of hope back in her life, though I continued to be concerned about the money.

Newspaper Articles

As the trial dragged on, we had to consider other financial possibilities: what would we do if the trial ended in a prison sentence? When the judge decided to prohibit Dr. Shalom from speaking in my behalf, Mr. Martino pointed out to me that this was a legal point on which we could appeal the verdict if I were convicted. However, if I were to be imprisoned, I would not be drawing a salary. It wasn't comforting to think about possible avenues for appeal, but a lawyer's job isn't to be comforting. He was exactly right in what he told me.

The reader needs to understand some realities about prison in order to comprehend the stress of awaiting a verdict, and the temptation to plea-bargain. Life in prison for a man or woman convicted of child abuse is not a matter of simply being locked up. Likelihood of violence at the hands of other convicts is extremely high. For out-of-shape Ph.D. types, the probability becomes a certainty. Rapes and beatings are commonplace.

A local newspaper story published around the time of my trial described a young man who, at age sixteen, joined a gang while in jail, for his own protection. Gang membership requires commitment. In that article, a young prisoner was assigned to inflict injury upon a new inmate who was convicted of child molestation. The young man said that gangs routinely attack those who commit crimes against children or women. The young man was given a blunt instrument to use when attacking the new inmate. Several inmates held the man through the bars of a cell as they beat him. Then they sprinkled him with baby oil and water and set him on fire. The young man then returned to his cell and cried, because what he had just done was so contrary to his upbringing.

Not all of Rev. Jake's congregation obeyed his every wish like puppets. A group of men from that church helped Darcie and me move from our house to a rental condo during the pre-trial months. Had I been falsely convicted, she would have been unable to continue making the house payments by herself, so we prepared for the possibility. The condo was much more secure; there was much less likelihood of a crazed zealot surprising us with a terrorist act there.

I encountered a number of people from Rev. Jake's church, usually at supermarkets, both before and after the trial. Only one of them treated me like a suspected child molester.

One of my very best friends in the church, intimately familiar with my children's ministry, summarized my ordeal with a classic line, worth quoting. His summary: "How unfortunate." It's an understatement to say that this man doesn't get it; he's still a follower of Rev. Jake.

When my friend asked him why he hadn't supported me, one man expressed the attitude common in that church. His response was "All I know is what I read in the papers." I had spent time praying for that man on one occasion, and solicited help from a couple of others once so the three of us could pray for a special need of his wife's. When his seventeen-year-old son got into trouble and had to move out of state, I wrote a short letter of encouragement to the boy, who had occasionally been my Sunday school assistant when I taught the ten-to-twelve class. The man's young stepson was under my care Sunday evenings. I doubt that the family had any suspicion of me, but it illustrates the lack of consideration.

Eventually, all of our friends from Pastor Dave's church ended up leaving Rev. Jake's church, but a few lingered much too long for our liking. In addition to Kate and Gary coming to the trial, where Kate testified for me, a couple of other families from that tiny group showed up to be supportive during the jury deliberations. The only financial contribution from anyone in Rev. Jake's church came from a family in that group. Otherwise, there wasn't a penny. Besides this small group, there were three others who had left Rev. Jake and came to the final court date. Also, a Christian couple from another church attended on that date; God bless them for their support.

Remember the Friday evening prayer group that met at our house for a year? Of all the people who shared those many intimate hours with us, only one individual contacted us to offer support. This happened to be the only individual from that group who no longer attended Rev. Jake's church. Our worship leaders in that group were a couple who married during those months that our group met. They're divorced now. We never heard from either of them or from any of the others — not a word from any of them, except that one man. We couldn't believe it.

Besides Rev. Jake's followers, newspaper articles were the other things that made it impossible for us to continue living in that community. One of the earliest articles had a headline saying that I might plea bargain. But the only fact was that the state had made an offer. The writer of that article had never met me, and therefore had no idea whether I was actually considering a plea bargain. The first offer was two years in a minimum-security prison, and I immediately rejected it. Again, I deeply regret that I cannot quote from the article verbatim. I wrote the book with actual quotes, then found out just before the book went to print that I had to paraphrase.

After the first day of the trial, the larger of the two area newspapers, the one based in the town where I was employed, ran an article which said that Elisa could not look at me during her testimony. The same article said that Joan took Elisa to the hospital after Joan became alarmed by the redness in Elisa's vaginal area. This is very misleading. The implication that Elisa's erythema was the reason why her mother went to the hospital is false. As far as the incorrect assertion that Elisa "could not" look at me, I don't know whether the author intended to use the word "did" rather than "could." If he wrote what he intended to, I think that could be a case of criminal misrepresentation. The implication is that a frail three-year-old was too terrified by her attacker to face him, which was absolutely untrue. Elisa was asked to point out her teacher. Until then, she had a pretty good time with the questioning, because she knew all the "right" answers, which she had been taught, however subtly or unconsciously. When asked to point out her teacher, she scanned all the people in the courtroom. She looked right at me at least two times, and her gaze quickly passed on. She did the same with everyone else. Did the author of the article project his own fears onto Elisa by saying she couldn't look at me? I don't think so. This word changes from "could" to "did" in subsequent articles in that newspaper, so I suspect it was just a mistake. Regardless, the newspaper articles made our lives miserable.

The next day, the same writer changed a key word, by saying that Elisa "did not" face me, rather than stating that she "could not" face me, as the earlier article had stated. In this article, Phil was quoted as saying that I was considered an upcoming leader in the church.

Friday's newspapers (the larger one in the town where I worked, and the smaller one in the town where we lived) both said that deliberations had started, that the jury had asked to hear Elisa's testimony and mine played back. I felt that it was a positive sign that the jury had asked to hear mine, but guessing what goes through a jury's mind is usually futile. I was one of the few who thought O. J. Simpson would be convicted, after I heard that his jury had quickly reached a verdict.

The larger newspaper in our county has a reputation for being biased; that's the way I would describe its coverage of my trial. They never even mentioned Joan's nightmare. A trivial detail that readers wouldn't care about? I don't think so. Bear in mind my former friend's statement: "All I know is what I read in the papers." Media misrepresentation can ruin a person's life.

There was no article in the Monday newspapers. On Friday, the jury asked to hear Joan's testimony again. When it was played back, I could just about hear the word "Liar!" ringing out from the heavens as she spoke. I assumed that someone on the jury was swayed by the accusation and wanted to hear Joan's testimony as a means of firming up his or her argument for a "guilty" vote. During those days of deliberations, I noticed that I was receiving warm smiles from some of the courtroom personnel. Quite a few people are involved. They, and the judge and lawyers and state inspector, and my supporters, and Elisa's state-appointed attorney — one of the smilers — were all required to remain in the courtroom, where my supporters kept up their silent prayer efforts. My friends in Kansas City, in the Ozarks, in our home county, and in other places were also praying a lot, individually and in church groups. The personnel and facilities and associated overhead make it extremely expensive for the state to hold a trial like this. A man in the audience — I don't even know who he was — spoke to me once during a break in the deliberations. He told me that "pretty much everyone" who witnessed the trial was on my side. Not only do I think he was right, but I am also sure that the prosecutor and state inspector knew for a fact that I was innocent. But there are no *Perry Mason* endings in real life; the community requires the prosecution to do everything possible to get a conviction at trial, just as defense lawyers are ethically obligated to get the best deal for their clients, even when they think those clients are guilty. The appeal to emotion, which was the basis of my case, is something I consider underhanded and morally wrong; trial lawyers seemingly acknowledge it as one of the most powerful tools used in courtroom arguments.

It wasn't a logical analysis of the situation that gave me the ability to cope through the days of deliberations. It was faith in God, and nothing else. Everything I know about God indicated that He would not allow me to be convicted. When my key witness was not allowed to testify, it became evident that everything was stacked against me. Two expressions that describe my state of mind during those bleak hours are: "I know that my Redeemer lives" (Job 19:25), and "You will keep in perfect peace him whose mind is steadfast, because he trusts in You." (Is. 26:3.) I know my Christian friends who were praying for me had similar thoughts, with myriad verses coming to their minds. I was also confident that even if I was falsely imprisoned (like Joseph, in Genesis 39, 40, & 41), God would still take care of Darcie and me somehow. It makes all the difference when a person under stress has such a worldview. In my pre-Christian days, I never could have made it.

I beg my readers: give your lives to the Lord if you haven't already done so. Obviously, it doesn't mean your life will be fun all the time. But I'd much rather endure the ordeal we went through and end up with Him, than have an easy life and never know Him.

In Tuesday's newspaper articles, the smaller (more responsible) newspaper said that the jurors would only tell the reporter that they voted 5-1 to acquit on the second charge, and that they would not identify the holdout juror. This means that when the jury was asking about the (disallowed) split-ticket vote, they had voted 6-0 on the sexual assault charge, and 11-1 on the Risk of Injury charge. Seventeen of eighteen votes cast were in my favor. But the only thing of legal significance is that the state had to decide whether to try me again on the Risk of Injury charge. By that time, the prosecutor's office was no longer misled by Rev. Jake; they knew all about the case and they knew they had no case. Unfortunately, that doesn't mean they couldn't win in court.

Once, during the last day of trial, I left the courtroom during a recess. Elisa's court-appointed attorney was on the phone.

I heard her say, "Yeah, he was parading a few more of his friends today as character witnesses." I was a little upset that this lady felt that way about me, but later I realized that she was talking to Joan, and simply telling her whatever it took to pacify her and keep me on the front-burner of her imagination as a villain. Finding out the truth was not the goal of all these people; it was placating a very angry woman. After the jury gave its verdict, according to the aforementioned newspaper article, the judge expressed his opinion that the case could possibly be settled after a short recess. The judge apparently hoped the prosecutor would drop it, as should have been done. But the prosecutor intended to call Joan and get her approval. She did not approve.

Outside the courtroom, the judge said something to my lawyer, to the prosecutor, and to others at that time: "This man has suffered enough already." The reader should realize that the judge knew with certainty that I was innocent. Weeks later, one of the courtroom personnel, a woman who had seen the entire trial, said to me, "Sometimes we get cases that never should have come to trial." These people not only concluded that I was not guilty; they liked me personally. I'm grateful that this was revealed to me.

Tuesday's article in the larger-circulation newspaper had a quote that I love. It said that I took part in a group prayer after my acquittal on the more serious charge. Sadly, the article then went on to repeat old news, stating that I had made remarks to Joan about Elisa's appearance, and that Joan once saw me try to conceal an erection when I was trying to seat Elisa on my lap, etc.

Dismissal of the Lesser Charge

If something is Scriptural, I believe it, and will continue to do so unless evidence compels me to believe otherwise. One Scriptural subject the reader might be interested in concerns the existence of angels, a topic of interest among Americans during the 1990s. As far as I'm concerned (based on Bible study, not on anything else), when the Bible uses the word *angel* it could, in some instances, have originally meant nothing more than "human messenger." Sometimes, but not usually. As the trial drew near, I was absolutely convinced that I would be under the protection of a large number of angels. The only aspect of the trial that I looked forward to, except for getting it over with, was seeing if I would be able to discern their presence. It would be a great story, but the fact is that I could not see or hear them (but I was still convinced they were there). Several people told me, prior to the trial, that they had visions of a great many angels protecting me, shoulder to shoulder, as far as the eye could see.

The last court date was Thursday, three days after my acquittal on the first charge. The prosecutor had contacted Joan, hoping she would thank him for a good try and let him off the hook. Instead, she told him she would put Elisa back on the stand and this time they'd get a conviction. The prosecutor knew how foolish it would be to have another trial — after all, they have a lot of real cases to deal with — so his best option was to make a face-saving speech. He did a fine job. In court, he talked about how such an allegation was much too serious to ignore, and how he had agonized over the decision for three days, but ultimately decided that he did not want to put Elisa through the stress of another trial. Joan was more than willing to do it. Did the prosecutor think he understood Elisa's welfare better than her own mother did? No, he was just using the child for an excuse. Think of it: both Joan and the prosecutor claiming to speak for Elisa, and nobody allowing Elisa to speak for herself. Isn't that the essence of cases like mine?

A couple of my Christian friends — not followers of Rev. Jake — were in court with me that day. Their daughter, who turned three on the day Rev. Jake took the stand against me, was with them. Not long after the accusation, when she was barely two, I stopped by to see these friends. At the top landing before I got to their door, she came running to greet me, so happy and excited she could hardly contain it; the only audible sounds at that scene were little gasps of pure joy. That little measure of reality helped me cope with the abandonment of all of Rev. Jake's followers. Occasional small doses of appreciation are all the encouragement some teachers get. But teachers' efforts are in a worthy cause. When the prosecutor saw my friend's daughter smiling at me in the courtroom, I guess he didn't want to look like a phony when he made his sham of a speech. So he told my lawyer that his offer to *nolle* the case had a precondition: my young friend could not be in the courtroom when he made the offer. He had the right to prosecute me again if he wanted to, so it was not in my interest to argue with his request. My little friend got booted out of the courtroom for the duration of his speech. In it, he said — and the newspapers dutifully published — that I would not be leaving the courtroom having been exonerated by a jury (in other words, I was still an accused child molester in the community). He then made the state's offer to *nolle* my case, meaning they would not prosecute me again, but they had the right to do so any time within the next thirteen months if new evidence arose. I was going to accept the offer, of course.

One Christian man came to support me at this very last court date. This is one of the most mature, stable people I have ever met. He is not prone to talk much about visions and miracles; such talk doesn't come cheaply with him. He said that when the *nolle* offer was made, he looked at the judge and saw the Lord's host swarming around the judge, compelling him into action. Tears come into his eyes immediately when he tells of this vision. The judge's mouth flew open at that time, and he stumbled on his words, then asked an extremely unusual question: "Uh, are there any motions?" Mr. Martino, who appeared to be unaware of the possibility until that time, asked for a moment to confer with the prosecutor. He did so, then returned and made a motion for dismissal. Immediately the judge said, "So ordered," then walked out of the room. I didn't know what that meant; Mr. Martino explained it to me: I didn't have to endure thirteen months of discomfort. The judge had dismissed my case outright. Legally, that means there was no more child molestation charge hanging over me; I was legally vindicated.

According to all the evidence I saw, this victory came from one source only: God's protection. It certainly was not due to any fancy legal maneuvers. Some will think I'm wacky for all this talk about God and angels; let each person judge for himself.

The newspaper articles the next day didn't vindicate me at all. The prosecutor's phony speech was quoted. It would have made him look foolish had he made his speech about agonizing over how to protect kids from me when my young friend was in the courtroom, obviously demonstrating fondness for me. He got what he wanted from a point of favorable coverage. In the newspaper with the larger circulation, a woman who had never attended my trial wrote the article. She had been on vacation. The man who wrote all the previous articles was in the courtroom on the last day, but the woman nonetheless wrote the last article. She simply restated sensational portions of previous articles, like the claim that Elisa did not look at me during her testimony. She also quoted the prosecutor. In a three-column article, the dismissal was not mentioned until six lines before the very end. A friend of mine wrote a thoughtful letter to the editor about how sleazy this treatment was; they didn't publish his letter.

The other newspaper wasn't as bad. However, in order to be "fair to both sides," they too quoted from the prosecutor's speech, thus smearing my name forever. A friend who had come to our Friday evening prayer gatherings, the only friend we ever heard from among that group, wrote a letter to the editor of this newspaper. It was published. He praised Darcie and me, and lamented the witch-hunt.

Nine months later, the prosecutor (Assistant State's Attorney) in my case was designated as *the* prosecutor for a new office dedicated to prosecuting sexual assault cases, the first such designation in the state. When the state inspector was fingerprinting me, seven months before my trial, she told Mr. Martino she was very thankful to be getting out of sexual assault cases and back into gambling investigations. But in this news article, she had been designated as the assistant to the prosecutor in the new sexual assault office. Those were the two who sat right next to me for a solid week as they tried to destroy my innocent life. I guess this was their reward for doing such a good job of carrying out societal demands.

I would like to believe that some lessons have been learned, and that the prosecutor and his assistant have changed their sloppy investigation procedures. However, an article about a different case, from the newspaper with the larger circulation, published precisely one year after my trial began, revealed the lack of progress. A man in the neighboring town who had been accused of raping a three-year-old girl was found innocent. His case should never have gone to court. The charges against him were identical to mine. His prosecutor was the same as mine. The jury deliberated less than two hours in his case.

The child's mother had accused the man of molesting the girl when he babysat for her and two other children. In the article, the man stated that "they" had subjected him to a hellish life for the last fourteen months, and that he had been deprived of "decent" sleep for the last two months. The man said he planned to try to forget about the experience and concentrate on his work, which involved electronics. Just like me, all he wanted was to get the witch hunters off his back.

During the child's testimony, she recited, like a parrot, that the man had sex with her, but was not able to identify him in the courtroom. The man testified that he never touched the child. He testified that the child's mother and an aunt had made the accusation because they didn't want to pay him back thousands of dollars that they owed him, and because they were afraid he was going to report them for using drugs.

Assuming the last sentence is fact (and that's how the jury saw it, apparently), this implies that the ticket that allowed these two women to use drugs and escape thousands of dollars of debt was simply to accuse an innocent man of molesting a young girl. Apparently the prosecutor handled the case in the same way, putting a well-rehearsed child on the stand and depending on emotion-based manipulative arguments to convict the man. This is abusive exploitation of children for adult purposes. Until there is public pressure to stop such practices, they will continue. And with each case like this one, the public will become a little more skeptical the next time they hear of child molestation charges. That is not in the best interest of children.

Considerations of Legal Action

The reader has perhaps wondered whether Rev. Jake got away with all his crimes. On the surface, yes, but I have no doubt that his day of reckoning is coming. As this book goes to press, Rev. Jake's lies and other misdeeds — my case just a small portion of the whole — are being revealed in a seemingly endless stream, and he is busily trying to control the minor uprisings. Maybe he'll finally give up and resign next week; maybe it will take another year or even longer. His demise is coming.

I do not regard the people at Rev. Jake's church as a cult, despite such cult-like practices as supporting Rev. Jake through anything that should ever arise. This, I believe, is common among all types of organizations with clearly defined leaders. It grieves me terribly to see it happen in a Christian church.

I think Rev. Jake longs for the good old days, when his group was very small and he didn't have to contend with issues that come up in larger churches. As it turns out, nearly all of his original followers have left him. They didn't move away from the area; they simply chose to wash their hands of Rev. Jake. Sadly, unsuspecting newcomers have taken their place.

According to Scripture, leaders who commit unacceptable deeds must undergo correction while someone else assumes leadership. But in Rev. Jake's case, he simply keeps all authority to himself, and argues with any attempted opposition. Who is more to blame, Rev. Jake, for taking advantage of his position and his manipulative skills, or the congregation and its so-called "leaders," who allow him to get away with it? In one aspect of my situation, I criticize my own behavior: I didn't pay attention to the ungodly signs present in my church leadership. Darcie is very upset with herself for failing to notice the warning signs in Rev. Jake, because in her profession she deals very successfully with con men. Rev. Jake seems like a harmless little guy when he's on stage, joking about everything. Scripture warns us about con men, and the fact is that we were temporarily duped. Saint Paul writes, "Satan himself masquerades as an angel of light. It is not surprising, then, if his servants masquerade as servants of righteousness. Their end will be what their actions deserve." (II Cor. 11:14-15.) I'm thankful that Darcie and I had never thought of Rev. Jake as an exemplary man of God. However, some of his followers hold him in high esteem, and I am concerned about the impact of their disillusionment when they realize how wrong they have been.

In Rev. Jake's denomination, forgiveness is a topic of major emphasis. I think the reason is that the emotionally wounded who make up the bulk of this organization — which is just the way Jesus wanted it to be — typically have a lot of emotional baggage that they need to get rid of. "Release it; just give it to Jesus" is the admonition heard regularly. I have no criticism of this. Unfortunately, it offers a tremendous opportunity for the leadership to be abusive, and the former denomination of Rev. Jake's church is now seriously confronted with such problems of abuse perpetrated by leadership. Correction of leaders in the denomination, not just in Rev. Jake's church, is inadequate.

After killing his brother Abel, Cain tried to ignore his sin, but God didn't simply shrug it off. Instead, God said to Cain, "What have you done? Listen! Your brother's blood cries out to me from the ground. Now you are under a curse..." (Gen. 4:10-11.) Rev. Jake's followers will have to answer to that same God.

The result of the oversimplified concept of forgiveness is that many of the people in that denomination define "forgiveness" as denial, simply forgetting that a problem exists. Jesus, Paul, Peter, and other leaders in the Bible certainly did not ignore sin in such a simplistic way. Powerful examples are found in Matt. 11:15, I Cor. 5:5, and Acts 5:1–5. The notion of ignoring ongoing sin in the church is unscriptural. In a Bible study on the topic of forgiveness — both Old and New Testament — one aspect is nearly always part of the process: the offending party confesses wrongdoing and asks for forgiveness. This is the very essence of our relationship with God. "If we claim to be without sin, we deceive ourselves and the truth is not in us. If we confess our sins, he is faithful and just and will forgive us our sins and purify us from all unrighteousness." (I John 1:8-9.) I could have forgiven any of my attackers if they would have confessed wrongdoing, but they remain in denial. This is a defining characteristic in cases similar to mine; witch-hunters never seem to apologize. I can't pray, "Father, forgive them, for they do not know what they are doing" (Luke 23:34) because my accusers knew exactly what they were doing; they even lied to make sure their schemes would work. And they haven't changed. If one of them ever repents, I'll be glad to forgive him or her. Until then, I'm not going to be deceitful by pretending that I hold no grievance against them. I don't spend my time feeling hateful toward them; I'm just relating the historical facts so others can learn.

Books on the topic of spiritual abuse have appeared during the last few years. If this topic strikes a chord, I suggest that the interested reader look for the books by Ronald Enroth. My personal favorite for wounded Christians is Bob Sorge's *The Fire of Delayed Answers*, a most insightful book dealing with life's confusing aspects of how God works during our times of affliction, often much too slowly for our liking or comprehension.

I concluded that Rev. Jake could and should be made to account for his crimes in a court of law. But it would have required much effort and $30,000 that I didn't have just to legally show his guilt. And even if I were to do so, his followers still wouldn't be likely to grasp the truth. If anything, I suspect that they would probably become all the more protective of him. I feel the frustration that parents feel when their adult children live in a cult. Adult children have the legal right to do so if they wish, and only a revelation from God can remedy the situation.

Similarly, I think that pastors and priests who have molested kids or vulnerable adults should be held accountable by our legal system if the church hierarchy fails to act. Every Christian should be outraged if they learn that their church leadership has been ignoring certain abuses. If the church doesn't do God's will, why shouldn't He use others to do so? "What then will the owner of the vineyard do? He will come and kill those tenants and give the vineyard to others." (Mark 12:9.)

There are probably many people who prefer to believe that Rev. Jake was merely confused, and not guilty of intentional wrongdoing. This is a classic case of denial, inspired by its convenience. If he had raped their wives or children because he was similarly "confused," would these people feel the same way?

I would have done Rev. Jake's congregation a big favor by bringing legal action against him, but I don't think they would realize it. They must be the ones to correct the problem if they are to benefit. Also, consider what the newspaper articles would be like in a very long legal battle between a man who had recently been arrested for child molestation and his former pastor. Do you think God would be glorified? Do you think the articles would be more concerned with facts than with sensationalism? I'm convinced that the harm to the worldwide family of Christians would outweigh the benefit of exposing one person like Rev. Jake.

According to my interpretation of Scripture, the proper way to fix an ugly situation like Rev. Jake's spiritual abuse is to do it through the denomination. A friend of mine in that church had once come close to suing Rev. Jake for slander, not long before my accusation occurred. A lawyer convinced her that it wasn't worth the effort. As an alternative, she wrote to the head of the denomination. The leader gave Rev. Jake a warning. Rev. Jake was furious with my friend, but his behavior toward her improved greatly. The system worked, on that occasion.

I decided that I should do the same thing (Matt. 18:17). A denomination shouldn't be condemned for failure to correct wrongdoing if it never gets the opportunity to do so. A Christian trial lawyer in my state, acting as my friend, offered to help me with the correspondence. It took more than half a year because he was utterly convinced that my letter would be thrown away if it was more than three pages long. Based on Rev. Jake's atrocities described herein (and there are many more), how could I confine my complaint to three pages? I ended up with a three-page letter plus two pages of appendices. I sent it by certified mail to the leader, the same man who had acted properly in my friend's case. I sent a copy to Rev. Jake. I doubt that he showed it to anyone.

As far as I know, the leader never even saw the letter. He had stepped down from his position of leadership, letting younger people take over. The man who responded to my letter is now the head of all churches in the denomination, which, the last I heard, had 650 churches worldwide. He telephoned my friend, the Christian attorney, which I had requested that he do. He acknowledged that the denomination instructs its pastors to get release notices to prevent confidentiality from being legally challenged, and that Rev. Jake failed to do so. He promised that he would personally look into the matter. The manner in which Rev. Jake broke the law put his denomination at serious risk.

We did not threaten a lawsuit; we just asked the leader to correct the spiritual abuse. Six months later we had heard nothing, but my lawyer friend was convinced that the denominational leader would come through, and that it was too early to re-initiate contact. A few months later, a friend of ours in that denomination encountered the leader at a conference and told him how important he thought it was that they attend to my complaint.

It turned out that the denomination had chosen to ignore (hide from) the situation. Subsequently, they failed to return repeated calls from my lawyer friend, who mentioned to me the fact that, if the denomination were to confess wrongdoing by one of its pastors, they would be open to liability in a lawsuit that could then be directed against them.

This sweeping crimes under the rug rather than dealing with them reminds me of the troubles the Catholic church has experienced in recent years due to some priests having sexually molested various young parishioners, and the allegations that a number of their peers chose to ignore the abominable behavior. Dealing with the problem is very painful; pretending it doesn't exist must be a great temptation to the leadership. Again, this goes back to the parable of the Good Samaritan, in which the priest and Pharisee turned their heads and walked on the other side of the road. I hope the reader has faith that God sees all these things, and will eventually bring every perpetrator to judgment. Due to the abominations alleged to have occurred within its leadership, financial losses in the Catholic Church have been astronomical; I hope that wasn't their primary motivation for finally acting to correct the problems. I identify strongly with those who have been molested by a priest; typically, nobody believes the victims when they try to tell their friends of the evil the priest has done, just as Rev. Jake's followers refuse to listen to criticism of him. Lest the reader assume otherwise, I generally have great respect for Catholic priests, and I wish the best for them.

I don't feel right about pursuing Rev. Jake's former denomination with a lawsuit. In Christianese, "I just don't feel led" to do so; I don't feel that the Lord desires or instructs me to do so. My conscience would have no problem dragging Rev. Jake into court, but the cost vs. benefit makes it an undesirable choice. Readers might gnash their teeth at the thought of this little manipulator going unchallenged, and the decision, for me, was and is extremely difficult. In the end, I've decided to trust that God will take care of the situation without legal action on my part. As for Joan, cost vs. benefit is also the problem, plus my unwillingness to inflict economic hardship on her innocent kids. The others I'd love to sue are the police and the newspaper.

My lawyer friend showed me an article about a case in which someone tried to sue a newspaper for irresponsible reporting that destroyed his reputation. The point of the article was that such lawsuits are almost impossible to win unless you can *prove* that they intentionally misstated the facts in news accounts of you. The fact that they printed news without checking the source's credibility, destroying an innocent life as a result, is insufficient to win in court. The inability to make them behave responsibly is what happens when a country has a free press, and a public that loves shocking news stories. I believe in the First Amendment. I'd rather have a free press than a government-controlled press, so my "solution" is for the public to learn to disregard irresponsible news reports. But I have no logical reason to believe that will ever happen.

We see no modern-day examples of people being struck by lightning (etc.) immediately after committing a heinous crime. I think the more common chastisement (found in several Scriptural locations) is stated in Romans 1:28: "...since they did not think it worthwhile to retain the knowledge of God, He gave them over to a depraved mind, to do what ought not to be done." In other words, God's punishment is to turn the ungodly over to themselves. In contrast, "The Lord disciplines those He loves." (Heb. 12:6.) I have chosen to trust Scripture as I await justice. The punishment of Rev. Jake's followers may simply be that they still have Rev. Jake.

As far as the police handling of my case, they were essentially just doing what society demands. My case was not pursued with the tenacity with which the "Satanic Ritual Abuse" cases were. Still, my conscience would have no problem suing them; it's just that my likelihood of winning isn't high enough to make the risk worthwhile. Recall that the police told the newspaper that the child had symptoms consistent with sexual assault — an intentional distortion of the facts. They planned to conduct my trial without ever having informed me of the fact that Joan had lied about her dream. Fortunately, I found out through other sources. And using a child whom they knew had been recently molested as a key witness, without letting me know this, was despicable. Still, they weren't nearly as deceptive as Rev. Jake was.

One of the many ironies of my case is that I was accused of abusing my spiritual position to satisfy sick desires by using a helpless victim. In reality, Rev. Jake has been guilty of committing that very deed on a number of occasions.

It was bad enough that the newspapers would make our lives unbearable in that community due to slanted coverage; the distorted account also could have made it more difficult to get an "impartial" jury. People read the papers and talk about sensational stories with others who don't read them. For that reason, Mr. Martino filed "Motion for Order Restricting Pretrial Statements." The judge denied our motion at one of our many pre-trial court dates, so the newspapers were free to print whatever they chose. Their source of information would continue to be the police.

God appears to be bringing down Rev. Jake's reign, but much more slowly than I'd like to see. I believe there are godly reasons for correcting the situation so slowly. Quick fixes don't seem to have the impact that gradual, long-term ones have. We should be thankful for the man who is a criminal one day, and proclaims the next day that he's born again and living his life for the Lord; we should be thankful, but we should also keep a close eye on him. Rev. Jake has an extensive criminal past — mostly drug-related, I believe — and is fond of telling how long-time acquaintances of his family refuse to believe that he became a pastor. Denominations have got to keep a watchful eye on their pastors, and this denomination has not done so. The denomination, I have been told, has a reputation among mainstream Christians as being basically immature. The denomination is tiny by the standards of Baptists, Methodists, et al. The reason many people learn about its existence is because of the music that has come from some of its members.

Not long after my trial, Rev. Jake said a number of bad things about Carl, a man in his church. He told many of the leaders throughout New England that Carl was incapable of leading in any manner, including Bible studies. I barely knew Carl, who started going to our church just before the accusation. I loaned him some videotapes of our visit to Nicaragua, for which he was very grateful. To my perception, he clearly was a leader.

The things Rev. Jake told people about Carl became so extreme that Carl ultimately complained to the top leadership of the denomination. I'm sure Carl didn't realize that my friend and I had also recently brought complaints to this level. In all three cases, our complaint was the same: Rev. Jake was slandering us. The leadership's response to Carl's complaint was the same as to mine: nothing. Or so it seemed at the time.

Rev. Jake's church is no longer in the denomination. Supposedly, he chose to withdraw from it. This happened not long after my friend urged the denomination leader to take action concerning my case. It was also, I think, around the time that Carl brought his complaint. Rev. Jake withdrew his church from the denomination without consulting the congregation. They just showed up one Sunday (Easter, 1996) and were told, with no discussion, that they were no longer in the denomination. The reason was never explained to the congregation. All they knew was that it was something "the leadership" had very quickly decided to do, somehow related to a disagreement of "the leadership" with the direction in which the denominational leadership was headed. As I've said before, I think the important change that needs to occur is for Rev. Jake's followers to start discerning truth from lies. And there's no more effective way to learn something than doing it at great cost. I think they will understand as time goes by; some need more convincing than others.

The list of people who have left Rev. Jake's church to attend another local church is truly a "Who's Who" of the more mature individuals. A few who seem to be fairly levelheaded still attend. I think they will eventually leave. But new people keep coming to fill the vacancies, unaware of all the complaints that people have made about their pastor. I've never seen any other church with nearly so fast a turnover rate.

As of May 1997, a year after Rev. Jake became officially accountable to no one, his followers adamantly claimed that he was actually under the authority of a different denomination, which was considering the admission of his church. The truth is that the church is not in that denomination, yet his followers believe Rev. Jake is under authority. As my friend Andrew says, "people basically believe what they want to believe."

This book is about witch-hunting. Rev. Jake occupies more space than I intended. However, the two situations, pastoral abuse and witch-hunting, share a common problem — and solution. In the church scenario, a group of people allows one skillful manipulator to get away with serious abuse, too intimidated to stop him. In the case of America in the '90s, people are too afraid to tell witch-hunting zealots that their tactics are harmful; nobody wants to be labeled "insensitive to the huge problem of child abuse." In both cases, the solution is to do the right thing, and forget about misguided peer pressure. Most of all, society must become motivated to stop the zealots from defining the rules.

I don't intend the term "zealot" as derogatory. I use it to denote people who are irrational on the topic of child sex abuse. There are perfectly valid reasons why people can become this way. If I had a child and somebody abused my child, leaving lifelong emotional scars, I would probably be a zealot myself.

III. Surviving the Trauma

Supportive Friends

There weren't very many things that helped us survive the agony of our witch-hunt. I would do anything to assist anyone else who goes through a similar false accusation. In fact, just to know that there are others who completely understand what it's like is in itself greatly comforting to the accused; it helps reduce the "Wonderland" confusion. I hope this book will be a comfort to such people. Family members and close friends are the most likely to see past the deception and help the accused preserve his or her sanity. Unspecified blanket support — "I'm on your side no matter what" — is not particularly consoling. The only completely comforting words are "I know for a fact that you're innocent, and I'm outraged at the things being done to you." Only then do you know for a fact that your supporter grasps the complete truth. The ultimate desire for a victim of false accusations is for the truth to be known. That's why most falsely accused defendants choose to put their lives on the line rather than "get off easy" by plea-bargaining. Occasionally, parents, such as Betsy Kelly, from the North Carolina case involving Little Rascals day care, will grudgingly agree to plea-bargain to make sure that their children will not grow up parentless for too many years. I applaud Mrs. Kelly for her choice.

I can express Darcie's and my survival tool only thus: faith in God was, much more than any other thing, what enabled us to survive the ordeal. This support is available to anyone who seeks it. If anyone out there is going through the trauma of a false accusation, and the world is against you, but you're not a believer, I absolutely beg you to try to become one. I promise you, God will hear you, understand, and take care of you. Don't be concerned about technique; simply talk to your Maker. It will be the wisest choice you ever made. Actually, I recommend that to any unbeliever, falsely accused or not.

I discussed the details of my case with several dozen friends during the months preceding the trial. During all of my waking hours, actually. That was very therapeutic, because they were all supporters, but I can't say that it would be appropriate for every falsely accused individual to do likewise. Within Rev. Jake's church, some of the things I said became distorted and were used against me, making me realize I would have been better off not speaking to those people at all. My experience indicated that you might be surprised by who may turn against you if you are accused. But is the alternative to refrain from talking to anyone, in case they might turn on you? I couldn't have tolerated keeping quiet about my ordeal for a year; maybe others could. My lawyer would have demanded that I say nothing whatsoever about the case to anyone except himself, if he could have. What I've described as "therapeutic" would be called dangerous and unacceptable by most trial lawyers.

Outside the workplace, daily life entailed some paranoia for me. For example, I couldn't completely relax while I was driving. I was concerned that, were I to get a traffic ticket or be in an accident, the newspapers might run a story with a headline such as "Accused Child Molester Involved In Collision." Being at work was like a safe haven: I knew I was among friends, and I could relax.

If there is ever a time to get medical help, counseling, or psychological assistance, it is during an experience like Darcie's and mine. Counselors and psychologists may not believe in the innocence of the accused. If that happens, the individual should simply get help from someone else. By virtue of a zealous campaign waged during the '70s and '80s, many counselors have been led to believe that child molestation is such a rampant problem that all accusation other than those linked to spousal quarreling must be true. It takes time for them to learn to consider the possibility of false accusations and learn to recognize them.

There is a powerful survival tool that I didn't try. If the accused can convince a TV crew that the case is being handled in an outrageous manner, heavy pressure can be brought on the police to behave properly. There is a big danger to this approach: TV coverage can make the accused look guilty in the eyes of huge numbers of viewers, which can be extremely dangerous, and can cause the police to spend more money in digging up irrelevant dirt that can increase the likelihood of conviction. Kelly Michaels was an articulate young woman, and the TV coverage of her Satanic Ritual Abuse case was probably a good way to introduce viewers to the fact that false accusations occur. However, if viewers were to get a look at me on their TV screen, they would be likely to assume guilt and dismiss the matter. At least one of my friends in the church, whose children had been under my care for two years, immediately embraced the accusation against me by saying, "Yeah, he had *that look*." Not everyone is likely to benefit from TV coverage.

One of the things I noticed during the months preceding my legal vindication was that I was very much "in touch with" my childhood feelings. I experienced feelings that had been gone from my life for many years. I'm pretty sure this was because some common elements of childhood were thrust upon me: My future was completely dependent on the judgment of other people; there were no alternatives; and I felt I had to prove my innocence to others. Until the accusation, my life had been comfortable for many years; I had everything I needed, with alternatives to any difficulties that might have ever arisen. Prior to the accusation, I wouldn't have been particularly concerned if anyone chose to think badly of me. The strange experience of becoming hopelessly dependent was not entirely negative. Pastors regularly discuss this topic, exhorting us to put our trust in God alone rather than in ourselves or in anything else in the world (e.g., II Cor. 1:9). Ideally, one wouldn't have to be forced into this childlike dependence in the manner that Darcie and I were.

Things the Jury Didn't Know

As I said earlier, I felt dizzy with the pace of the trial. I think this was largely because I could see that the jurors were never told many salient facts pertaining to their upcoming verdict.

For example, they were not told about:

1. My complaint-free history while having had authority over approximately 2000 people during my life.
2. Joan's admission that she lied to the police, "because she was afraid that no one would believe her, otherwise."
3. The fact that, having worked with nearly 200 kids during my time in that church, there were only two (both boys) whom I ever escorted into a restroom.
4. Rev. Jake's wife, too, taught with the door closed, and there were times when she had no assistant, and thus had been left "alone" with the four-year-olds.
5. The fact that every time Joan dropped Elisa off, adults were in the room with me, less than ten feet away, leading the singing. For the remaining forty-five minutes, I had at least one other adult helper for probably seventy-seven of the eighty classes I taught, the other three times having been due to a lack of volunteers.
6. The fact that I cannot recall having ever been with Elisa when other adults or older children weren't present.
7. The fact that Elisa's erythema, if caused by me, had to have been induced no less than seventeen days prior to the examination, which makes it extremely unlikely that I caused it.

8. The fact that, regarding the medical report, it would have been more accurate to say that the results were consistent with *no* sexual assault having occurred, according to Dr. David Shalom, one of the foremost children's advocates in New England.

The Most Damaging Thing I Did to Myself

One of the realities of cases like mine is that people are likely to reach hasty conclusions of how the witch-hunt came about. "If only you'd been more argumentative with Rev. Jake," or "If only you had shown more emotion," or "If only you hadn't offered to leave the church," or "If only you wouldn't have speculated about what the mother must have been thinking." I'm convinced that the first three notions would have made no difference at all. I'd like to address the fourth.

When I guessed, within hours, that Joan must have conjured up visions that I had fondled Elisa's genital area, I was 100 percent correct. Is it improper to guess at something of grave importance, among friends, when you are pretty sure you have figured out the explanation?

I have explained the size and layout of the room, and all the circumstances. I have narrowed the time intervals of "opportunity" down to a few minutes of the many months that I taught the two- and three-year-olds. During those few minutes, I had articulate four-year-olds — Phil's daughter and Elder #2's daughter and several more — still in the room with me. Even when Joan envisioned the "erection," Brittany (age ten) was just a few feet away from Elisa and me. Other than improper fondling, I still can't think of any sexual deed that anyone familiar with the circumstances, as Joan was, could imagine.

Based on common sense, I knew from day one what the accusation was likely to be. On that day, my own pastor asked me to go to his house to see what "we" should do. "If only you hadn't gone to his house," some second-guessers may think. I disagree. My accusers would have become all the more suspicious had I suddenly refused to talk to the very people I had spent all my "free" hours with for the past three years. Plus, I was never so eager for anything as I was to see how my "friends" thought we should handle the false accusation. I needed their support then as never before. If anyone had suggested that I treat Rev. Jake and his elders with apprehension, I simply wouldn't have listened.

Once I was at Rev. Jake's house, I was asked, point-blank, what I thought had happened. I was pretty sure I knew the answer, so my choices were to either treat my "friends" with suspicion, using only diplomatic dialog, or be completely forthright, as I was with all my other friends. Dr. Shalom and one of my co-workers criticized me severely (as I'm sure many others do) for not limiting my comments to a simple "I don't know." I have described how beneficial it was to be able to talk with all my friends and co-workers about every aspect of the case. The notion of treating some friends diplomatically is just not how I choose to live my life. No lawyer, no criminal, no high-level manager, or politician, or child-care professional would have been as open as I was. So is "right" behavior to withhold information from some of the closest people in your life? Sometimes we have to make concessions because there is so much evil in the world, so maybe the answer to the last question is yes. But I choose to enjoy life rather than be paranoid about my everyday surroundings.

The Impact of the Primary Accuser

"I don't know if at the time it was suspicion. I was teaching at a Sunday night — and Paul came in and he was — and I didn't know he was in the building. And he came in and he sat down, looked around and laughed. And later I found out that he was with the kids that night, and it just struck me as odd. I just, I just — at that point I continued to kind of hold that in my mind that there was something strange about that. It didn't make sense to me. And so from that point on I kind of had a tickler in my mind."

The above was Rev. Jake's response to the simple yes-or-no question, "Prior to the accusation, did you ever entertain any suspicions about Paul Grey molesting the children?" Rev. Jake was surely the main reason the police chose to pursue my case. Some of his tactics and their impact will now be discussed.

Earlier, I stated that one Sunday night, Phil specifically requested that I take the youngest kids into the room in the corner of the basement to protect them from the dodge-ball game. The policies I followed, of having the door closed and being alone in a room with young children, were not of my own making; they were sanctioned by the #2 leader in the church. At least, they were sanctioned on that one occasion, and no one ever told me that it deviated from official policy.

Contrast this with the written statement Rev. Jake gave at the police station the day after the accusation: "...we address the issue of safety, for the adults, the children, and to avoid the appearance of evil. We always have had another adult in the classroom as well as a child helper so no one would be placed in a compromising situation. However, since this has occurred, unfortunately, I can state that within the last two months there have been times when this system has not been carried out correctly by Paul Grey. Also, there is down time after the service where everyone is milling about without structure, and Paul would possibly have the opportunity to be alone with a child."

The reader can see the attempt to place all blame on me and none on the church. Rev. Jake wouldn't have been able, on his own, to identify the "opportunities" he talks about. He learned of them from his conversations with me. The "problem" was that I was meticulously honest with him. Rev. Jake's point about "after the service" was not an issue concerning Elisa, because Joan always picked her up very promptly, before my helper(s) left.

Rev. Jake told the investigator that I didn't need to keep the door to my classroom closed, because the church had stretch-gates available. Anyone who has worked with four-year-old boys knows that a stretch-gate cannot contain them (a few of my boys did occasionally try to sneak out of the room). The third alternative was to just keep the doors open, but can anyone claim that they could keep track of ten to twenty roving toddlers in a room with two open doors? Nevertheless, the police could only infer, based on Rev. Jake's words, that I was indeed a suspicious character. If they were to ignore such warnings from a pastor, and the public found out about it, the police would pay dearly.

I assisted Phil on a number of occasions, at morning and evening services, when he instructed kids to get on my lap. But after the accusation, Rev. Jake told the investigator that there was a church rule that was "published and well known" forbidding kids to sit on their teacher's lap. Rev. Jake was simply lying. With the possible exception of Rev. Jake's wife, none of the teachers knew of any such rule. After the accusation, some teachers expressed concern to Phil that they had never been informed of the "rules" Rev. Jake was accusing me of violating. Phil gave the response Rev. Jake demanded: such actions by the teachers "cannot happen." The church would be liable if any problems resulted from such actions, so the church intended to deny all responsibility for any occurrences.

Earlier, I quoted from a fax Rev. Jake sent to the police not long after Joan's original accusation. In the fax, he said a "second mother now believes that Paul Grey also molested her daughter." Put yourself in the position of the police. A pastor makes this statement to you. Given the demands of society, do you have the option of dropping such a case? As I said earlier, the second mother never materialized. However, the damage done by Rev. Jake was permanent.

Many took up the mantra "Rev. Jake was just protecting the church." They had been led to believe that, as the ultimate protector, he was taking all necessary steps to protect the children from potential abuse. The reality was that, to protect his church from a lawsuit, he simply used me as a scapegoat to draw attention away from the church's responsibility. He did it without asking my permission. It had nothing to do with protecting children.

How despicable it was that nobody in the church did anything to reimburse any of the financial losses that Darcie and I incurred, except for a generous contribution from one family.

The police statements by Mary and by the wife of Elder #2 were made not long after they had learned "the facts" of my case from Rev. Jake. Furthermore, the police insisted on getting all church information from Rev. Jake rather than from Phil. The reason is obvious.

On the witness stand, Rev. Jake testified, "He could have thought he was coming in 'cause kids weren't singing the right songs." He was claiming that I had no idea why I had been called to his house immediately following the accusation and that to his knowledge I didn't even know there had been an accusation of child sexual molestation. Yet his own brother-in-law, his long-time Children's Church leader, had called me that very morning and told me of the accusation. Was Rev. Jake truly ignorant, for the ten and a half months preceding my trial, of Phil's conversation with me?

In the New England state where all this took place, there is a law that states: "A clergyman, priest, minister, ... shall not disclose confidential communications made to him in his professional capacity in any civil or criminal case ... unless the person making the confidential communication waives such privilege herein provided." Rev. Jake flagrantly broke the law and has never suffered any consequences for doing so.

Joan was the one who started the process, predicated on a lie she later acknowledged, but Rev. Jake caused the vast majority of the damage. Recall that I telephoned my friend Kate to see if she would testify as one of my three allotted character witnesses, and that I was a bit leery about doing this because I hadn't heard from Kate and Gary for many months. *After* the trial, *after* six strangers had rendered a verdict, Kate told me she had actually entertained a bit of doubt about me *based on things that Rev. Jake had told her*. His impact on my trial was all encompassing, in ways that the jurors knew nothing about. Hence the chapter title "Can I Get a Witness?"

Prior to the trial, the prosecutor told my lawyer "Your client is going to have a real hard time, *based on things this pastor has told me*." The childless man who never set foot in Children's Church for three years took control of my case and, by virtue of being a pastor in title, caused tremendous damage. When I say that Rev. Jake knew nothing I am being very accurate. He didn't even know who Joan was when she accused me. He had never spoken with Elisa. Yet the things he told the prosecutor were what caused the case to be perpetuated.

During the phone conversations I had with him (he would call me at work), Rev. Jake frequently asked me who my best friends in the church were. He then contacted them, and that was usually the last I ever heard from them. He even called Darcie when I was at work, and suggested that the two of them "network." Unlike Rev. Jake's followers, Darcie didn't allow him to set the agenda, and he soon stopped trying to talk with her. She was pretty much demonized in the gossip circles at church from then on. "She's so angry and bitter, God can't possibly break through to her with the truth." "Why did they leave the church, anyway?" "She's so drugged up, she doesn't have any idea what's going on." (Darcie's occasional need to take Imitrex to help her survive her migraines is what prompted them to express this last notion. We know of at least two people, formerly good friends of ours, who passed along this bit of slander). When we asked Rev. Jake why he wanted to know where we started going to church after we left his church, he said, "Oh, I just thought I'd network with the leaders there." Obviously, he wanted to poison their minds just as he had with all our friends in his church, but didn't want to admit it.

The behavior of Rev. Jake's followers was the exact opposite of Paul's admonition: "Carry each other's burdens, and in this way you will fulfill the law of Christ." (Gal. 6:2.) Instead of looking to Scripture for guidance, they looked to their pastor. It was very poor judgment on their part.

How reprehensible it was for Rev. Jake to try to turn my own wife against me in my moment of greatest need, by calling her when I was at work. Rev. Jake is not merely guilty of becoming scared when an accusation was made; his crimes are much deeper than that. And, as long as they claim that their church was blameless, his followers also have blood on their hands. Rather than be upset about their lack of repentance, I bear in mind that these people paid a heavy price for their self-imposed denial: they wasted some of their prime years subjecting their families to Rev. Jake's spiritual leadership, and eventually learned what a tragic mistake it was. Sadly, some of them haven't learned this yet. I assume that the longer it takes each person to learn this reality, the more painful the realization will be when it occurs.

Recall that in the letter he sent out "To Leaders, Workers, and Advisors in the Church," Rev. Jake stated, "We've heard all sides of the story and feel as though we can convey the positions of each side effectively." Rev. Jake officially designated himself the spokesman for Joan, the police, the kids, their parents, and me. Needless to say, I would have preferred a different spokesman for myself. His tactics were successful: all our friends at church heard nothing but Rev. Jake's representation of events.

The police did what Rev. Jake wanted. Even though the jurors seemed to eventually grasp how unreliable his testimony was, Rev. Jake manipulated those in his church with impunity. His misguided story that two experts had confirmed child sex abuse was probably a very effective tool for turning my friends against me.

In the fax that Rev. Jake sent to the police, when referring to Joan's dishonesty about her nightmare, he said, "Personally I find the introductory contradiction disturbing as I've taken such a hard line in favor of the mother's account." He followed it up by assuring them that he still had his suspicions about me. The police were presumably quick to reassure him about this concern. Rev. Jake was not merely "caught in the middle" of events, trying to protect his church. Although he designated himself the spokesman for all parties, in fact he sided strongly with Joan. Rev. Jake gives vivid meaning to the term "the devil's advocate."

Psychology: Joan

The reason for Joan's behavior seems perfectly clear to me. She is fearful that men want to perform sexual acts on young children. I have no idea how she developed such a fear.

At the time when Joan's suspicions about me were building, her husband was not living with the family. Did I pay a price for any resentment she might have felt toward him? Did a poor marital relationship make her prone to having nightmares? I don't know.

In several decades of listening to countless sex-related conversations among men, I never heard any man say anything that implied a sexual interest in toddlers. Parents should certainly keep a close watch over their children, but suspicions directed toward "strange men" are often misguided. I assume that readers can see from the cross-examination concerning the nightmare just how much Joan was willing to distort the truth. Also, she most certainly never told me she had any objection to Elisa sitting on my lap, as she claimed during the trial.

The question "Did anybody in the church suggest to you that you should speak to Paul Grey," posed to Joan during the trial, should interest Christians. It concerns one of the most frequently quoted Scriptural passages among those who study the Bible: "If your brother sins against you, go and show him his fault, just between the two of you. If he listens to you, you have won your brother over. But if he will not listen, take one or two others along, so that every matter may be established by the testimony of two or three witnesses. If he refuses to listen to them, tell it to the church; and if he refuses to listen even to the church, treat him as you would a pagan or a tax collector." (Matt. 18:15–19.) Rev. Jake's church never even considered suggesting what I had asked for all along: a chance to talk to my accuser, especially with Elisa there to be my witness. After I became aware that Rev. Jake was turning my friends against me, I went to him with three other men. He argued and argued, then stopped me in my tracks by telling me he had inside information that my arrest was imminent, whereas I still assumed the case would be dropped. Rev. Jake did not change his ways at all as a result of that meeting. I complained to the denomination rather than to the courts, because I didn't feel right about legal action. The above passage of Scripture was my reasoning. The reader may disagree with my unquestioning acceptance of Scripture, but it explains why I do certain things.

Psychology: Reverend Jake

Rev. Jake is not a typical example of witch-hunt psychology. Even more so, he is not a typical pastor. I don't think he can be placed in a simple psychological category.

The reader may by now envision Rev. Jake as being such a jerk that no reasonable person would ever want to interact with him. In fact, he was gifted in a number of ways. He had a good sense of humor, he could sing and play guitar quite well, he could convince, he read many Christian books, he could emote, and he had the ability to make new believers feel comfortable. I liken his situation to that of Bill Clinton: both were quite gifted and could have achieved great things had they used their gifts purely for good.

Here's my best-guess summary of how Rev. Jake's actions can be explained. I don't think he disliked me or felt threatened by me prior to the accusation. Afterward, he wanted to be in complete control, both because that's his nature, and because his church was potentially threatened with a lawsuit. With nothing but Joan's lie to go on, and his own poor judgement about me, he quickly led the police to believe me guilty, thereby establishing control over my situation. I think that he then realized the error of his ways (and learned of Joan's lie), but did not want to look foolish. Rather than confess, he tried to save face by getting others to join him in agreeing that I looked suspicious, and then, with victory nearly in hand, he tried to get his people to stop talking about the matter altogether. Nothing would have served his purposes better than a willingness to plea-bargain on my part. By the time of the trial, he was obsessed with trying to prove my guilt. I don't know if this was due to fear of my lashing back with legal action, or for some other reason.

I am convinced that Rev. Jake was afraid of a lawsuit being brought against his church. I think this prompted him to go the extra mile to make sure he stayed on good terms with Joan and, more importantly, the police. Remember that he has a criminal record in that community.

When, after the accusation, I interacted with Rev. Jake for nearly fifteen hours (usually by phone), he didn't show the repulsion symptomatic of someone who believed I had actually been molesting children. I could sense that repulsion in other people whose minds had been poisoned by the accusation and by the subsequent gossip. Rev. Jake's goal seemed to be simply to prove that he was justified in his questionable treatment of my case.

One of the men in Rev. Jake's congregation once said — and Rev. Jake repeated, from the pulpit — that nothing is quite as strong as Rev. Jake's "need to be right." Recall that Rev. Jake asked those of us in my previous church to refrain from criticizing "his" church for a year. He seems hypersensitive to criticism; I have no idea why. I was definitely critical about how my case had been handled, and I shared my criticisms with everyone I spoke with, including Rev. Jake's followers. If those people had believed the things I told them after the accusation, without being thrown off course by the lies and rumors that were fed to them, it would have made Rev. Jake look very foolish. Perhaps this touched a nerve. I believe that Rev. Jake's sensitivity to criticism is the main reason why he acted the way he did.

Recall that when Sunday night services were initiated, many children showed up, and there was no one other than Phil to watch them. I was the only consistent volunteer to assist him. In theory, he would have violated church policy — being "alone with the kids" — had I not helped. Theoretically, my assistance made it possible for a Sunday evening service to even exist. I helped Phil, Rev. Jake's own brother-in-law, *every Sunday night for about two years*, and went upstairs to join the adults only when I had the chance. In light of these facts, think about Rev. Jake's incredible testimony about me: "I was teaching at a Sunday night, — and Paul came in and he was — and I didn't know he was in the building. And he came in and he sat down, looked around and laughed. And later I found out that he was with the kids that night, and it just struck me as odd. I just, I just — at that point I continued to kind of hold that in my mind that there was something strange about that. It didn't make sense to me. And so from that point on I kind of had a tickler in my mind."

My refusal to plea-bargain took away the convenient argument Rev. Jake would have been able to use to justify his actions. Mr. Martino's question had been "Prior to the accusation, did you ever entertain any suspicions about Paul Grey molesting the children?" The correct answer to the question was a simple no. After all, if he did harbor such suspicion, then wouldn't it be criminal negligence that he failed to look into the matter? Why did he make such statements in court rather than merely answering no to the question?

A month or two before the accusation, Rev. Jake confided to a group of new people in the church that he has a quirk that makes him dislike college-educated people. I've mentioned that I have a Ph.D. I never flaunted it before him or anyone else.

Rev. Jake has said from the pulpit that he is very fearful of losing his job, "because I'm not qualified to do anything else." From the pulpit, he sometimes described situations in his daily life in which he felt hateful toward some stranger he encountered (in a store, for example), then realized it was just a trigger mechanism going back to his earlier years, with the reason for the hatred no longer relevant. Does he have an unusually long list of such trigger mechanisms?

The real (Brittany's) child molester in Rev. Jake's church apparently ended his case by plea-bargaining. I think Rev. Jake wanted me to plea-bargain to end the criticism he had encountered concerning his treatment of my case. I think the many pieces of misinformation he fed me (about anatomically correct dolls, Christian child abuse experts who had examined Elisa, etc.) were designed to pressure me into plea-bargaining. And remember, he was telling me all these things before I figured out that he was trying to get me convicted.

Consider the fact that when I allowed Rev. Jake to call me at work, thinking he would eventually realize how wrongfully my case was being handled, I used to remind him of the fact that, since I had done nothing wrong, there were no witnesses to my doing anything wrong. His response was "There were all sorts of witnesses." There's only one logical explanation why he would say this when he knew it was untrue: he was trying to get me to agree to plea-bargain. Most pastors would want it proven that their Sunday school teacher was innocent; Rev. Jake apparently wanted the exact opposite.

About the time of my trial, Rev. Jake fired Phil as Children's Church director. A year before that, he had fired one of his three elders, after the man had become quite popular with the Sunday night crowd. From the 1993 cast of elders (when the accusation occurred), that leaves only Elder #2. Rev. Jake fired him in 1998. Elder #2 then had the good sense to leave the church; the others didn't.

A married couple had prominent positions of leadership. I think her title eventually became "Assistant Pastor," and he became an elder after the trial. They led numerous programs in that church. Rev. Jake got rid of both of them. One of the many deposed elders described Rev. Jake's methodology by saying, "He had a plan for getting rid of every one of them."

One day I went to visit a Christian friend who was trying to create a Christian hangout in a downtown location. This brother intended to have Christian bands perform there, and do all the usual things done by Christian outreach ministries nationwide. It was a special opportunity; he already had the building, because his business was located there. Rev. Jake stopped by while I was visiting my friend. When my friend went into his building briefly, I asked Rev. Jake if we could pray for the man and his ministry before we left. Incredibly, Rev. Jake asked me why we should do so. I told him it was because the man was trying to serve the Lord. Then he asked me how I knew that was really the case. At the time, I was very confused about Rev. Jake's odd behavior. I should have taken it as a warning sign.

My best friend, a recently converted Christian, wanted to help a Christian endeavor by selling a food item at a huge, once-a-year festival. Rev. Jake pummeled my friend with irrelevant questions about city codes, and kept saying, "I'm just trying to find out what's going on." I told myself that Rev. Jake was legitimately confused. Actually, it was another warning that I should have taken to heart.

Rev. Jake treated his testimony as if he were the one on trial, rather than myself. Do you remember how Beaver Cleaver, a 1960s TV character, would, whenever he was called to account for his misdeeds, shrug his shoulders and say things like, "Yeah, well, kinda, gee, but sorta"? That is precisely the impression Jake conveyed as he testified. He really was shrugging his shoulders, and readers can review the testimony to see what I mean.

The abominable things Rev. Jake said to my friends about me, that he had "caught me lying to Darcie," that the accusation against me did not merely involve one child, etc., successfully caused them to drop their support of me. I think there is no defense against such slander other than a lawsuit.

One could pose the question: How could Darcie and I be part of Rev. Jake's church for so long, with extensive involvement on my part, and not recognize his emotional problems? Recall that I had it drummed into my head during childhood that I was a great person. I don't identify with those who are insecure about themselves. I don't think like them, I don't see issues the way they see them, and I can be oblivious as they struggle with their inner torments. Recall the communication gap between Rev. Jake and me at the meeting at his house. I perceived myself a trusted Sunday school teacher meeting with my trusting pastor, and he apparently perceived himself a prosecutor collecting evidence against an accused child molester. Chances are, I go through life assuming that I fully understand the things that others speak or write, when in reality I miss their meaning entirely. Maybe part of the reason I so seriously misjudged Rev. Jake was my Scripture-based reluctance to criticize my own pastor. Don't entertain the notion that Scripture is wrong; it doesn't tell us to do foolish things, like sticking with the same pastor regardless of serious faults. In practice, Darcie and I should have recognized Jake's problems and changed to another church. On the other hand, I think God decreed that I go through this ordeal as a part of Rev. Jake's church, for reasons I can only try to guess.

There is a technique that voters can use to judge candidates for political office: don't get sidetracked by the things they say when they're campaigning; just check their voting records. Likewise, the only thing that really matters about Jake's conduct is his testimony, not the manipulative things he said to his followers about my case. Jake said very damaging things about me in his testimony; Phil did not. There's only one solid criterion by which Rev. Jake should be judged: his testimony before the jury was extremely damaging to me. The jurors, and no one else, were the ones who would decide my fate. Rev. Jake knew this, and he will answer to God some day for his behavior. When that day comes, God will not be swayed by Beaver Cleaver shoulder shrugs.

Scripture presents a convenient measuring stick for distinguishing between good and evil. "The fruit of the Spirit is love, joy, peace, patience, kindness, goodness, faithfulness, gentleness and self-control." (Galatians 5:22–23.) I pointed out to Rev. Jake that three years of observing the fruit of the Spirit in my life should have indicated to him that the accusation was untrue. He knew that the accusation was built on a lie. He also knows I Tim. 5:19, "Do not entertain an accusation against an elder, unless it is brought by two or three witnesses." And yet he just argued and argued. His response to that verse was "there were all sorts of witnesses." Of course he was wrong, but his followers heard only his version of all the events. Distorting

Scripture to achieve personal goals is quite common; Satan himself did it while arguing with Jesus (Matt. 4:1–11).

Flashback to Salem

Rev. Jake had a predecessor in this country. Reverend Samuel Parris (1653-1719) was a key player in the Salem witch-hunts. *Dictionary of American Biography*, ed. D. Malone, Scribner's Sons, 1934, says the following about Parris:

> "His daughter and his niece became subject to curious attacks which physicians and ministers both attributed to 'an evil hand.'...The situation got out of his hands when...a member of his church gave his West Indian slaves instructions as to how to discover the 'witches' and soon the jails were filled with the accused. Parris...accepted 'spectral evidence' (*the witch-finding methods of the day*) contrary to the advice of the Boston ministers. He often acted as court clerk and sometimes as a witness. His testimony against several condemned members of his parish caused disaffection among their relatives, who...drew up a list of grievances against the minister." (Italics mine)

Reverend Parris had a regular pattern: his supporters did not get accused, and his enemies did. From *A Delusion of Satan*, by Frances Hill, (Doubleday, 1995), 193: "If the witch-hunt was shown to be a sham, [Rev. Parris'] livelihood was in jeopardy and his future at stake."

Some might say that the spirit of Samuel Parris lives on in New England in the person of Rev. Jake.

Psychology: Others

There is a logical reason why my status in that church shifted so suddenly from trusted teacher to child molester. It is Joan's lie. When she telephoned Phil, even before calling the police, she told him that Elisa had awakened, "screaming," from a nightmare, and that the reason for Elisa's disturbance, Elisa said, was that I had molested her. My case was not one of "kids say the darndest things." It was purely a false accusation. The people in that church could think of no logical reason why Joan would make up such a story.

Many of the adults in that church claim to have been sexually abused. During one of my meetings with Rev. Jake, when we were discussing Joan's allegation of child sexual molestation, Rev. Jake asked me, "Have *you* ever been abused?" When I told him no, he said, "Well I have." I thought I had finally learned the source of so much of his inexplicable behavior. But I later learned that Rev. Jake claimed he hadn't been *sexually* abused. He told one of my friends that the "abuse" he endured was that his father didn't spend enough quality time with him.

Darcie and I could observe on a daily basis the way Phil's mind oscillated between the truth and the positions that brother-in-law Rev. Jake demanded he take. Since Rev. Jake had daily access to Phil, and supposed authority over him, the battle for Phil's innocent mind was one we were destined to lose. It was a clear example of Matt. 13:19, in which the seed of truth is immediately snatched away by the enemy of God.

Key Ingredients for a Witch-Hunt

Fear is certainly the biggest reason behind the witch-hunting tendencies in America today. This fear has several consequences: trigger-happy accusations and convictions, intense prejudice (assumption of guilt) toward the accused, and fast-fix "solutions" based on political correctness. The number of accusations and arrests has increased dramatically over the last two decades, as the public has become more "educated" on the subject of child sex abuse. This education has often produced fear in individuals that was not there before the education process took place. The question bears asking, Who has been in charge of this education process? Do you suppose it was unbiased professionals?

Going over Joan's preliminary thoughts that led to the accusation, the question arises: What caused her to be so suspicious of me from the very beginning? The fact that she was highly suspicious, yet would continue to place Elisa in my care one hour per week for the next seven months, was all it took to seal my fate. Could her suspicions have been due to "education" she had received on the topic? Was it due to watching sensationalized TV stories, or reading newspaper or magazine accounts that overstated the problem? Something placed the notion in her head that all men have a desire to molest toddlers. That fear was all it took to ruin our lives. Child abuse is a real problem, but fears like Joan's are out of proportion. Such fears tend to be directed, in scapegoat fashion, against those outside the family unit, whereas the vast majority of child sex abuse, according to professional journals, takes place in the home.

When fear dominates an individual's attitude toward a person suspected of child sex abuse, one result of the fear is intense prejudice. This hypersensitive prejudice can cause the fearful individual to see and hear things that didn't happen. Today there are laws against prejudice based on age, race, gender, physical handicap, religion, and sexual orientation, but it is still permissible to have prejudicial attitudes toward persons accused — but not convicted — of child abuse.

Joan had been suspicious of me for seven months, and it appears that she questioned Elisa about me on at least one other occasion during that time. This is evident in the following passage from the warrant, in what Joan told the state inspector:

> The mother further gave me the information that while brushing her teeth one night, she asked her daughter if her teacher ever kisses her, and her daughter said, 'Yes,' and then demonstrated with her tongue the way the teacher kissed her. That the mother has no explanation as to how her child would know this.

I can't determine when this exchange between Joan and Elisa took place. The warrant was dated ten weeks after the accusation. It could have occurred at any time up to that date or any time as much as seven months before the accusation. Was Elisa conforming to Joan's repeated suggestions? Did Joan envision a tongue sticking out the same way she had envisioned an erection, or the way she envisioned Elisa's patting of her genital area? We'll never know. The jury was not informed of this exchange.

Consider this similarity: Joan was fearful that I was in the classroom with an erection, doing improper things with Elisa, which is why she left the service early that last day. When she got to the classroom, she saw precisely what her hypersensitive, prejudiced mind had envisioned, even though there was no erection. Similarly, Rev. Jake apparently believed I was guilty when he first heard the accusation. Subsequently, the first time he saw me, he saw — just as Joan had seen — exactly what his accusation-prone mind had envisioned: a guilty child molester whose lies could be cleverly discerned by analysis of a hand gesture and by the molester's having unwittingly disclosed "details" of the alleged crime. Both Joan and Rev. Jake saw exactly what their distorted, fearful minds had envisioned. I think Joan's fear was genuine, while Rev. Jake's actions were largely governed by a desire to seize an opportunity to gain control. When I innocently went to his house the evening after the allegation, he wasn't even in the same ballpark I was in, as far as communication is concerned. Speaking to such a person is a no-win situation.

Joan's fears fed on themselves. In contrast, the other three who wrote police statements had never entertained the notion of accusing me of any wrongdoing until Joan made her accusation. In all three cases, it was *after* the accusation that their underlying fears took over. The result was intense prejudice, which caused all three of them to re-interpret past events. None of this would have happened without the accusation; it greatly boosted the level of fear that lay within them. Joan was a different situation: she never heard an accusation from any other person, but in her own mind had accused me from the very first time she ever met me. Joan never went through the phenomenon of reinterpretation; she was the only one who believed in my guilt even before the accusation.

After the accusation and subsequent conversations with Rev. Jake and the police, Brittany's (and Dottie's) mother re-interpreted everything she knew pertaining to me. Remember that I had worked with Dottie every week for nineteen months. One of the re-interpretations by Dottie's mother was that Dottie must have been crying on that Sunday during my final month of teaching because she was reluctant to go to my class. Dottie's mother originally assumed this incident had occurred because both parents had been preparing to leave the country for two weeks. Her original interpretation was correct. Even my cat recognizes immediately whenever Darcie and I start making any travel-related preparations. Dottie is a very astute child; of course she felt threatened by the prospect of being abandoned by her parents.

I don't believe the rest of the church re-interpreted everything about me (Brittany and a few other legitimate victims may be exceptions). The church did not abandon me due to fear or intense prejudice; it was just a case of a congregation doing what their pastor directed them to do. The intensity of underlying fears concerning child sex abuse merely made it very easy for them to be manipulated into obeying Rev. Jake's wishes. A few of the women, who listened to Joan tearfully relate her story, probably identified with her and began to entertain doubts about me. If anyone had earned the trust of the women, it was Phil and myself. The man who showed them for three years that men can be trusted was branded by Rev. Jake as a wolf in sheep's clothing. What does that do to these women's attitudes toward men in general? Within a few days, Rev. Jake undid my three years of demonstrating Christian servanthood. In the eyes of God, that is an abomination.

Joan will probably argue until her dying day that her fears were justified. Actually, I recall praising Elisa's behavior; not just her "awesome cute" looks. From a teacher's viewpoint, she was one of the least stress-causing kids under my care. My friend's daughter who would "play Sunday school" all week long was another such example. These were kids whose behavior never caused me any grief. As a worn-out teacher, I appreciated them. They were fun, not burdensome, to work with. My adult assistants also enjoyed our non-stressful times with the kids quite a bit. Elisa had big red cheeks; she was cute the way a puppy dog with big ears is cute. If any child in my class could have been called beautiful in a more grownup sense, it clearly would have been Phil's daughter. She was a dear little friend, and I regret that she is no longer in my life.

Speaking of "worn-out teacher," I do recall being very weary on my last day of teaching, because of my two-year-old visitor's nonstop attempt to open doors. In the final fifteen minutes of class, I probably got a rare chance to sit down. When I did so (though I don't recall the event), it's likely that Elisa took advantage of the situation, making a beeline for my lap. My aunt in Saginaw has a dog that jumps into her lap, landing there even before my aunt is fully seated. Elisa was getting to a stage where I probably should have started to insist that she stay more focused on the classroom tasks. In my final weeks of teaching, Elisa loved to get on my lap. On the other hand, Joan had made the "We don't treat them according to the way they look" remark to me several weeks earlier, and I had become leery of her. As fate would have it, moments after I sat my weary body down, Joan walked in the door and saw Elisa getting on my lap. Joan's written police statement that "when he saw me he stopped and put her down," was probably accurate. But her perception that I was *placing* Elisa on my lap in the first place was erroneous.

I think the remarks I made about Elisa's appearance that caused Joan's fear are best put into context by the following: for every word I ever uttered about Elisa's appearance, I have uttered 10,000 words of praise about my cat's appearance. I happen to think puppies are absolutely adorable, even "awesome cute." It has nothing to do with sexual desire. Sunday school teachers with ugly thin beards and slightly crooked smiles are merely convenient receptacles of fears for people like Joan. Statistically, these fears are misplaced.

Recall that in Joan's written statement to the police, she said that I tried to hide an erection with my left arm. In court, she said I tried to hide it with some paper. In the arrest warrant, the state inspector, quoting Joan, said I tried to hide it with my hand. I don't know if the change in terminology was for manipulative purposes; I suspect it was. I assume that readers understand how extremely unlikely it is for someone to get a glimpse of a seated fully clothed man and discern that he has an erection. The fear that placed that notion in Joan's head is the same fear that caused Rev. Jake to perceive my innocent hand gesture as a graphic demonstration of a finger being inserted into a child's vagina. His notion was far more violent, I suspect, than any that Joan ever entertained. In both cases, the conclusion of what they had "witnessed" was nothing but a reflection of the fear itself. Without the fear preceding the event, they wouldn't have seen these things at all. This truly is the essence of what happens in a witch-hunt. Many Christians would refer to these two instances of fear-induced visions as "demonic." Joan's dream also belongs in that category.

It is fairly common for people to see and hear things that do not exist or are terribly out of proportion. I vaguely recall during childhood, after going to bed, entertaining the fear that there was some kind of harmful person or creature in the room with me. Fear of the bogeyman is a time-honored tradition among kids. Adults too are subject to needless fears. In psychiatric institutions, it is very common for patients to hear voices that no one else hears. Many would label these as demonic. Whatever their origin, they are absolutely real to the patient. With the possible exception of Rev. Jake, people who perpetrate a witch-hunt to convict an innocent person are entirely convinced that they are behaving rationally. Is this the same phenomenon as the bogeyman?

In 1999, an official in Washington, D.C. lost his job. The reason was his use of the word "niggardly" at a meeting. The word has no racial connotation at all, but he was nonetheless accused of being a racist, due to the misunderstanding of those around him. That's exactly what happened in my case: Joan observed my innocent friendliness and misinterpreted it, then 1990s political correctness allowed her to punish the "perpetrator." Abuse of the country's sensitivity to racism is called "playing the race card." Politicians in the '90s have also overplayed the "for the children" card. Along the same lines is the "get tough on child molesters" card. All these are means of political manipulation using current societal fears.

In the '90s, the major television networks focused heavily on anything that would arouse intense emotions among viewers. One would suspect that this was to be competitive. After all, the "lively" TV talk shows had great success. Network newscasters (Barbara Walters, Diane Sawyer, etc.) appeared regularly on hour-long shows featuring emotional topics. The networks had successfully adapted to the times. For example, on the cover of *TV Guide* in September 1999, the title was "How Women Took Over the News." The subtitle was "Powerful journalists like Katie Kouric have changed the face and focus of the stories we care about the most — and the revolution has just begun." The technique of stirring up emotions in American news presentations is reflected by a term that originated in the 1990s: "infotainment."

The networks also helped shape the times through their influence. For weeks after the shooting rampage by two boys at a school in Littleton, Colorado, you couldn't flip through the channels for weeks without seeing special presentations about Littleton, and about how dangerous guns have become in our schools. This was greatly agitating to children and parents throughout the country. Kids everywhere expressed fear about going back to school.

I think there were two reasons why this incident received so much coverage. First, it was intensely emotional; therefore it attracted lots of viewers. Second, it offered the networks a convenient means of promoting gun-control legislation. Perhaps I am cynical to suggest such a thing, but I am convinced it is true. The tactic is to scare society into making a change that the news network feels is "for the better." This is the same technique used by the more zealous proponents who "raised the awareness" of the child abuse problem in America today. For the record, I have never owned a gun. I was required to shoot a rifle on three or four occasions when I was in the Air Force. My point is that emotion and political manipulation dominated television in the 1990s, and I think the impact of TV on our society is obvious.

Bowing to public pressure stirred up by TV productions, the '90s produced a flurry of "hate crime" legislation for which the penalties were greater if the lawbreaker's motivation was deemed to have been hatred of homosexuals, Jews, blacks, women, or other groups who had been overly victimized in the past. Such legislation was the epitome of the '90s, and I believe it helps explain how the seeds of my witch-hunt were sown.

Consider the parents who neglect discipline of their own children. They try to substitute threats as a replacement for consistent discipline. They resort to occasional outbursts, thinking this a quick-fix solution to their children's misbehavior. It doesn't work. Nonetheless, that's how America tried to solve problems in the 1990s. Consider the school principal who tries to solve a problem by increasing the threats of what will happen to anyone who breaks the rules concerning the problem *du jour*; and by creating more supplemental rules to make sure the bad guys don't get off on a technicality. The result is that innocent people are harmed by the new quick-fix policies. In Illinois, a seven-year-old was suspended from school for bringing toenail clippers to school. The reason was that the clippers included a 1.6-inch-long nail file, and his school was trying to make sure that no violence — such as the Littleton shootings — would happen at their school. That's how America tried to solve problems in the 1990s. The problems only seemed to get worse, and the victims of the new quick-fix policies were very often people like that seven-year-old boy and myself.

I believe that quick-fix policies are part of a more general key ingredient for witch-hunts: the willingness of rational people to let irrational people control the process. Being aware of zealots does not solve the problem. Rational adults must apply pressure to effect changes, counteracting the influence of the zealots. This pressure could take the form of letters to legislators, newspapers, the police, *et al*, and speaking to others about the need for change.

No Lessons Learned in the World of My Accuser

The Sunday school teacher who replaced me was a young single mother. Her son was about five when my three-year involvement in Rev. Jake's church began. I think there was at least one time when Phil told him to sit on my lap when he was misbehaving. His usual practice was to silently leave the area where the group of kids had assembled and watch from afar. He was usually smiling; it seemed to be something of a game to him. He would not usually obey when I told him to rejoin the group; I had to keep after him. I think he was just spoiled; his temperament was very peaceful for a boy his age. His mother didn't know me; we had only spoken on a few occasions — she's one of the few long-time adults in the church whom I never prayed for on a personal basis. She is a staunch follower of Rev. Jake. After she took over the job of teaching my two- and three-year-old class, my best friend encountered her in the supermarket. She shouted at him about how poor Rev. Jake had done the right thing, and God knew the truth about me; I wouldn't get away with it if I was guilty. What is the likelihood that my beloved little former pupils got nasty subliminal messages about me from their new teacher? It's a really unpleasant thought. I think they would be terribly frightened and confused if she or any of the parents who were influenced by Rev. Jake were to say bad things about me to them shortly after the accusation. Hopefully, it didn't happen.

If people had shown signs of having learned anything from my ordeal, I would be much more at peace. In Rev. Jake's church, it seems they didn't learn anything. No belated apologies, even though they could have been relayed easily through my friend

Skip. Mary was extremely sympathetic about all the bother that poor Rev. Jake had to go through. After the trial, she told a friend of mine, "Paul Grey should get in front of the church and apologize for what he put us all through." When my best friend spoke of Rev. Jake's despicable actions in my case, one of the long-timers told him God would punish him for "speaking bad things about a pastor anointed by God." I think that remark gives insight into the psychology that enables Rev. Jake to manipulate his group so effectively. For the record, the Bible does not instruct us to blindly obey everything that every church leader says. Jesus criticized church leaders more than he criticized any other group. The problem in abusive churches — and cults — is when the congregation treats the leadership as though the leaders had been divinely chosen when it's not true.

A couple of months before the trial, one of the Sunday school teachers quoted Rev. Jake's teachings regarding the "lesson" the church had learned from my case: "These are evil times; you can't trust anyone." Scripture was abandoned in favor of Rev. Jake's opinions, and his followers never recognized when the abandonment happened.

Since Rev. Jake fired him, Phil has merely played his flute during Sunday services. That's a lot more enjoyable than working with kids, but the fact is that Rev. Jake destroyed a powerful ministry. Phil's replacement was a godly young man from out of town. Within two years, the godly young man abruptly left; Rev. Jake's followers were never told why. The man remarked that he was leaving "with a bleeding heart." This was just after the time that Rev. Jake made himself officially accountable to no one by pulling out of the denomination.

Readers might be curious about what draws people to Rev. Jake's church. The main reason is the music, which is what the original denomination is noted for. Other reasons are summer softball, lots of fun people, and a non-judgmental atmosphere. Of course, criticism of Rev. Jake *does* draw swift judgment. As long as an individual doesn't get on the bad side of "the leadership," it's a lot of fun. People usually don't leave fun churches. In my case, quite a few chose to stay even though they knew of Rev. Jake's misdeeds. They figured it was my problem, not theirs.

The music has three big draws: it's real fun music, the lyrics are about Jesus, thereby facilitating true worship, and Rev. Jake allows many different followers to occasionally get on stage as part of the worship team. Rev. Jake leads the music more often than anyone else does, and he makes all important musical decisions. His doling out of occasional "music ministry" (onstage) positions is a powerful tool that has kept many a person attending that church. The music sessions are a mixed bag of good (Ps. 92:1) and bad (Amos 5:21).

The importance of the music in getting people to attend that church cannot be overstated. If the guitarists and vocalists were suddenly replaced by one organist and one off-key vocalist, 99 percent of Rev. Jake's followers would no longer "hear the Lord telling them" to attend that church.

One of the local pastors articulated a community sentiment, I suspect, when a couple of my friends visited his church. He asked where they had been previously attending church. When they told him Rev. Jake's, he immediately said, "Boy, it was really something the way they sold out on their Sunday school teacher." It was inappropriate for him to say that to a visiting couple, but it shows what Rev. Jake's reputation is like among some of his peers. In late-1996, another local pastor threatened to inflict violence on Rev. Jake for saying so many nasty things about his friend, who was going through a very difficult period in her life. Still another local pastor remarked that Rev. Jake is "simply not a pastor" (meaning that Rev. Jake should not have a pastoral role). I could give more examples, but it's not necessary; the point is simply that Rev. Jake's reputation is not very good among his peers in that community.

Perhaps readers are curious about how Rev. Jake's church treated the news of my acquittal and dismissal. Not a word was spoken. After all the fuss, their #2 childcare servant had finally been legally vindicated, and there was no mention of it whatsoever in that church. I find it hard to believe that such a large group of people could act so strangely. My relations continued to be better than ever with all my acquaintances in the community, with the exception of Rev. Jake's church. The change they made in the church to protect against allegations like mine was to start requiring their Sunday school teachers to be fingerprinted. (My fingerprints have been on file since 1968, when I first got Top Secret clearance. I couldn't have held my job in Rev. Jake's community if I would have had a felony record such as sexual assault). Rev. Jake's new policy is, as usual, designed to protect him, not children or volunteers.

Even though my 100-odd adult friends from Rev. Jake's church never initiated any form of support for Darcie and myself, I think only about ten of them still believe Rev. Jake and Joan. Several others probably entertained doubts until they saw the newspaper articles when the trial was going on. The world-class slander job that had been done on me for nearly a year could finally be seen to contradict the facts. Still, the vast majority of them simply chose not to acknowledge the mistreatment of Darcie and me. As a matter of convenience, they simply denied the reality concerning the abuses perpetrated by their church.

Now that several years have gone by, what could these people say to me? I guarantee that if I were to go back there and encounter them in the community, their greeting would be the usual meaningless "Hey, how's it going?" Remember the Nicaraguan teenager who was so heartbroken after her sponsor dumped her because "she just couldn't handle" the girl's tragic story? I think the manner in which this Nicaraguan child was treated illustrates the basic survival technique — running away from unpleasant issues — of those in that church who knew me. For those who didn't know me that well, I think it just doesn't dawn on them that when their church ruins a person's life, they should do something about it. It *should*, but it doesn't.

Recall that there was a very mature man in that church who conducted the music sessions for my two- and three-year-olds both years that I taught them. He alternated weeks with Kate and Gary. His son was in my class the first year. He was in the same line of work I was in. We seemed much more similar to each other than we were to the rest of the church. But when the trial approached — ten months after the accusation! — and Mr. Martino's chosen investigator contacted him to ask him questions about the classroom circumstances in my case, he didn't even know which child was the alleged victim." To the man who worked shoulder to shoulder with me in the trenches for two years, I became a complete nonentity after the accusation was made. In contrast, some of my Air Force friends — from twenty-five years before the accusation — telephoned me and sent me $1000 and sent letters of encouragement. Once again, Rev. Jake's church provides a textbook example of how not to behave in a case like mine, whereas my supporters were models of proper behavior.

Several of the adults in Rev. Jake's church claimed to be victims of past sexual abuse. As the months passed and I talked about my case with virtually everyone, a few friends outside the church also told me they had been sexually abused when they were young. I used to think that such people were always likely to assume guilt, no matter what, when an accusation was made. I found out from these friends that this assumption of guilt is not automatic. Certainly they don't have the childlike presumption of innocence robbed from them long ago, but these friends of mine were capable of thinking quite rationally. Rev. Jake's most influential leader — a woman; the assistant pastor I mentioned earlier — described a friend of mine as "the worst case of abuse [she] had ever encountered." She had even called me and asked me to take this man's case as a special prayer project. I did, and he became my best friend. He earned a prominent place on the church's "most hated" list for his willingness to speak loudly and frequently in my behalf.

Another friend of mine was the Children's Church leader at one of the larger churches in our county when the accusation occurred. I called him, and he was extremely supportive, just the way all my Christian friends outside of Rev. Jake's church were. My friend told me that a fearful woman had tried to accuse one of his male teachers for "paying too much attention" to her daughter. My friend knew that the teacher was innocent, and stuck up for him. After some heated arguments with the lady and her husband, they reached a compromise: the child wouldn't be taught by that particular man for the remaining few months that both families would be living in the vicinity. The result was that no one's life was ruined. My friend ended our initial phone conversation by praying for my protection, which is how mature Christians behave in such situations.

In the final weeks that we lived in that community, I made friends with several other people, including a nice young Christian couple. They were not members of Jake's church. Meeting them was a pleasant way for me to end my days in that part of the country. Just before this book went to press, in the year 2001, I learned that Rev. Jake had told the husband of this nice couple that Paul Grey "would be in jail today, if that child would have identified him in court."

Regardless of the consequences of Rev. Jake's immaturity, I have no doubt that God orchestrated the whole ordeal, certainly not to punish me, but for reasons I'm not qualified to identify. Remember, God orchestrated Job's afflictions, the trials of Joseph, Jesus, Paul and Silas, Peter, and many others. It was not a mistake, as far as I'm concerned. That doesn't excuse the improper behavior, though. Dottie's mother and Mary are also primary guilty parties in my case. Suspicions are one thing; a written police statement is another. Their actions are an essential ingredient of witch-hunting.

If any reader is bothered by the question of how God could allow innocent behavior to be met with such evil, and by the lack of any good coming of the ordeal, consider where Darcie and I might be today if it hadn't happened. We might still be deceived, allowing a very evil con man to be our pastor. No thanks; if God's enemy is prominent in my life, I prefer to know where he is. There was a huge price to pay, but that's because of evil people, not because God chose for the people to *be* evil.

IV. Ongoing Problems in America

Examples of Modern "Solutions"

I believe that the definition of sexual assault is being broadened in an overly simplistic effort to accommodate the country's political eagerness to deal with a major problem. The definition of sexual harassment — a different subject — has certainly been broadened. Recently, a twelve-year-old boy was suspended from school for sticking out his tongue at a girl. The teacher called it sexual harassment because of connotations that go with the tongue. The boy and girl both claimed they had no idea of any sexual implication that went with his time-honored gesture. The blatant cases ("Sleep with me or you're fired") that initially prompted our country's modern-day efforts to deal with sexual harassment are now less common. Presumably the would-be perpetrators have learned the new rules and have changed their behavior to avoid prosecution. Clearly, the number of sexual harassment complaints has increased ever since the subject first became a politically active issue, despite the fact that women (and men) are not being sexually harassed any more than they used to be.

A woman won a sexual harassment case because her male co-workers displayed a *Playboy*-type calendar in the workplace. Their behavior was unacceptable, but did America really want sexual harassment laws to include such behavior? Definitions are being broadened regarding what constitutes sexual harassment; that's why the number of cases keeps increasing. In a similar manner, definitions have been broadened as to what constitutes a child abuse allegation worthy of legal pursuit.

Recently a six-year-old Delaware girl was reprimanded for "inappropriate sexual touching" of her teacher. She had patted her teacher on the bottom, and the teacher reported the child's "misdeed" to the principal. The child's mother, shocked by the reprimand, said that the girl really loves this teacher, and was merely expressing it in the form of a love pat. This breaks my heart; I'm sure this child will remember the hurt of this incident — anger and rebuke in response to her love — for the rest of her life. *That* is real child abuse, in my eyes.

On a school playground in 1996, a six-year-old boy kissed a little girl on the cheek after she asked him to. The teacher reported the incident to the principal. The boy was charged with sexual harassment and suspended from school. Even the pronunciation of the word has been changed in accordance with political correctness. In the military and elsewhere, one can get in trouble for using the old-fashioned (correct) pronunciation, because it sounds like "her ass," and some zealots want to make sure no one utters such offensive speech. This is just like the incident I mentioned earlier, involving the word "niggardly." The zealots need to be constrained; they have gained too much political power.

Parents are being taken to court for a variety of questionable reasons. There is an organization dedicated to assisting such parents. VOCAL (Victims Of Child Abuse Laws) can be reached at (303) 770-5096, if the reader knows of a parent or other individual with such a problem.

I suspect that the rejoicing among some black Americans when O. J. Simpson was acquitted after his criminal trial, and the encouragement of witch-hunters like Joan, are caused by similar conditions: in their minds, years of seeing white men treated more favorably by our legal system "justifies" today's legal absurdities. This backlash effect is likely to claim some innocent men like myself. Older black Americans can probably identify with the injustices I've described in this book; the root cause being intense prejudice. Recall the plot and theme of *To Kill A Mockingbird;* it fits my case perfectly, and shows how morally wrong today's witch-hunting behavior is.

Maybe it is human nature to assume that we know better than our predecessors did about every aspect of life. We are led to believe that our new discoveries about the prevalence of child sex abuse have made us more knowledgeable than our precursors. I'm skeptical about how much "better off" we are with our modern-day attempts to solve this problem. In my case, the heart of the problem — besides the fears that initiated the process — was that irrational people were given too much authority. Joan should not have been allowed to cause so much taxpayer money to be spent on her fears. If it were her own money, I wouldn't object nearly as much, especially if she had been required to reimburse Darcie and me for our immense losses. I don't think society will allow people like Joan and Rev. Jake to control child abuse investigations for too many more years; numerous other programs are competing for the tax revenues involved. Plus, lawsuits brought by victims against zealots will start to curb the abuses and increase general awareness of the problems. Until such changes are made, other innocent victims will be brutalized.

When the police bend the rules to achieve their goals, most of us are willing to tolerate it, thinking that the result will be the conviction of a few more criminals. But we fail to see the danger: criminals are the first to adjust to the new unwritten rules because they are the ones most motivated to learn them, while innocent men and women get trampled by the police before they figure out what's going on. Similarly, while the police can easily generate a "case" out of nothing but word-twisting against an innocent person, criminals are too guarded to allow any such thing to happen to themselves. If a case has no evidence, and the police need to get a conviction in order to look good, their easiest targets are the most innocent members of society. Obviously, most police don't stoop to such tactics, but the practice is not so uncommon. My simple-minded assumption that the police would treat my case with honesty and competence ended up damaging me terribly. It grieves me spiritually to learn that getting a good lawyer, rather than being honest, is the key to success in America. And the trend toward ever-increasing litigation doesn't seem to be slowing down.

Americans today look back at seventeenth-century Salem and ridicule the society of that time for allowing witch-hunts to happen. The Salem residents are ridiculed for their foolishness, for believing in such "nonsense" as witches. Other than the fact that the standard of living has increased dramatically, in what way is America in the 1990s more mature than seventeenth-century Salem? There, the suspects were hanged. Today, the only reason why people convicted in cases like mine don't get hanged is because we don't hang anyone for any crime. If we did, convicted child abusers would be the first to get that punishment. In what way is our society wiser than that of seventeenth-century Salem?

Other Sunday School Scapegoats: Akiki & Fijnje

Young Bobby Fijnje was an innocent lamb who helped his church's Sunday school efforts while in his early teens. He was subjected to a full-fledged witch-hunt in Florida, 1989 through 1991. Bobby was indicted and tried as an adult, and the state refused to release him on bond. State Attorney Janet Reno gave her approval to that arrangement, and she insisted on being in court when the verdict was reached for fifteen-year-old Bobby. Her office had pointed out to Bobby that he would be imprisoned, where he would be subject to beatings, rape, and possibly death from mistreatment by prison inmates. Or, he could avoid it all by plea-bargaining. He didn't plea-bargain.

Bobby was a juvenile diabetic. They questioned him for hours. After seven hours of having eaten one bite from a sandwich, Bobby said to his interrogators, "It just happened. Now can I go home?" This "confession" wasn't taped and he didn't sign anything. His blood sugar was dangerously low at the time of this so-called confession. I'm convinced that Bobby did what most innocent defendants who plea-bargain do: he just said whatever he had been led to believe would secure his release from the agonizing ordeal. It was along the lines of, "OK, you're stronger than I am; now can I go?" Coercion such as that used on young Bobby Fijnje is practiced by dictatorships throughout the world.

"Trial by Therapy," a *National Review* article dated 6 September 1993, also contained the following information: Miss Reno's office told Bobby's family that he "would have AIDS within a week of entering prison." Furthermore, Miss Reno saw to it that young Bobby "was held in solitary confinement for much of his stay at [Miami's] Dade County Juvenile Detention Center." After he had been in jail for nearly two years, the moment finally came when his jury was ready to announce the verdict. A guilty verdict on any of the seven counts against him would have led to a mandatory life sentence. With his "heart trying to jump out of [his] chest" (Bobby's words, *Frontline*, 27 October 1998), everyone had to wait two and a half hours because Janet Reno wanted to be there. That is one of the cruelest forms of torture ever perpetrated on a youngster.

Miss Reno represents political correctness. Despite her abusive techniques in Florida (Bobby Fijnje's case was not the only one), she was appointed to head the Justice Department for the Clinton Administration; she became the nation's #1 law enforcement official, and held that position for eight years. I have heard it said that the Clintons selected her because she claimed to be such a staunch advocate for children. (Janet Reno has no children of her own.) Clearly, one of their goals was to select a woman. For those who do not know, First lady Hillary Rodham Clinton played a major role in decisions concerning domestic issues.

When the Branch Davidians had a standoff with the FBI near Waco, Texas, Janet Reno resisted the use of force. The

FBI then persuaded her to change her mind by telling her that children were being abused in the Branch Davidian compound. She did indeed reverse her decision, and the federal government proceeded to attack the compound, resulting in the deaths of dozens of children and adults. Janet Reno is a representative witch-hunter. Everyone seems to think that she "means well," but her zealotry has led her to make some misguided decisions. What one child thinks of Janet Reno: Referring to the excessively cruel sentence she tried to impose upon him — at great expense to the state of Florida — Bobby Fijnje asked, "Why would you even think of doing something like that if you're a crusader for children?" (*Frontline*, 27 October 1998.)

Bobby Fijnje's lawyers were very pessimistic during his trial, because their favorable expert witness was not allowed to testify, while expert witnesses for the prosecution were. I can identify with their feelings: Mr. Martino was truly in shock when the judge ruled that Dr. Shalom could not testify. Despite his lawyers' pessimism, Bobby maintained his confidence. He spoke with his parents on the telephone every evening and read his Bible. I am humbled to have been through such an experience that links me, to a small extent, with anyone who has such character. God bless my younger brother in Christ, Bobby Fijnje.

Dale Akiki was an innocent lamb of God who was a teacher's aide for three- and four-year-olds at his church near San Diego. In "Trial by Therapy" (*National Review*, 6 September 1993), I note that three mothers from that church "had gotten together and talked about common behaviors in their three- and four-year-olds, such things as bed-wetting, nightmares, and aggression. They decided 'Mr. Dale's' odd appearance might be frightening their children," and the initial witch-hunt seeds were sown. A mother who saw her daughter crying in the hallway questioned the child for an hour before the child finally said, "He showed me him's penis."

We'll never know the questions the mother asked her child during that hour. I believe that the mother projected her own fears into the child, then conducted the interrogation accordingly. Perhaps the mother was overly "savvy" due to education she had recently acquired concerning the rampant problem of child sex abuse.

As the California judge denied bail to Mr. Akiki, he spoke these classic words: "This is a very, very serious case. *I have to assume there is truth to these charges.*" So much for the notion of innocent until proven guilty in this country. The last portion of "Trial by Therapy" follows; it concerns Mr. Akiki's case, and is very revealing:

> Dale Akiki, who has passed three wedding anniversaries, two Christmases, and two birthdays in jail, said his ordeal has not weakened his faith in God. "When I'm not in court, I spend a lot of time reading the Bible and praying," Mr. Akiki said. "I pray for my wife and mother and my family and I pray for the children and their families. But I can't say I pray for the therapists or the prosecutors. That would be a lie."

Dale Akiki was acquitted after a massive witch-hunt and a seven-and-a-half-month trial; he spent years in jail even though he was never convicted.

God protects his servants. Job was allowed to be tormented for a season, but he emerged victorious. So did Bobby Fijnje. Dale Akiki's fellow inmates would have put him through torture, but the sheriff's deputies protected him. I truly look forward to meeting Dale Akiki in heaven. God bless him, and his wife and their families.

One of the best ways of describing the psychological assistance that God gave me was penned by King David: "You are a shield around me, O Lord; you bestow glory on me and lift up my head" (Ps. 3:3). The difference it makes when you know you've done the right thing is priceless. This peace of mind applies not only to Christians (Matt. 7:21); it is a very common phenomenon among innocent defendants in witch-hunt cases, presumably representing a variety of spiritual beliefs.

Innocence Lost

When *Frontline* did a two-part TV special called "Innocence Lost," the title they chose was extremely appropriate. There are several areas in which innocence is lost when an accusation of child molestation is made:

1. In real cases, the child suffers lifelong damage, including difficulties with sexuality, a diminished ability to trust adults during the remainder of childhood, and underlying fears during childhood and adulthood that can cause a wide variety of problems.
2. In cases like mine where the child is merely programmed to believe that bad things happened even though they never did, will the child exhibit the same problems as if it were a real case? It breaks my heart to think a happy child like Elisa might grow up to be like her mother, but I suspect that's exactly what will happen.
3. Innocent defendants and their families lose the "child-like" trust in people that they may have formerly had. After their acquittal, parents accused of abuse often become more reserved in their physical contact with their child because of their fear of the witch-hunting society around them. The child suffers the consequences the most. Some of the most dedicated childcare workers, after their acquittal, refuse ever to be near children again. Zealots may claim victory in this matter, but the fact is that children lose some of their best advocates this way. In contrast, real perpetrators, after their release from prison, tend to strike again when the opportunity arises. Increasing numbers of convictions won't solve the problem.
4. In cases involving false accusations, deep-seated animosity between the two sides, those who believed innocence vs. those who believed guilt, is likely to remain forever. In communities nationwide, name-calling and shouting matches occur when individuals from the two rival groups encounter each other. Many rivals today were best friends

> before the accusations came forth. I see no other solution to this problem than long-term education; I think the zealots should be challenged rather than encouraged or ignored. This is unlike me; I am as non-confrontational as anyone you'll ever meet, but I now realize that passive acceptance of false accusations is just as damaging as active participation in a witch-hunt.

In 1997, *Frontline* presented a follow-up story, in which the dismissal of all remaining charges in the infamous Little Rascals day care case was announced. In October 1998, *Frontline* presented "The Child Terror," focusing on the abusive techniques employed by Janet Reno's office in Miami before she became U.S. Attorney General. *Frontline* has been the leader in revealing the witch-hunting abuses of the last decade. I am grateful to the producers for the tremendous service they have done for our country. We need all the media, especially television, to do likewise.

Allow me to belabor a point. As the year 2000 arrived, a zealot, Janet Reno, was the head of the United States Justice Department, chosen for the position for reasons of political correctness. Most people think she means well. She has never acknowledged any wrongdoing concerning her witch-hunting techniques, such as the atrocities she perpetrated against fourteen-year-old Bobby Fijnje. Janet Reno is not the problem; it's the society that sees nothing wrong with her zealous quick-fix solutions to the problem of child abuse.

After all of the modern-day Satanic Ritual Abuse witch-hunts had been thoroughly discredited, and the charges against nearly all the falsely accused defendants in those cases overturned, the people in Wenatchee, Washington proceeded to make the exact same mistakes. More than 100 adults were eventually falsely accused. The two primary accusers were foster children who lived in the home of the lead investigator, Bob Perez. Children who had no accusations to make were forced to undergo "memory recovery therapy," with Mr. Perez given near-unlimited authority in directing the process.

Newspapers and TV stations were more than happy to publish/broadcast the horrendous charges. Years later, now that this case has been proven to have been nothing but another sham witch-hunt, and the convictions overturned, at least one person still refuses to acknowledge the truth. U.S. Attorney General Janet Reno, the most powerful law enforcement individual in the nation, continues to say that she sees no indication of official misconduct in the Wenatchee case. She's merely denying reality. Readers who research this case will see how blatant was the official misconduct.

Detective Perez is a classic example of a zealot who should not have been allowed to run the show. Like Rev. Jake, if Mr. Perez's superiors had kept him in check, the witch-hunt would not have been allowed to get out of control. Lawsuits are pending against the Wenatchee Police Department and against Mr. Perez. Battles in the courts will obviously be difficult as long as the people in authority — like the U.S. Attorney General — wish to deny wrongdoing. TV coverage is probably the only hope of achieving justice against such odds.

My Friend Andrew

Andrew, a friend with whom I mingled at work on a regular basis, ended up having the most amazing story of anyone I've ever known. As the weeks passed, and he heard me engage in dozens of conversations about my case, he felt a disturbance inside himself that he couldn't understand. After about six months of being subjected to conversations concerning my case, he started pondering why he had been so withdrawn back in his school days. As an adult, he was extremely likable; he didn't enjoy being the focus of attention (nor do I), and he was categorically pleasant and considerate. Months went by, and his inner disturbance continued and grew. Finally, just as my trial was beginning, he started remembering his nightmare of a childhood. He had been sexually abused for many years by multiple perpetrators.

Andrew has two siblings. Both claim that they can't remember *anything* in their lives from childhood. Sound suspicious? Andrew says the childhood abuse experiences of his siblings and of their cousins were more typical cases of pedophilia than was his own. Among his cousins, pedophilia was a way of life; consistent attempts were made to convince the children that the whole routine of abuse — their little "secret" — was actually pleasant. Assuming that they really believe this misguided concept throughout childhood and into adulthood, could this be why pedophiles raised under such circumstances don't ever seem to demonstrate heartfelt repentance after they are caught?

Andrew knows who the perpetrators were in his family, but he does not seek vengeance. He is glad that so much of the confusion that had plagued him throughout his adult life has been cleared up. When he was a toddler, he was forced to pose for hundreds of pornographic photos. Today, when he hears an adult make an innocent remark about how a cute child "should be a movie star," it causes him to become tremendously suspicious of that adult. He has a long list of trigger mechanisms; that particular one happens to be very strong. Andrew does have one trait that is probably utterly lacking among all of our professional child proponents: he is completely at ease around pedophiles. He would never let them go unreported if he had any suspicion that a child was being subjected to abuse, but he is devoid of the repulsion most of us feel when dealing with known pedophiles. I wish his special gift concerning this untouchable group could be put to good use.

Andrew does not support our country's current methods of solving child abuse problems. One of his main conclusions is that the social workers who are supposedly protecting our children are merely venting their own pent-up emotions. In his case, he endured ten years of extreme abuse before disclosing it to a teacher. The social worker made it clear to him that since he had already made the disclosure, all he had to do was say some specific words about the abuse, and both his parents would go to jail for life. The problem was, he didn't want his parents to go to jail, and he didn't want a new set of parents; he just wanted the abuse to stop. He had to walk a tightrope of word selection to keep his parents from being thrown in jail, and he succeeded. The abuse quickly tapered off and then ended after that. But his point is that the state had only one solution: throw the parents in jail. Andrew feels that the state's only available solutions are designed to satisfy the emotions of the child proponents, rather than provide the children with what they really need. I think he has a valid point; it is politically incorrect and not allowed for a child to choose to stay with parents who the state believes may be sexual abusers. The state's desires can be forced on the child in such cases. The state's expanding definition of what constitutes child abuse further aggravates this issue.

In recent years, therapists have led patients to recover lost memories. This is a very controversial area of research, because the recovered memories are sometimes manufactured by suggestion and untrue. For the false "repressed memory" cases, irate adult kids have sued their parents for abuse that never happened. Disagreement about which cases are real and which false is bound to continue throughout our lives. "Repressed memories" have been successfully brought back to adults by therapists. Again, sometimes the memories are real, and sometimes they are merely manufactured by suggestion. This phenomenon seems to be quite similar to the child suggestibility issue I discussed earlier in this book. Obviously, therapists should proceed with caution and professionalism when probing such areas.

Those who have heard of repressed memory cases may be tempted to place Elisa in that category. I disagree. The only similarity she has with such cases relates to those in which the repressed memories were completely false, entirely generated by suggestion. Elisa's case was nothing more than a little guiding and word twisting. I suspect that no one asked her incredible questions — "Did the perpetrator make you watch while he killed babies?" — as did the therapists in the Satanic Ritual Abuse cases. My guess is that the questions posed to Elisa would not have been particularly unpleasant to her. Repressed memory cases are not like that. Whether true or false, the probing questions lead to great suffering.

This issue of "true vs. false" discernment reminds me of an observation Dr. Ceci wrote about child sex abuse allegations. The stories the children related, some true and some fantastical, were filled with details. The scary part, Dr. Ceci said, is that he could see no difference in the way the child related the story, to distinguish the true accounts, based on actual experiences that the child had, from the false ones, which were shaped into existence by leading suggestions. It appeared that both the true and the false were equally true in the children's minds. This is why it is essential to investigate child sex abuse allegations promptly and professionally before any leading suggestions taint the child's mind and make it impossible to discern the truth. Once a child is contaminated by leading questions, there is no known dependable way of determining the truth. (I contend that Rev. Jake's adult followers were effectively brainwashed by this same mechanism.)

The child sex abuse investigation manual I referred to earlier agrees with Dr. Ceci's point. Unfortunately, the police are not legally obligated to follow anything in that manual. For each investigation, the vital question is, do the police want to know the truth or do they only care about getting a conviction? Societal pressure is what drives the answer. I suspect that, just as guided children come to believe the suggestions as staunchly as they believe the truth, repressed-memory adults do likewise.

What percentage of political candidates engages in demagoguery about how it's time to get tough on child molesters? As long as they think they can gain an advantage over their opponents by playing upon emotions this way, the rhetoric will continue.

It may seem hopeless for American society to see past the emotion and start looking at facts. But there are some glimmers of hope, such as the *Frontline* TV segment I mentioned.

In 1997, the jury in the "Nanny Trial" of the au pair in Massachusetts convicted the defendant, Louise Woodward, of murdering the infant in her care. The jury's decision drew a wave of protest. People had seen the entire trial on national TV, and many of them perceived that Ms. Woodward was not a child-shaking murderer, which might have been their only perception — via newspaper headlines — had the trial not been on TV. Education, rather than inflammatory sound bites, is the way to conquer our witch-hunting tendencies.

In the months following the trial, I would talk with Andrew for several hours each week. One of the greatest honors of my life was being supportive of this man, whose "Welcome to Wonderland" experience made mine look trivial in comparison. Psychiatric hospitals and prisons are filled with people whose childhood experience was much milder than Andrew's.

Andrew has no desire to put his parents in jail. Their denial of criminal abuse is extremely bothersome, but not fatal to the relationship. His attitude of forgiveness is perhaps the best example I've ever seen. He continues to recuperate from his many years of abuse and deception, and is trying to sweep away some of the old trigger mechanisms that hold him captive. He is free of malice. He's a truly great person. May God bless my friend Andrew and his family now and forever.

Andrew has no trace of pedophilia. If I had children, I wouldn't have any concerns about placing them in his care. But that couldn't happen, because he doesn't spend any time at all with any kids.

Andrew's hypothesis, that child social workers are more concerned about their own interests than about what is best for the children, is similar to the main point I have tried to make in this book: the zealots should be constrained in their ability to destroy lives. Putting state resources behind a woman who has a nightmare and then lies about it, assuring her that her lie is "no problem," is not merely a terrible waste of taxpayer money; it destroys people's willingness to serve as volunteers.

Andrew told me of another conclusion of his that I think is responsible for many of the difficulties we face today: "People basically believe what they want to believe." That certainly describes how Rev. Jake has been able to maintain control over his followers, and I think Andrew's point is valid.

Because he benefited from my ordeal by having gained understanding about himself, Andrew provided me abundant peace during my last year in that community. In Scripture, eventual benefits of the trials that various Biblical characters went through are ultimately identified, allowing us to see why God chose to act in such unpredictable ways. Concerning my ordeal, Andrew's "rebirth" is the only satisfying benefit that I can see, so far. It is frustrating that other benefits are not being made known at the present time; I look forward to seeing that change. It truly was an honor to be able to support Andrew as he staggered through his nightmarish Wonderland experience.

Another benefit arose through my ordeal, but it is not the type that would motivate many people to volunteer to suffer such torment. The benefit is that many of my friends across the country no longer automatically assume that scandalous accusations they read about in the papers are true. Furthermore, they are more aware of the dangers of working with children. I hardly think the latter point a benefit; I consider it innocence lost.

A Sobering Verse to Consider

Webster defines slander as "the utterance of a falsehood that damages another's reputation." The key word is falsehood. Some of the things that were verbally passed on about me in Rev. Jake's church were true, such as "Did you know that Paul Grey had a vasectomy?" Such a statement would by itself not cause anyone to think me a child molester. But combined with the fact that there was an accusation, that "witnesses" claimed I had "paid an inordinate amount of attention to the victim," etc., the result is a gossip package as damaging as slander. The Bible warns repeatedly against both these practices, e.g., Rom. 1:29–30.

Worse than gossip or common slander is an outright false accusation. There are few places in the Bible where the word "abomination" is used. One is in Proverbs 6:19 (King James Version), which refers to a false witness as an abomination.

One of the other aspects of the accusation against me is particularly reprehensible, according to Scripture. In Matthew 12:24, the Pharisees label Jesus' casting out of demons, which was the work of the Holy Spirit, as being demonic in itself. He didn't merely rebuke them; he referred to their blasphemy against the Holy Spirit as being the unpardonable sin. We should tread carefully in matters of this nature, regardless of political correctness. In my case, serving the kids was the purest form of God's work that I've ever done in my fifty-plus years. And it wasn't I, who would have preferred to stay home and watch football, but God himself who orchestrated it. To attribute this work of the Holy Spirit to a carefully concealed demonic motive is a most serious charge, according to Scripture.

More about Mary

Mary had little if any impact on my case, but she provides some insight into the psychology and practices of witch-hunt participants, so I will discuss her a little further. Mary's statement may have sounded benign to the reader, but remember that the police had absolutely nothing to use against me except for written statements by four adults, plus God only knows what verbal statements from Rev. Jake. Mary shouldn't have gone to the police to make any statement at all concerning a child sexual assault case because she really didn't know anything. On my final teaching day, she was a visitor who hadn't been to the church for ten months, and had never met Elisa.

Given that the police were committed to pursuing the case, the result was destined to be a courtroom attempt to use every possible thing they could against me. Recall Frank Lee's "Welcome to Wonderland" warning: "What you consider innocent statements, photos, love notes, etc., can and will be used against you in ways you never dreamed possible."

Consider this portion of Mary's statement: "I will never

forget the first time I met him at the church, I saw Paul go up to a retarded thirteen-year-old boy in the sanctuary and ask if he could pray with him. The boy left the room with Paul for about three minutes, then I saw his mother go and get him. I had a bad feeling about that at the time, but didn't think of it again until now."

The HOLA leader had an adopted son with Down's Syndrome. Doctors had told the parents that the boy would probably live to age fourteen, when the two holes in his heart would take his life. Until then, his body would compensate, causing other problems. When the HOLA leader came to our house every Friday evening, the boy would come with him and participate in both worship and prayer time. One of his favorite songs was I Tim. 1:17: "Now to the King, eternal, immortal, invisible, the only God, be glory and honor forever and ever. Amen." Friday evenings, we prayed for him frequently, usually for his heart to be healed.

Mary's description of the first time she supposedly met me, which left her with "a bad feeling" that she recalled after the accusation, was an occasion when I was able to briefly escape from my downstairs duties. There were four men that I used to try to see, individually, on those Sunday nights. In each case, I had to arrange it around brief opportunities, because of the lack of volunteers downstairs to help Phil and me. On the occasion Mary described, I recall that I was indeed praying for the boy's heart. The last I heard, he was still alive. He must be about twenty-two years old now. Once she got to know me, Mary never gave my prayer for the boy a second thought until after a shocking accusation was made; then she re-interpreted everything about me. That is classic witch-hunt psychology.

Another excerpt from Mary's police statement: "Paul sponsored a boy there, and my brother, [John Doe], mentioned that Paul went off with that boy while in Nicaragua. Paul's wife was not on the trip." The notion of my molesting a sixteen-year-old Spanish-speaking boy — who had more maturity than the average American adult — is a good example of the bizarre notions people start to entertain once a witch-hunt starts. Despite the fact that my case file had an embarrassing lack of substance, Mary's brother's statement was too far-fetched for the prosecution to use; it was never brought up in court.

Mary's last sentence is accurate: "I never saw Paul kiss a child on the mouth or do anything inappropriate." Certainly, I never kissed Elisa on the mouth, cheek, or anywhere else, and I never hugged her. That doesn't mean I never had any hugs or kisses from any of the kids. I did on a few occasions, but not from Elisa. My main concern was to make all the kids feel wanted, and I didn't need to exert any extra effort in her case; she had enough lap time. Many adults might be shocked at a situation in which children hug or kiss a grown man who isn't in their family. That shows the sickness that has overtaken America. Regardless of what I think is wrong with our society, it is impermissible for anyone working with kids to do things of which society disapproves, and I never did anything with the kids that I wouldn't have done in the presence of their parents. Elisa's case was a little different because I was leery of Joan. I never felt that way about any of the other parents I ever dealt with. If I had had perfect foresight and discernment, I would have demanded that Joan stay with us during class sessions, until her ground rules were perfectly understood and obeyed by both Elisa and me. But I left it to Joan to voice any objections she might have. When she eventually did so, she just didn't do it in the way I would have expected.

Teachers keep their distance from kids these days, in deference to political correctness, and Joan never gave me permission to act otherwise. One of the closest people in my life, a teacher, realized after my trial that she would have to stop routinely checking to see if her young handicapped pupils had soiled their pants, which often happens. These days, the kids have to fend for themselves. If they hurt themselves, teachers don't hug them like they used to. I don't know of any drop in the child sexual abuse rate that accompanies our new way of treating kids, so where is the benefit? Incidentally, for every hug I ever got from a child at that church, I probably received twenty from various men, and probably even more from women. Some people may criticize me for having had too much physical contact with the kids, but I believe that my behavior was appropriate.

Webster's definition of the word *hearsay* is "rumor, gossip." Mary's quoting a statement made by her brother was hearsay, which is not permissible in a court of law. In the police statement of Brittany's mother, the damaging words were clearly in the realm of hearsay. Further, Rev. Jake made numerous incredibly damaging hearsay statements about me in his written statements and on the witness stand. Recall Frank Lee's words from "Welcome to Wonderland" on the topic: "You were also told ... that hearsay evidence cannot be used against you. *Know this*: None of the above applies in your case."

Mary's statement that Elisa was "new to the class" was poorly worded. Elisa had been in my class for seven months. But Mary had not attended the church for ten months, so Elisa *was* new relative to Mary's viewpoint. Mary didn't know anything about my case and shouldn't have written a police statement, yet the police used her as much as they could in their effort to convict me.

There were seven children on the final day. Mary knew and dearly loved five of them. One was a boy who was visiting for the second time. Finally, there was Elisa. Since I knew for a fact that Mary cared very deeply about the kids in that class, I knew she would want to know who the regulars were. Elisa was the only regular she didn't know.

The only part of Mary's statement that the police even tried to use was: "... when I got back, he had a little dark-haired girl on his lap. She was new to the class and I can't remember her name, but Paul told me what her name was and said she was a very special little girl." For having written these words, Mary was commanded to leave Nicaragua to attend my trial — a high price to pay for her misguided meddling.

The child on my lap whom Mary referred to was, indeed, Elisa. Here's why I made the "special child" remark. Whenever any child is in my presence and I speak about that child, I choose my words in a way that will encourage the child. My statement that "this is a special child" was nothing unusual. More significantly, I was making the point to Mary that Elisa had been in the class for quite awhile; that she was not merely a visitor. If Mary had continued to be my assistant, Elisa would by that time have become like family to her.

During that brief encounter with Mary on my last morning teaching, I followed my "special child" statement by saying, "Mary, check these cheeks out." I knew for a fact that Mary would be swooned by Elisa's incredible cuteness. Sure enough, Mary reached down, tweaked her cheeks and said, "Oh, aren't you adorable?" Elisa was apprehensive about this, and wasn't smiling. When I heard, a few days later, about the accusation, I wracked my brains about how such an allegation could possibly have been imagined. The only thing I could think of was that Elisa might have been referring to Mary when she made the alleged statements about being touched by her teacher in a bad way. I strongly suspect that Rev. Jake relayed my thoughts on this subject to Mary in greatly distorted fashion, perhaps implying that I had attempted to shift blame from myself to her, thereby making Mary suspicious about my credibility. I could be wrong in believing that Rev. Jake influenced Mary to write a statement to the police, but I'd bet he played a role in it. For what it's worth (this is hearsay), a friend told me that Mary had indeed claimed that Rev. Jake caused her to go to the police.

The frenzy to imprison men who utter words like "special child" shows a real sickness in our society, as Jesus indicated in Matt. 19:13–15. When His disciples criticized the people who brought children to him, he told the disciples they were wrong to do so. Many Americans today might think my practice of allowing kids on my lap was strange and wrong, but my conscience is 100 percent clear on this: offering a lap to a fatherless child who requests it is the morally right thing to do. But, because there is much evil in the world, sometimes we have to concede morally right behavior in order to live at peace in our communities. Clearly, the kids are the ones who lose.

A verse from the same chapter (Matt. 19:5) is one of my favorites; Jesus quotes from Moses and attributes the words to God. Calling the Bible "God's Word" is not a modern-day invention. I encourage the reader to look up these verses.

Brittany's Contribution Revisited

Recall the definition of hearsay. A court will not allow a witness to testify "so-and-so told me such-and-such." Evidence must be presented by the original witness if the jury is to use it as a basis for judgment. When Dottie's mother said, "Brittany told me that Paul Grey held Elisa on his lap all the time," she put Brittany in a very awkward position. This was the one portion of the statement that the police wished to use. After all, I was charged with molesting Elisa, not molesting Dottie (Brittany's sister). The police used this particular hearsay by Brittany's mother to claim that "witnesses" had stated that I paid "inordinate attention" to Elisa. Actually, there was one other such witness: Joan herself, who never spent any time in our classroom. For lack of significant evidence, the police tried their best to make much of the two corroborating witnesses. This "evidence" that made me look suspicious was rampantly spread around the church.

Until my last teaching day, Brittany had not been my helper for about six months. I don't think the police were ever told that. It makes clear that her concept of "all the time" was subject to cross-examination. I doubt, however, that the prosecutor cared about what was true or false; he just wanted incriminating statements to bolster his flimsy case.

Prior to those final six months, Brittany had assisted me several times. She knew more than half my regular kids well, which is to be expected of an elder's daughter in a small church. She was a good girl; her parents should be proud of her.

Apparently, Brittany thought that I taught Sunday school for the enjoyment of it. As an eleven-year-old, she didn't understand me. I think she suspected that I was holding another child — the youngest in the class — instead of her own sister because I preferred Elisa to Dottie. To combat this notion, I requested that my lawyer ask every witness, "Did you ever see Paul Grey deny his lap to any child?" (I never did). So, perhaps Brittany condemned me for paying less attention to Dottie, while their mother condemned me for my "weirdness" in using Dottie's name as my computer password. When accused in a case like this, you're attacked from every angle.

The perception expressed by Brittany, that I held Elisa on my lap "all the time," is incorrect. Since Brittany had not been my assistant for six months, her statement was based on one Sunday school session, during which Elisa asked to get on my lap two times. The first was during worship; the second was moments before Joan arrived. Chances are she stayed on my lap for a good part of the half-hour worship session; I don't remember. During the teaching, I was walking around, frequently trying to keep our second-time visitor, the two-year-old boy, out of the supply cabinet and in the classroom. It was not a relaxed class session. So, Brittany's statement about "all the time" was based on part of a half-hour interval. It was a hasty generalization by an eleven-year-old.

Who's the abuser here, anyway? Brittany endured great stress because witch-hunting adults pressured her to take the stand against a friendly Sunday school teacher whom she had known for three years. I assume that they did this in the form of an invitation rather than a threat; still, Brittany wouldn't have gotten involved at all if it weren't for the adults. They did this because they didn't have a case against me. It was immoral to use a child in this manner. I don't know whether the decision by Brittany's parents to allow this abuse was their own or if Rev. Jake persuaded them. And I never was told that Brittany had recently been sexually abused until I heard privileged information several months after the trial was over. I wasn't supposed to ever find out. Until recently, child witnesses like Brittany weren't allowed to testify in court. My case illustrates the problems that the new rules and political correctness have created.

One man who sat through the entire trial concluded that Brittany must have escorted Elisa to the restroom and been a bit rough with the wiping assistance. I don't think so. That is based on the premise that something happened on that last teaching day to cause the accusation. I believe the only significant event was Joan's decision to question Elisa. When you consider what made Joan begin the interrogation, you can conclude that the fantasized erection and subsequent nightmare were the only things that made the last day, and therefore Brittany, unique. I think the key from then on was suggestibility.

Consider the man's point, though. Elisa did refer to her "teachers." They did take her to the restroom, and they did use their fingers to touch her booboo. Incidentally, my understanding of Elisa's terminology is that her genital area, according to Joan's testimony, is called her "privates," and anything that hurts is a "booboo." If the state had been truly interested in learning the truth, they would have looked into my various assistants' interactions with Elisa. But they were apparently interested in nothing more than placating Joan, for political reasons.

Misguided Policies

I think my case provided a good example of how such an accusation should not be handled. Elisa was three years and one month old when Joan made her accusation. Compare this fact with the late-nineteenth-century opinion of the Supreme Court. In an aside to *Wheeler v. United States*, the Court's opinion included the following: "No one would think of calling as a witness an infant only 2 or 3 years old." That Supreme Court wisdom was completely disregarded in the 1990s.

The cruelty inflicted on victims of false accusation can be as psychologically devastating as that experienced by victims of child sexual abuse. The Amirault family of Massachusetts was victimized by false allegations that began in late 1984. The mother — at age 61 — and daughter were imprisoned in one location, the son/brother at another. Mother and daughter were given an offer almost too good to refuse: just "confess" and they could leave prison for good. Both chose to serve out their twenty-year terms rather than confess to something they didn't do. This illustrates how heavy the psychological pressure is, which leads to plea-bargaining from defendants, and why many people would like to see plea-bargaining removed from the legal process.

Exceptional cruelty is shown in this quote from *The Boston Globe*, 19 March 1995:

> Both Cheryl and Violet were close to being released two years ago when the judge who presided over their trial decided that they had served enough time, revised their sentences and ordered them released. But the prosecutors succeeded in getting the courts to overturn the order as an unconstitutional intrusion into the power of the parole board, a maneuver unprecedented in Massachusetts legal history. The women's possessions were packed in boxes and they were literally walking down the corridors of MCI-Lancaster believing they were on their way to freedom, when they were notified that the order had been reversed.

That is psychological torture at its worst, and the root cause was misguided, unchecked political correctness, and its power in the '90s. Mrs. Amirault, still awaiting vindication, died at age seventy-four.

On 12 June 1998, a new trial for Cheryl was ordered by Judge Borenstein, who remarked, "We now know much more than we did fourteen years ago about how small children can easily be influenced and manipulated through improper procedures, and to do so to them in order to have them divulge unreliable stories about events including abuse."

On 18 August 1999, Judge Borenstein was overruled by the Massachusetts Supreme Judicial Court, and Cheryl's conviction was reinstated. Then, in the week of 17 October 1999, the prosecution agreed not to seek Cheryl's return to prison for the remaining twelve years of her 1987 sentence. So Cheryl was free, and never had to "admit" guilt. But her innocent brother, Gerald, is still in prison.

A recurring theme unifies the current wave of false accusations, whether a given case involves day care, repressed memory therapy, facilitated communication, or, simply, "expanded awareness" of child sex abuse, which has saturated the American media over the last decade. That recurring theme is: a trusted individual, who assumes that abuse actually occurred, transfers all of his or her assumptions into the mind of the client by way of suggestion, until they become the reality of the client. The alleged victim embellishes the suggestions, and becomes completely convinced that he or she truly experienced everything in the embellished package.

The alleged victim can swear to the truthfulness of the imagined events as much as to any genuine memory. Both are memories; they are the client's reality, and, when physical evidence cannot prove otherwise, there is no known way to distinguish the true from the suggestion-induced memories.

Witch-hunts tend to be led by one or two key individuals who have tunnel vision and who manage somehow to get authority over the case. Without checking into the facts, newspapers print the stories as related by these accusing individuals, then the community believes what is printed in the newspaper or seen on TV. My case and others — all the way through the nationally known Satanic Ritual Abuse cases — share a common element: they wouldn't have gotten so out of hand had an investigation been done with professionalism. The accusers tend to be extreme and irrational, which explains why nearly every one of these cases has eventually been overturned. Police decisions in the poorly handled cases are not decided among a team of truly competent professionals. Society can do better. Hopefully, police departments are starting to learn some lessons concerning these cases.

A few years ago, a former prosecutor told me that if the police get by with bypassing *some* rights of a suspect, they'll proceed to trample his rights altogether. This is something that contemporary American society is willing to tolerate. When it comes to a child sex abuse allegation, the police are capable of getting away with more abuses than usual.

When a police department puts its own slant on the "evidence" against a child sex abuse suspect, and newspapers print the police account, it's obvious who's on the losing end. The notion that innocent behavior will speak for itself is totally misguided. The police will squash the suspect's rights and get the conviction they're after, unless a lawyer holds their abuses in check.

One of the major aggravating factors is that politics is heavily mixed into these cases. The temptation of an elected official to try to look like a hero, saving society from a monstrous villain, is undeniable. The case of Richard Jewell falls into this category. Remember the bomb that disrupted the 1996 Olympics in Atlanta? Richard Jewell put his own life in danger to usher dozens of people away from danger. The government desperately wanted to show how efficiently it could deal with terrorists, so a prime suspect had to be identified, and quickly. Based on a handful of people saying that Richard Jewell was rather strange, he began to be demonized in the national press. This demonstrates two facts: the police don't need to have any solid evidence in order to treat a person like a scoundrel; and the news media are more than willing to broadcast the defamation to sell their product. Aggravating this is the fact that America has an insatiable appetite for stories about deviancy. It's unlikely that the country's desire for fantastic stories will change, so, if this situation is going to get better, the police and the media must become more ethical rather than merely looking after their own short-term interests.

Political correctness is the reason why Richard Jewell was nationally disgraced, and it is the reason why police departments are so willing to put extra effort into allegations of child sexual abuse. When politics are involved, these are politely referred to as "high-profile cases." Lawyers told me that the police would not drop the accusation against me simply because it was a high-profile accusation.

Where does it end? Must we start installing video surveillance systems in public restrooms to protect against wrongful allegations? I used to think a video camera would be a foolproof means that a church could employ to prevent false accusations. I see now that it wouldn't have made any difference in my case. I would have needed two cameras below the table and two above, and seven months of videotape to be able to categorically prove my innocence. And that's exactly what a defendant must do in these cases. The notion of "innocent until proven guilty" is absolutely, undeniably irrelevant in today's cases involving child sex abuse. Political correctness has the higher priority.

It's just common sense that statements of toddlers concerning criminal charges should be interpreted with great caution. As Dr. Shalom pointed out, what if Elisa had said that JFK had put his finger in her private? Should we then disinter and put him on trial? When we occasionally had an extra few minutes at the end of class, we would sometimes just let the kids play. There was a play kitchenette in the room next door. The girls would often grab a spatula and skillet, then look at the adults around them to share the joy of the moment. I usually asked them, "Did you make me some pancakes?" Every single time, the answer was "Yes." What if I had asked them "Did my helper put crayons in your private when you went potty?" It is extremely easy to manipulate kids into making untrue statements. As child expert Stephen Ceci said during the 27 October 1998 *Frontline* segment, "They want to give you the answer that they think will make you happiest. And especially if the first couple times they resist this and say no and you keep bringing it up, they start to get the message that, 'Well, maybe I've been giving the wrong answer, and I should switch.'" But what good is acknowledging the reality of children's suggestibility if juries such as mine are not allowed to hear it?

The most serious part of Joan's written statement is when, according to Joan, Elisa says her teacher uses his finger and it hurts her. Contrast this with what Elisa told the nurse when

Joan took her into the Emergency Room to be examined. The nurse asked her if it hurts her when her teacher touches her. The nurse noted that Elisa thought for a moment, then replied "no." The burden was on me to point out this inconsistency during the trial, which we never did. One of the most definitive aspects of today's witch-hunts is that the police simply ignore evidence that contradicts the charges. And it's easy to get a jury to do likewise. The prevailing sentiment that governed every jury that voted for convictions in the Satanic Ritual Abuse cases was: "I know some of this is untrue, even absurd, but there are so many allegations, there must be some truth behind it." And then they vote to convict the defendant, based on the sensational nature of the accusations, even though the prosecution's case may be filled with inconsistencies.

"They broke every rule in the book" was the way child abuse expert Dr. Shalom described the police handling of my case. He was referring to a thick manual titled *Investigation and Prosecution of Child Abuse* as "the book." It was written by the nation's foremost experts on the topic. The intent behind the creation of this manual was to provide the police and child experts with guidance on the subject, to overcome the irresponsibility that is so rampant in these cases. Remember how O. J. Simpson's lawyers were able to get the jury to condemn the police for doing a few things sloppily? In a similar manner, there is a risk of child molesters having their cases dismissed due to police sloppiness. Dr. Shalom refers to the aforementioned manual as *the* Bible on how these cases must be investigated. Unfortunately, as I mentioned earlier, the document is not legally binding. In my case, the police chose to ignore the collective guidance of the country's experts so that they would be unhindered in the pursuit of my conviction. For this irresponsible handling of my case, they paid no price whatsoever, and the jury never heard about it. Residents of that state must force the police to use this manual, if they expect it ever to happen.

From page II-20 of the manual:

> Throughout the investigation and during your interview with a child, consider alternative explanations for the charges that would indicate there was no abuse or that someone *else* was responsible or that other, perhaps additional, perpetrators were involved. As you talk with the child, look for sufficient confirmation of the people involved and circumstances described so that you can rule out any possibility of deliberate falsehood, misinterpretation of innocent contacts, or coaching by someone else.

Clearly there was no consideration in my case that perhaps there had been no molestation. Consider that adults — Kate and Betsy — had escorted Elisa to the restroom, and touched her "boo-boo" with their fingers, and that younger helpers had done likewise. Can you think of any good reason why this possibility was not explored at all by the police?

After a few questions directed to Elisa, the state inspector chose to stop trying to get information from her because it was obvious she was not giving a credible account of molestation. In child sexual abuse cases, inconsistencies in the children's testimony are simply disregarded. That practice is unfair to defendants, but it happens regularly.

Here's how the inspector's questioning went:

And then I (the inspector) said, "Did your teacher ask you to touch him?" And she said, "On the butt." And then I asked "Did he touch you anywhere else?" and she said, "My teacher touched my boo-boo." And then I asked "Did this happen a long time ago, or did it just happen?" And she said, "A long time ago." And at this point, I felt — I wasn't really sure how much of the additional questioning she was understanding." Notice that Elisa responded to every question even when she appeared to have no understanding of what the inspector was saying — another reason why children must be interviewed by competent professionals. And where did "on the butt" come from? Joan had to have planted those words in Elisa's mind during her personal questioning. Look at Joan's police statement again; she asked Elisa the same question but got a different answer.

Note that the approach used by the inspector was designed to lead the responses. The question "Did this happen a long time ago, or did it just happen?" makes it easy for the child: just pick one of the two. In the inspector's mind, Elisa made the wrong choice; therefore, she questioned the child's understanding concerning that particular question. The most important rule when trying to get a child's testimony about alleged abuse is that the child cannot be led in any manner. And you certainly don't interview a child when she is sitting on the lap of a dedicated accuser.

When you ask a toddler whether the correct answer is A or B, the child is much more likely to choose the option spoken last (thus more fresh in the mind), option B. From the documented examples, the inspector consistently made option B the one that incriminated me. In the words of child expert Stephen Ceci, children "tend to like the second one, the last one that you say." (*Frontline*, 27 October 1998)

The inspector's technique of posing questions to Elisa and defining the only two possible answers for her epitomizes the way the interview should not be done. For example, if Elisa had chosen the other possible answer — "it just happened recently" — to the last question cited above, then that "evidence" would have been used against me with great ferocity.

Another question the Inspector asked Elisa was if her teacher touched her "on the outside, or on the inside?" When Elisa made the "correct" 50-50 choice — "on the inside" — it was deemed, according to the warrant, a solid reason for declaring "probable cause" and arresting me. The notion of "disclosure," in which an intimidated child finally overcomes the shame and tells an adult the awful secret about coercive sexual abuse he/she has been subjected to, was a joke in my case. The imaginations of Joan and the inspector were the only things that were disclosed. The prosecutor didn't try to get Elisa to say these things during the trial. They just wanted her to say, "My teacher touched my private," and then point me out, knowing that a typical jury would then be moved to convict.

Investigation and Prosecution of Child Abuse is highly influenced by many of the most zealous child protection leaders, whose techniques destroyed many innocent lives in the Satanic Ritual Abuse cases. *Satan's Silence* discusses the authors and also gives an overview of these phenomenal cases, which interested readers might wish to see. Despite the influence of such authors, *Investigation and Prosecution of Child Abuse* offers a lot of good advice. In my case the police ignored it. One technique they didn't ignore was the intentional avoidance of videotape. Tapes have exposed flawed techniques in numerous cases, resulting in a number of overturned convictions, so the authors recommend to the police not to tape the interview with the child or the "confession" of the defendant. This amounts to hiding the truth. Hopefully, legal pressure will be able to overcome this unfair manner of prosecution. Elisa's interview could have been videotaped very easily. The police chose to hide the truth and appeal to emotions instead.

To discern true accusations from false, child sex abuse experts place their strongest emphasis on the manner in which the child initially disclosed that abuse had occurred. The initial disclosure is described in detail in Joan's police statement as follows: "Then I asked her if he touches her anywhere? She said yes and patted her genital area." Joan guided Elisa's so-called initial disclosure, rather than allowing Elisa to speak for herself. And the interpretation that Elisa patted her genital area in direct response to Joan's question was subject solely to the interpretation of Joan, who by that time was obsessively intent on proving my guilt. Nobody ever questioned Joan about her interpretation of Elisa's "patting" motion in the middle of the night. The police tactic was to prevent responsible child sex abuse experts from reviewing my case, in hopes that they could coerce me into plea-bargaining. The police know full well that most people of good community standing would do almost anything to prevent their names from making headlines in a case of alleged child molestation. Since the newspapers get their information directly from the police, this gives the prosecutor a powerful advantage in coercing plea-bargaining even when there is nothing more than bluster behind the state's case.

Technically, the police must have "probable cause" to arrest anyone. In my case, written statements by four adults supposedly constituted sufficient "probable cause." That doesn't mean their logic in determining probable cause must be persuasive. Politics greatly influences the likelihood of an arrest. Nobody would ever get arrested for bank robbery or arson were the "probable cause" as flimsy as it was in my case.

Witness tampering is a crime. President Clinton was impeached for several reasons, one of which was that he made suggestive, false statements to his secretary, such as "Let's see, I was never alone with [Monica Lewinsky], right?" For doing so he was accused of witness tampering, i.e., obstruction of justice. Contrast his behavior with the power of suggestion Joan had over Elisa. Joan's impact on the witness was far greater. She could and did write any script she chose for Elisa to repeat. And she showed a willingness to lie to make sure I would be convicted. Where does our legal system correct such witness tampering?

I was lucky that Joan and the police didn't guide Elisa's beliefs more than they did. Joan testified that she didn't like discussing the accusation with Elisa, because, in Joan's erroneous thinking, she didn't want to upset her. That's the only thing that saved me. Usually, zealots don't let such considerations stop them. Did Joan really want to take care that Elisa would not get upset? Remember that she wanted to put Elisa back on the stand to make me undergo another trial.

Rational Policies

To summarize some of the most important points I have raised:

1. Yes/no questions should not be used with toddlers as a basis for charging anyone with a felony
2. Irrational zealots should not be given control of these cases

3. If we think someone is a good person, we should not change our opinion based on what someone else says, and we should be especially skeptical about what the police — and therefore the news accounts — say.

How can a church protect itself from being harmed by this societal fear? Some friends of mine said that in their church, the teachers — minimum two per room, and no husband-wife teams allowed — would grant permission for a child to go to the restroom. The child would then go unescorted while one of the two teachers watched from the top of the horizontally divided door as the child went down the hall and into the restroom, and then would keep watch until the child emerged and arrived back in the classroom. For children who need assistance, parents must be contacted. That policy sounds pretty good to me.

Dr. Shalom pointed out a significant clue in Joan's statement to the police. It was the fact that Elisa laughed after her "wiggle, wiggle, wiggle" statement. While Joan was focused on fears that she had been entertaining about me for seven months, Elisa's laughter revealed a very different story. Incidentally, according to some women friends of mine who have raised daughters, an adult finger forced into a child's vagina would be excruciatingly painful; laughter is the exact opposite of excruciating pain.

Where does "wiggle, wiggle, wiggle" come from? Whenever a child was on my lap, over 95 percent of the time it was during worship, when I was just sitting by the door. For the last forty-five minutes of class I was almost always standing. The unspoken rule was that any child could sit on my lap whenever they wanted to; I never denied my lap to any child. Whenever a child was on my lap as we sang our Sunday school songs, I wanted to impress that child in some way with the significance of the song. So, I would usually sway them back and forth and/or gently bounce them in time with the music, and always positioned them so they faced the musicians. In that way, the child was always aware of the song. It was a happy time for the kids.

Three-year-olds don't use the terminology, "swaying back and forth." They just say, "wiggle, wiggle, wiggle."

Other Elements of Witch-Hunting

The kids I had worked with for nineteen months were not allowed to be my witnesses. Rev. Jake and his followers chose to do the speaking for them. It was like a dream; children who had been so close to me for so long were treated as if they didn't exist. Darcie too was treated as completely irrelevant. When you consider all the toddlers in that church, and total all the hours I spent with each of them, you get a huge amount of data in the form of a character reference. And whom did the church and police accept as my spokesman? A man who had never seen me with kids.

Failure to listen to the children is a common feature of modern-day witch-hunts. Zealous adults choose to do the speaking for them. This reality helped inspire the title *Satan's Silence,* a book that is vital reading for anyone seriously interested in contemporary witch-hunts. What I wanted all along was a chance for Elisa to demonstrate what she thought of me. Just put me in a room with her, with the world watching through two-way mirrors. Let Elisa demonstrate whether she was fearful or trusting of me. Given that opportunity, there's no doubt in my mind that she would have immediately climbed onto my lap and shown affection toward me. But she was never given that opportunity. Joan, the police, and Rev. Jake did all the talking for her.

Even if I had had one or more adult helpers every Sunday, there still could have been occasions when two different kids needed to use the restroom, a minute apart, and both my assistants would have been gone, leaving me alone with the kids for a minute. I wouldn't have been able to state with 100-percent certainty that this never happened, so the police still would have had their societal mandate to pursue my case. Even if Darcie had been with me every moment that I taught, the result would have been charges against both of us. Sunday school teaching is simply a very dangerous activity if a parent or child chooses to make an accusation.

Child workers claim that there are cases in which an adult does not molest kids in general but singles out one victim. I don't doubt that this happens sometimes. However, now that I've seen how these cases go, I suspect that many defendants have been labeled in such a manner simply because there was only one accuser. Those defendants who choose to accept plea-bargaining are in all likelihood listed among the "established" cases of this selective pedophilia phenomenon, even though innocent defendants plea-bargain for a variety of reasons. In the 1990s, no matter how extensive and spotless one's reputation was beforehand, suspicion never abates once one is accused. Even denial of guilt is used against the accused, because initial denial of the charge has been labeled a tactic used by guilty people.

In a Reuters story dated 4 May 2000, two people were killed by a witch-hunting mob in Guatemala. The mayor of the town said, "Let it be clear that (the attack) was a confusion caused by a rumor that satanic rituals were going to be performed and that children were being kidnapped to have their hearts stolen." From the same article: "In 1994, U.S. journalist June Weinstock was beaten almost to death by hundreds of angry peasants ... who thought she was trying to steal a baby."

What happened in Guatemala? Clearly, some people stirred up fears, and society didn't correct the false rumors. Every time that I have mentioned politics in this book, I have been alluding to a main thesis: the American media and the politicians have, at the recent turn of the century, used fear-mongering as a means of achieving social change, the fear-mongering largely directed at women voters. It has worked very effectively. The outcry against guns at the turn of the century was very much a women-driven issue. That outcry came even as the statistics were getting progressively better. If you study the way that women were mobilized to change gun laws, I believe you will see the exact same techniques that mobilized them to pressure their communities to do the things that ultimately create unnecessary witch-hunts like my own. Campaigning for political change is fair game, but playing on fears is risky: it often leads to laws that damage society. Political correctness is the easy approach for a candidate to take; voters need to learn how to see past quick-fix promises.

Women in the 1990s were empowered as never before. Bill Clinton was twice elected specifically because of the women's vote. I surmise that elected officials, eager to serve the interests of this emerging bloc of voters, have offered fast-fix laws in order to gain political benefit. There is no good reason why the total number of laws should forever increase. Just get rid of the bad ones and enforce the good.

Suggestibility of Children and Adults

The way we saw adult minds — especially Phil's mind — oscillate between the truth and the distortions made it clear to Darcie and me that children aren't the only ones susceptible to suggestion. The research by Ceci, Bruck, and others shows how unreliable children's testimony may be if there is any possibility of their having been led during previous questioning. The most dramatic example in one of their studies is a girl, four or five years of age, who was visited by a supposed doctor, who touched her wrist, stomach, and foot. The entire visit was videotaped for the experiment. After the visit, the child was asked to demonstrate with a doll how the doctor had touched her vagina. The child correctly answered that the doctor had not touched her vagina. But a few days later, when Professor Bruck and the child's father brought up the topic of the visit, the child related a very different story. She said that the doctor had choked her, tightly, with a ribbon. After the father asked her what the doctor did, his daughter responded that the doctor had put a stick into her vagina. She then demonstrated, with the anatomically correct doll, how the doctor had hammered the stick into her vagina, and had looked into her rectum. But all this never happened, and there were no suggestions planted other than the one mentioned above. Professor Bruck found, in her well-conducted research, that when dolls were used, fully half of all the kids who had never had their private parts touched claimed the doctor had touched them. The resounding conclusion of this, and of a number of other research efforts, is that children can be led in subtle ways, with the result that they firmly believe detailed accounts of events that never happened. With a little occasional reinforcement, the belief becomes absolute reality in the child's subsequent years.

I suspect that Elisa will probably grow up to be like Joan, very fearful of men's intentions, even though I provided her with an environment of trust that would cause her to know better. Hopefully God will reveal enough truth to break the cycle of fear in her family. Elisa spent over thirty hours in my class; those positive experiences are in her memory somewhere, even though they may be masked.

In the trial, recall when Elisa said, "Make me do that again, right?" Doesn't that make it clear how she had been coached for the trial? She asked this question before she was asked to point to her "private." From my understanding of kids, you can get them to say anything you want, with very little coaching. In her mother's own words, Elisa didn't know that her story was causing me any harm. I think she viewed the whole thing similarly to the way she learned to say her A-B-Cs.

Darcie and I saw the phenomenon of suggestibility work efficiently with adults, also. She has considered writing a book on that topic alone. After Rev. Jake made his dramatic announcement to the congregation that "It looks like a wolf has gotten in among our sheep," the minds of his followers were made fertile for details about the accused. Rev. Jake then planted seeds in those suggestion-hungry minds he had created. Probably the most reprehensible lie that circulated about me was that Rev. Jake had caught me lying to Darcie. He actually claimed this; I have written notes from the investigator quoting Rev. Jake firsthand, saying "Paul Grey lies to his wife." When people heard this, they could either believe that their own pastor was lying or that I had been caught lying. And if I would lie to my wife, then I must be lying about the accusation. Rev. Jake manipulated his followers masterfully, and most of them have no clue that he did so.

The tactics used by Rev. Jake are probably familiar to those who have studied cult psychology. Even when there is a set of established rules, such as the Bible, a skillful manipulator can learn how to circumvent those rules. This is similar to crafty lawyers who can warp the minds of jurors. Christians must measure their leaders against Scripture, with the Holy Spirit bearing witness by giving them inner peace in the matter, and they have got to refuse to accept persistent wrong behavior. Remember the warning signs about Rev. Jake that I ignored? God speaks to us; often, we just do a poor job of listening.

An individual who is greatly trusted (typically, a therapist) can easily create in the client a set of beliefs. The therapist/client relationship is extremely similar to the pastor/parishioner relationship. Readers wishing to read more about therapist/client sessions gone awry, and the resulting false "repressed memory" cases, should consult Reinder Van Til's book, *Lost Daughters*, and Mark Pendergrast's book, *Victims of Memory*.

Virtually all the Satanic Ritual Abuse cases have been discredited, and the convictions overturned. In these cases, it has been discovered repeatedly that a few over-zealous adults — psychologists, prosecutors, etc. — who believed the validity of the accusations, led the children in questioning until eventually the children repeated some of the words the adults wished to hear, thereby confirming the accusations. Outlandish things the children said during these interviews were simply ignored due to the burning desire to achieve convictions of the accused. The children's ridiculous statements included rides in space ships, being forced to drink the blood of slaughtered babies, being on a ship with trained sharks swimming around it, having an adult's head inserted into a child's private part, and many more. The scope of allegations in all these cases seemed to grow without limit as the fears of the adult interrogators grew.

The probability of a person getting accused increases greatly if he has already been identified with an accusation. That's why it is extremely appropriate for people like myself to move, once the trial is over, to a community that doesn't have the preconceived notions. For those who have been falsely convicted, and now are required to register with the police in their community, it is probably best to minimize their social contacts and stay far from kids. I hope the police keep track of all those who have been released after serving prison time, but I suspect that police budgets don't generally allow that luxury. One thing is clear: we can't let the zealots take sole responsibility for monitoring those who were convicted or chose to plea-bargain. Maybe electronic monitoring can help provide a reasonable solution. In the case of clear-cut guilt, I believe there should be no release from prison. But despite this preference of mine, we can't change the rules after a person is already incarcerated; we can't change a five-year sentence to a life sentence, despite political pressures.

Reflections

I would not want anyone to be so frightened by this book that they avoid doing God's work in any form. Even after the hellish years Darcie and I went through due to my mini-witch-hunt, I have no regrets about having done the right thing. Our days on Earth are very short, but our time with God will last forever. Our relationship with our Creator is much more important than any earthly trials. My guess is that most readers of this book will belong to future generations, and that they will read this account with the same amazement that Twenty-first-century Americans read about the events of seventeenth-century Salem.

In any group led by a skilled manipulator, followers are likely to argue as they are encouraged to do, even if their encouragement is based on lies and distortion fed to them. Recall the lady who wrote to the editor to protest my community's ignorance of the dangers of child abuse. I didn't quote the part where she complained that I was allowed to stay out of jail for a mere

$10,000 — which, she didn't realize, I never had to pay. She claimed that one of every four girls will experience sexual assault by the time she reaches her eighth birthday. The problem is that this lady, and millions more like her, will treat such lies that they have heard as truth, perhaps until their dying day.

I suspect that such deception as was exhibited by this lady is not a forceful brainwashing of the listener's mind by the manipulator. Rather, I think the listener embraces it to suit his or her convenience. By the way, most assuredly, one of every four girls will *not* be a victim of sexual abuse by her eighth birthday. *Satan's Silence* identifies many of the origins of such exaggerated statistics. Those who spread such statistics should be held legally accountable for the problems that they create.

I once made a list of all the thirty-seven adults in that church whom I had encouraged to get involved in helping Children's Church in some capacity. When the accusation occurred, only five or six of them were actually helping. Another three or four had helped for a brief interval, then stopped. One who helped out for two or three weeks summarized the church's attitude when she told me why she intended to stop: "I don't hear the Lord directing me to keep doing this." It's not hard to see through the Christianese terminology and discern the real meaning behind her statement. Clearly, Rev. Jake cannot be blamed for all the problems in that church.

One of the men in the church described the manner in which some embraced Joan's nightmare. He said he had been told that Joan had a dream about me molesting Elisa, and that her subsequent questioning of Elisa "confirmed the dream." In Christianese, "confirmation" means a God-given sign showing something otherwise not visible to the one who receives it. The implication is that God gave Joan the dream to show her that she needed to protect Elisa from me.

This subtle statement shows how new believers can be led astray by too much fascination with "signs and wonders." A few individuals may have treated Joan's dream as if it were precognitive, like the ones experienced by Old Testament Joseph and New Testament Joseph. Most readers can see precisely where Joan's dream originated, but some in Rev. Jake's church treated it reverentially. Remember that most of the people in that church had recently become Christians. Fellow-Christians, don't let yourselves be swept away by emotions so that you abandon sound reasoning. For the record, I believe that God speaks to us in dreams, but I also believe dreams are often just a result of our waking concerns and fears.

Not long after the accusation, Rev. Jake gave me a book about child sex abuse: *When Child Abuse Comes to Church*, by Bill Anderson. The book is about a Minnesota case involving a twelve-year-old who molested many young children in Sunday school. When, about a year before my accusation, Rev. Jake's church brought in a speaker to teach on this topic, I really wanted to attend but couldn't find the time. All who attended the class read this paperback. The book has no relevance at all to the accusation against me. On page 35, Mr. Anderson states, "Pastors and parents of victims should resist the inclination to conduct an investigation on their own." The very reason why I was arrested was because Rev. Jake blatantly ignored this advice.

My favorite sound in the world is Darcie's laughter. Whenever I hear it, I know that all is well in my world. Rev. Jake and the other perpetrators managed to kill that beautiful sound for years. This sentiment is described in Jer. 16:9: "I will bring an end to the sounds of joy and gladness and to the voices of bride and bridegroom in this place." We would have preferred death to the ordeal we had to go through.

Those who have dealt with witch-hunt cases advise defendants to never accept plea-bargaining. I was unaware of all the bad things that happen to those who do accept it. In the early days following the accusation, I believed in my naïve innocence that society wants only to make sure suspects are kept under watch and are willing to become educated about sexual assault. I envisioned an offer to drop my case if I would simply take some classes. For a case as incredibly weak as mine, and given my squeaky-clean background, it seemed the logical thing for society to do. But I was unaware of the things Rev. Jake had said about me, and of how society now demands blood when an accusation is made; so my notion of what was logical was completely out of touch with reality. In confidence, I told Rev. Jake that if the police made such an offer as I just mentioned, I would have to consider taking a few classes and be done with the whole ordeal rather than going through the time, effort, expense, and adverse publicity of a court case. His response was to tell the prosecutor and others that "Paul Grey wanted to plead guilty, but his wife wouldn't let him."

In the prosecutor's final statements and in the local newspapers, Elisa was quoted as having said that her teacher put his finger in her private. Look at the actual quote and you'll see that her words were "Just his finger." All the other words were generated by the prosecutor. Ask any woman who was sexually molested as a child whether that is the response a recent victim would give. And why couldn't the newspaper quote her accurately? She spoke only three words. Editors will never admit it, but they have an agenda of their own.

Phil should have left Rev. Jake and started his own church long ago. His one big failure is that he subjected himself completely to such a misguided individual. Rev. Jake was able to plant false notions in his head, against Phil's better judgment, just as therapists were able to distort the realities of the children in the Satanic Ritual Abuse cases. Phil's blind obedience of his misguided brother-in-law has spoiled his true calling. "No servant can serve two masters." (Luke 16:13.)

Bad things happen to innocent people because there is much evil in the world. We can expect to suffer unjustly sometimes. Scripture even tells us to make concessions to the sinfulness so that nonbelievers can find no fault in us. For example, suppose the speed limit is 55, but all four lanes along your route are traveling bumper to bumper at 70 mph. If you must use that highway, you will endanger the lives of others if you insist on strictly obeying the law. In this case, it is appropriate to concede to others' disregard for the law, for the common good.

Likewise, we must be aware of societal fears (e.g., of men interacting with children), even when society makes bad choices. Occasional concessions to society's backward thinking shouldn't be too hard to endure. After all, Scripture also tells us that this world is temporary.

Perhaps some readers assume that I became dispirited as a result of the witch-hunt. I don't feel that way; I don't think of myself as a victim. The witch-hunt happened several years ago. My life has actually been blessed; this ordeal was the only severely bad time I've ever had in my fifty-plus years. I've never gone without food or shelter, or had a broken bone, or serious bouts of depression or sickness. I've had a very luxurious life, by world standards. Just to be born in America is an incredible blessing. I've still got my sense of humor. I'm enjoying life, including the small things, but I do not enjoy witnessing destructive behavior. Such behavior is not unique to witch-hunts. Since the trial, I have felt that my primary purposes in life are to take care of Darcie and to enjoy life as it passes by.

The Bible (Mark 11:22) tells us that we must live by faith. I chose to work in a high-risk ministry — with children, in a church of known immaturity, in Nicaragua — with the faith that God would provide for all my needs. You never know if you can or can't do something until you try. I gave it my best effort and trusted God to do the rest. The results were very good for several years, until the accusation. I regret that a few people turned my effort into a witch-hunt, but I don't regret that I made the effort to serve the church. I hope that readers will not be weakened in their faith because of my experience.

Parallels in the Political World

The Bible makes it clear that God abhors dishonesty. Those who aspire to political office must, it seems, learn to ignore this fact, and to artfully manipulate the populace, or else have no chance of getting elected. The polite expression for such artful deception is that the candidate "knows how to connect with the American people."

During the tenure of President Bill Clinton, I was greatly disturbed to see many similarities between his political tactics and those employed by my accuser, Rev. Jake. The level and frequency of dishonesty, the abuse of authority, the ability to verbally manipulate, the demonizing of opponents, the unflinching support of many women, the never-ending denials of guilt, the destruction of friends in order to protect self-interests, and the willingness to send legions of followers into dangerous battles to achieve personal goals, were the main similarities between the two. And, I had to acknowledge the painful reality that the country, for the most part, didn't mind the character flaws. Polls consistently showed that about 80 percent of the country thought Bill Clinton had committed perjury, yet his approval ratings were consistently above 70 percent. This is why I'm not particularly optimistic that America will turn away from its witch-hunting way of thinking any time soon. I don't see the desire for change. As my friend Andrew said, "People basically believe what they want to believe."

In the 1990s there was extensive political pandering to voters' demands for immediate gratification. Before television, I think people were more realistic in their expectations, but as technology grew and more and more people learned to use the Internet for diverse purposes, they increasingly expected immediate responses to their needs and desires. This way of thinking may have been the reason for the creation of various quick-fix solutions to societal problems. For example, groups in the 1990s advocated giving taxpayer-funded clean needles to drug addicts to help prevent the spread of AIDS. Other groups advocated giving taxpayer-funded condoms to schoolchildren — fifth-graders were the youngest target group I heard about. Both these policies were implemented in a number of large American cities. Such quick-fix political solutions would have been soundly rejected in the past; in the 1990s they were accepted by many, with the advocates simply claiming to be "champions of the little guy." The theory was that since the behavior would continue regardless of consequences, society would be better off dealing immediately with the behavior rather than focusing on efforts to stop it. Early in the twentieth century, prohibition of alcohol was repealed using identical logic.

In the 1990s the news media, especially television, favored one political party over the other. Political correctness was defined by the media and presented to the public. The media advocated quick-fix solutions, thereby giving an advantage to politicians who used demagoguery. Political candidates who advocated fiscal restraint were demonized by their opponents; they were accused of wanting to hurt the downtrodden. The media chose not to expose such wrongful and harmful demagoguery, in fact they bolstered it on a daily basis because it served their own political preferences. It also kept the news "lively," which, they claimed, kept more Americans interested. When a person is taught from childhood that American TV newscasts are unbiased and that only the evil countries of the world engage in propaganda, it takes a long time, if ever, to recognize that the assumption is wrong. It is extremely confusing. I think people are slowly learning the reality. Month by month through the 1990s, the big network news programs lost viewers.

A sickening tool has dominated American politics for the last few years: the shameless political pitches that have been made under the guise of doing everything "for the children." In the 1990s both parties tried to outdo each other in the way they introduced legislation, and then tried to stir up voter support by claiming that the legislation was needed "for the children." A large book could be written to discuss the many examples of this tactic. For example, when the federal government figured out a way to generate massive new revenues by increasing tobacco taxes by more than 100 percent, it was done under the guise of preventing teen smoking. Whatever the proposed legislation, one party claimed that more taxes were needed to protect the children, and the other side said that fewer taxes were needed to protect the budgets of families and children. Such pitches were directed primarily to women voters. In accordance with his phenomenal political skills, President Clinton made the pitch more persuasively than anyone else.

This disgusting, yet highly successful, attempt to stir up emotions among otherwise apathetic voters was one of many such examples of scare tactics. In the 1990s everything discussed in the political arena by Congress and the administration seemed to be called "a crisis." Lack of sufficient federal oversight concerning childcare for working parents was a crisis; the popularity of large sport-utility vehicles was a crisis, and so on, *ad nauseam*. One political party claimed that the other party intended to cut benefits to senior citizens so they couldn't get the medication they needed. The intent was perfectly clear: scare enough voters so the proposed legislation could be passed or defeated. This method of scaring people to achieve political gain is the same phenomenon that has made so many Americans so fearful about child sex abuse (combined, of course, with the real dangers that exist). I see no reason why political candidates will cease to make references to "getting tough on child molesters" in an attempt to win voter approval. As long as the voters can be easily manipulated, our lawmakers will continue to engage in scare tactics. There is no substitute for an educated populace. People have got to learn how to discern truth from lies when they hear or see stories covered by the news media. We must learn to recognize scare tactics.

Another thing that really annoyed me about the Clinton years: His famous "spin team" (professional liars) presented the argument "So what? Both sides do it" on a daily basis, until it became a mantra. Based on this misguided assumption that "everybody does it," they proceeded to slander all the great presidents in the country's history. Their purpose was to lower the standard by which their client would be judged. The result was that schoolchildren — and adults — were taught that President Clinton's lying under oath and other faults are actually commonplace among great men. This is a despicable lie. With the upcoming generation having been taught these false, immoral lessons, what will be the future impact?

Presidential elections in both 1992 and 1996 were decided by the women's vote. Were women audiences targeted in the 1980s and '90s by child advocacy groups? Did this bring about political pressure that led to a lowering of the threshold for determining "probable cause" in child abuse cases? One thing is clear: the manipulators did not act out of complete innocence; they lied intentionally, as a powerful political tactic to achieve their goals. I doubt that the witch-hunts in seventeenth-century Salem were based on intentional deceit to so great an extent.

Our Societal Approach Has Got To Change

I can't over-emphasize the importance of who gets to tell their story first: the accuser or the defendant. If I had put everything in this book that could be used to make me look bad at the beginning, without any rebuttal, some readers would have stopped reading, having concluded that I was guilty. That is how my case was initially presented to the police by Joan, to the jury by the prosecutor, and to our friends and to the police by Rev. Jake. That is how the newspapers presented it to the community. Once the slanderous seed is sown, the damage can be permanent. Once a mind is made up, it takes more than the initial amount of input to make it reverse its decision.

Sadly, many newspaper editors and TV/radio managers exploit this very phenomenon, making "news scoops" appear more sensational than they really are, taking advantage of scare tactics simply to boost sales. I hope my story has enabled some readers to see past some of the scandalous accounts that will be given by the media in the future. The proper method of scrutiny has been known for centuries: look at the facts only.

In our new hometown, a true monster is on the loose. He is a serial killer/rapist of schoolgirls. The community is extremely tense about it, and rightly so. Recently, the newspaper put a man's picture on the front page, with a headline meant to tag him as the prime suspect. This misguided headline was based on some benign hearsay statements made by a prisoner with whom the man had recently gotten into a dispute. A week or two after the irresponsible headline, DNA results proved the man innocent of the serial killings. This puts my community through great stress, as the people get their hopes up over nothing, only to have them dashed again.

The newspaper exploited the community's acute fears, and tied this man's picture to those fears in a despicable attempt to make it look like they had a big news story. In my opinion, the news media are the biggest contributors to today's witch-hunting practices. I suppose such irresponsible practices will continue until they become unprofitable. Maybe this will require a new level of community awareness, which will take many years to achieve.

In the year 2000 a young schoolgirl exploited the community's fears once again. She failed to return home from school promptly. She said that a black man in a white panel truck had abducted her, but she had managed to escape and hide in the woods for several hours. My community searched all over for the man, confident that the perpetrator's identity could be determined. But the girl had merely made up the story, taking advantage of the real fears that existed. Fortunately, the police identified no suspects in this occurrence.

Darcie's supervisor, two grades above her, and my supervisor, two grades above me, had something in common: they each had taught Sunday school for about twenty years. Is this a dying breed, as men become dissuaded from doing God's work while political correctness runs rampant? These two men knew for a fact that what happened to me could have happened to them.

I believe that the vast majority of Americans believe that a person is brought to trial only if the police have solid evidence of the person's guilt. Was my case a rare exception, concerning police abuse? Concerning child sex abuse cases, the answer is clearly no.

A child social worker who is employed by another New England state, and who was very supportive of me, was incredulous that the police in my state had pursued my case (she didn't know how persuasive Rev. Jake can be). She had an interesting observation about Joan. She said that sometimes women will maintain their silence while being in an abusive relationship, but it is when they begin to feel safer that they will make accusations. Did Joan find it very easy to accuse me since I was such a non-threatening person? It's a point worth pondering.

Recall the letter that the lady wrote to the newspaper editor in my county. She said that in our county the child is first interviewed by the police, then by a social worker, then by a child expert, and, if necessary, by a prosecutor. She claimed that our county has a team that includes all these professionals, and that this team bases its conclusions on a responsible evaluation. Then she claimed that less than 2 percent of all accusations are false. Concerning her reference to extensive interviewing by a multidisciplinary team, you now know — assuming I've been telling the truth in this book — that she is absolutely wrong. They *should* have employed a team of professionals but they didn't. Likewise, her statement that less than 2 percent of all accusations are false is enormously erroneous. The problem is that once somebody writes misinformation like this in an article, zealots are prone to keep quoting it, even long after it is proven untrue.

When the police apprehend anyone suspected of a crime, they check to see if he has a criminal record, which influences their suspicions. I would like to see a similar method used when allegations of child abuse or sexual assault are made. Does the accuser have a record of making accusations or of being a zealot regarding such accusations? The amount of tax revenues spent needlessly on flimsy allegations is mind-boggling. If we don't change our system so that the accusers must pay when they lose in court — as is done in Germany — we could at least improve the problem by implementing such a simple background check. To make it happen, the political correctness pendulum will have to swing back toward normality. I think this idea should be pursued: protect society from damage, whether by criminals or by zealots.

Societal rules have changed since I was a child. Back then,

people weren't frivolously accused of child molestation, and newspapers did not delight in carrying stories of such allegations, as they do now. Teachers used to hug their pupils. Now, teachers are strictly forbidden to initiate a hug. I remember being kissed by a teacher as late as the sixth grade. Back then, toddlers most assuredly spent time on their caretakers' laps. If society's new rules are here to stay, and if the newspapers continue to publish every allegation (as they probably will because of this country's insatiable appetite for sleaze), we'll reach a point when allegations of child abuse become so common that they no longer have the reprehensible stigma they had in the past. Perhaps that's the best way to continue the overall effort to reduce child abuse. Maybe the witch-hunt phenomenon is only temporary — while the rules and definitions are being changed and society learns to curb its automatic assumption of guilt.

I have tried to show the readers what happened at a detailed level in one particular case — details they never get to see in newspaper and magazine articles about such cases. I would like to motivate readers today to try to change our country's current policies, but I want also to document my case so that future generations can see how the country behaved in the 1990s.

I thank God that Darcie and I had no children of our own during this ordeal. The torment of children having to face their peers under such circumstances would have been sheer torture. I have thanked God many times that my mother and my father-in-law had passed away before the accusation was made. I thank God that my livelihood didn't involve working with kids; changing professions at my age would have been very traumatic. I'm thankful that we had a cat that never ceased to show us affection when even our church family abandoned us. We are thankful for our many friends and supporters, to whom this book is dedicated. I'm thankful, too, that we were given the opportunity to move away from New England. I'm very pleased that I still feel love toward people. Darcie and I are very comfortable around the people in our new community. We still love the Lord.

Witch-hunting discourages people from volunteering their services in the community. One of my co-workers was tempted to help coach a girls' soccer team at a local school when they invited him to do so, but after seeing the police handling of my case, he wouldn't even consider it. Another co-worker, with a heart of pure gold, was picking up his kids at an outdoor ice skating pond. A shivering young boy asked if my friend could give him a ride, too. With my case in mind, he reluctantly gave the boy a quarter and told him to call his parents. Our country is filled with such examples. It's abnormal, and I don't think the benefits of "getting tough on child abuse" are outweighing the drawbacks. I believe the key lies in society getting fed up with the existing overkill, and demanding changes.

A former prosecutor for the state told me that my case probably cost taxpayers well over $100,000. It also cost my county the services of one of its most dedicated child advocates. In the same state where my witch-hunt took place, one of my friends had a two-year-old who was suffering serious health problems. A good mother, she took the child to the hospital for diagnosis. The state, based on some guideline that some child "proponent" had written, concluded that my friend had been shaking the girl to punish her. The state took the child and placed her with foster parents, and told those foster parents that eventually they would probably be able to adopt the girl. They also took the child's older brother and placed him in a foster home. My friend and her husband, truly some of the most loving people you could ever meet, had to pay legal costs nearly ten times as much as mine just to get their kids back. Their children might be psychologically scarred for life, because now they know for a fact that they can suddenly lose their family, no matter how much they object. My friends' daughter was eventually diagnosed with a rare affliction. Did the state help the child overcome it? No, it merely heaped abuse on a loving, law-abiding family at their weakest moment. The foster parents who had temporarily cared for the girl also had their hearts broken, when they learned that they could not keep her. Perhaps they were led to believe that if the child were ever returned to her mother, that baby-shaking monster would once again abuse her. Many hearts were torn apart by this case, and my friends are now saddled with hundreds of thousands of dollars of debt, because of the state's arrogance and incompetence.

A key problem in my case was that nobody would stand up to Joan. Everyone in the chain was afraid of being perceived as "soft" on child-molestation accusations, and all Joan had to do was keep demanding that they get me. Remember that when the Inspector found out that Joan had lied in her initial report, her response was "That's no problem." Even if Joan had been released from a psychiatric institution the day before the accusation, I think it wouldn't have mattered. The police never questioned her integrity in the least. As the prosecutor said "She had no axe to grind." No one in the church came even close to advising her to speak with me, or suggesting that she might have gone overboard by making an accusation immediately after a nightmare. She simply demanded my blood, and society complied out of political correctness. Joan got the red carpet treatment from everyone, despite their knowing that she had intentionally lied about the allegation. Is that the kind of enlightened behavior we want for our society?

I am moderate in nearly all aspects of life. When I drive, I am not concerned about being seen by the police. It makes me angry when the driver in front of me suddenly slows down, and then I see a police car, which caused the driver to do so. That sudden braking puts me at risk of an accident. I don't suddenly slow down when I see a police car, because my driving habits are reasonable. I've driven in front of police cars when, on occasion, I was exceeding the speed limit. They're just not interested in me, because my behavior isn't dangerous. If the police had been told the truth about me concerning Elisa, they would have concluded that I was not a danger to society. But they were told a lie, because Joan was afraid that they would otherwise not have believed her — her own words. Joan was never penalized for uttering such a lie; her behavior has thereby been reinforced.

Mother bears have a reputation for being downright dangerous when they think their cubs are threatened. The problem isn't that there are people who exhibit mother-bear behavior. The problem is that society helps them destroy their perceived enemies, even after their stories have been discredited.

Readers might find it amazing that Americans in the 1990s could show such poor judgment. Unfortunately, there are also zealots who could read this book in its entirety, be convinced that it is a pack of lies, and wish that I had been imprisoned for life, or even executed. Such people simply see through different eyes, and are unlikely ever to be swayed by any argument.

Although a pastor perpetrated the witch-hunt described in this book, it would be a mistake for readers to over-generalize and become skeptical about the messages given in the Bible. It is wrong to blame our Creator for the cruel things that people do to each other. God loves my accusers just as He loves me; but He does not love the sins any of us commit. Does Rev. Jake deserve to go to heaven? Absolutely not, but then, neither do I. My thoughts and deeds have always fallen pathetically short of God's perfect standard. Grace is offered to each of us as a gift, not through any merit of our own. Each of us needs to be honest before God about our shortcomings, and recognize that His forgiveness is offered only as a matter of grace. No one can earn that forgiveness by good behavior.

A few weeks ago I heard someone on the radio describing a set of symptoms. As the newscaster listed them, I recognized those symptoms: they had troubled Darcie ever since Rev. Jake's followers abandoned us. The symptoms involved nightmares. The people the speaker was describing were victims of torture. Darcie's recurrent dream, which has tormented her since our abandonment by our church "friends," involves a cute bunny. Cruel people get their hands on it, put it on a board and drive nails through it. I'm no psychologist, but I can figure out what causes this dream. This is the product of Rev. Jake and his followers, and the placing of state police resources at the disposal of zealots. It is precisely the opposite of evidence of the Holy

Spirit: love, joy, peace, patience, kindness, goodness, faithfulness, gentleness and self-control. May we come to see these on Earth as in Heaven.

Afterword

After fifteen years' work in the areas of false accusations and trial consulting, I'm continually saddened by the resistance and ignorance of members of the professional community who fail to recognize the damage such accusations do to innocent individuals, their families and, above all, the children involved in these cases. No honest professional can deny the extent of the false alarms and intentionally untrue assertions that plague our society.

From the Mouths of Babes illustrates the emotional roller coaster lived by Paul Grey and his wife, Darcie. While I disagree with some of Mr. Grey's assertions regarding legal, psychological and societal issues, I feel his pain and understand why he feels as he does. Grey is certainly correct in his perception that kids sell, politically and materially: we all remember the absurd TV commercial showing a baby sitting inside a tire zooming down the street.

Certainly well-meaning, but over-reactive and without accountability, the Child Abuse Prevention and Treatment Act (CAPTA) awards every state financial benefit if:

1. Immunity is provided for those involved in the investigation and prosecution of allegations of child abuse;
2. A central registry is established by Child Protection, listing all who are accused of abuse (there have since been minor modifications to this provision);
3. Anonymity is preserved for those who make the initial report of abuse, thereby denying the accused in most cases the knowledge of who are their initial accusers.

Unfortunately, until accountability is established by removing immunity from those empowered to evaluate and investigate each claim of abuse, children who have been genuinely abused will fall through the cracks, and innocent families and children will continue to be harmed, if not destroyed, by false allegations. I applaud Paul Grey for sharing his experience; I'm certain this is the beginning of emotional healing for him and for his family.

For readers who are falsely accused, *From the Mouths of Babes* shows you that you are not alone in this painful experience: your thoughts, your confusion, your shaken beliefs and your disillusionment with the "justice system" are normal. You are okay! Make no mistake; you will be forever changed by your experience. It's up to you to decide what to do with the knowledge you have gained.

— Kimberly Hart, Executive Director
National Child Abuse Defense and Resource Center

Bibliography

ABC News 20/20. "From the Mouths of Babes." Transcript #1345, 22 October 1993.

ABC News 20/20. "Presumed Guilty." Show #1128, 5 July 1991.

Anderson, Bill. *When Child Abuse Comes to Church*. Minneapolis: Bethany House Publishers, 1992.

Armbrister, Trevor. "Justice Gone Crazy." *Reader's Digest*, January 1994, 33-40.

Bays, Jan. "Medical Diagnosis of the Sexually Abused Child." *Child Abuse and Neglect* 17 (1993) 91–110.

Ceci, Stephen J., and Maggie Bruck. "Child Witnesses: Translating Research Into Policy." Social Policy Report, Society for Research in Child Development 20, No. 10 (Fall 1993).

Ceci, Stephen J., and Maggie Bruck. "Suggestibility of the Child Witness: A Historical Review and Synthesis." Psychological Bulletin 113 (1993) 403–39.

Ceci, Stephen. "Cognitive and Social Factors in Children's Testimony." Master Lecture Presented at American Psychological Association, Toronto, 20 August 1993.

CNN Crier & Co. "Were They Really Abused?" Transcript #22, 31 March 1992.

CNN Larry King Live. "McMartin Trial Defendant Raymond Buckey." Transcript #95, 26 July 1990.

CNN Larry King Live. "Parents Unfairly Accused of Child Abuse." Transcript #200, 26 December 1990.

Cohn, Debra. "Anatomical Doll Play of Preschoolers Referred for Sexual Abuse and Those Not Referred." *Child Abuse and Neglect* 15 (1991) 455–66.

DeJong, Allan. "Legal Proof of Child Sexual Abuse in the Absence of Physical Evidence." *Pediatrics* 88, No. 3 (September 1991) 506–11.

Edwards, Gene. *Crucified by Christians*. Beaumont, TX: The Seedsowers, 1994.

Enroth, Ronald. *Churches That Abuse*. Grand Rapids: Zondervan, 1992.

Enroth, Ronald. *Recovering from Churches That Abuse*. Grand Rapids: Zondervan, 1994.

Finkelhor, David, and G. Zellman. Flexible Reporting Options for Skilled Child Abuse Professionals. *Child Abuse and Neglect* 15 (1991) 335–41.

Gardner, Richard. *Sex Abuse Hysteria: Salem Witch Trial Revisited.* Cresskill, NJ: Creative Therapeutics, 1991.

Gleick, Elizabeth, and Jamie Reno. "Free At Last." *People Magazine*, 13 December 1993, 83–6.

Goodman, G. S., and A. Clarke-Stewart. "Suggestibility in Children's Testimony: Implications for child sexual abuse investigations." *The Suggestibility of Children's Recollections*: American Psychological Association, Washington (1991): 92–105.

Hill, Frances. *A Delusion of Satan*. New York: Doubleday, 1995.

Holy Bible, The: New International Version. Grand Rapids: Zondervan, 1986.

Investigation and Prosecution of Child Abuse. American Prosecutors Research Institute, National Center for Prosecution of Child Abuse. 1033 N. Fairfax Street, Suite 200, Alexandria, VA 22314, (703) 739-0321.

Investigative News Group, Inc., The. (New York) Geraldo. "Wrongfully Accused of Child Abuse?" Transcript #901, 28 February 1991.

Johnson, David, and Jeff VanVonderen. *The Subtle Power of Spiritual Abuse*. Minneapolis: Bethany House, 1991.

Kermani, Ebrahim. "The U.S. Supreme Court on Victimized Children: The Constitutional Rights of the Defendant versus the Best Interests of the Child. *J. Am. Acad. Child Adolesc. Psychiatry* 30:5 (September 1991) 839–44.

Lee, Frank. "Welcome to Wonderland." *Newsletter from VOCAL*, November 1993, 2–4.

Lee, Harper. *To Kill A Mockingbird.* New York: HarperCollins, 1995.

Malone, D. editor. *Dictionary of American Biography.* New York: Scribner's Sons, 1934.

Mikkelsen, E., T. Gutheil, and M. Emens. "False Sexual Abuse Allegations by Children and Adolescents: Contextual Factors and Clinical Subtypes." *American Journal of Psychotherapy* 46, No. 4 (1992) 556–70.

Myers, John. "Expert Testimony Regarding Child Sexual Abuse. *Child Abuse and Neglect* 17 (1993) 175–85.

Nathan, Debbie, and Michael Snedeker. *Satan's Silence: Ritual Abuse and the Making of a Modern American Witch Hunt.* New York: BasicBooks, 1995.

O'Donohue, William, et al. "Perceived Credibility of Children's Sexual Abuse Allegations: Effects of Gender and Sexual Attitudes." *Violence and Victims* 7, No. 2 (1992) 147–54.

Pendergrast, Mark. *Victims of Memory: Incest Accusations and Shattered Lives.* Hinesburg, VT, Upper Access, Inc., 1996.

Rabinowitz, Dorothy (winner of the 2001 Pulitzer Prize for commentary). Various social commentary articles from *Wall Street Journal.*

Sauer, Mark, Okerblom, Jim. "Trial By Therapy." *National Review*, 6 September 1993, 30–39.

Sorge, Bob. *The Fire of Delayed Answers.* Canandaigua, NY: Oasis House, 1996.

Supreme Court of the U.S.; Syllabus. *Daubert et ux v. Merrell Dow Pharmaceuticals, Inc.* Court of Appeals for 9th Circuit. Argued 30 March 1993, Decided 28 June 1993.

Underwager, Ralph, and Hollida Wakefield. "A Paradigm Shift for Expert Witnesses." *Issues In Child Abuse Accusations* 5, No. 3 (1993) 156–67.

Van Til, Reinder. *Lost Daughters: Recovered Memory Therapy and the People It Hurts.* Grand Rapids: William B. Eerdmans Publishing Co., 1997.

Vorenberg, Elizabeth. "Diagnosing Child Abuse: The Cost of Getting It Wrong." *Arch Dermatol* 128 (June 1992) 844–5.

WGBH-TV (Boston) Frontline. "Innocence Lost - The Verdict, Part 1." Show #1120, 20 July 1993.

WGBH-TV (Boston) Frontline. "Innocence Lost - The Verdict, Part 2." Show #1121, 21 July 1993.

White, Sue, and K. Quinn. "Investigatory Independence in Child Sexual Abuse Evaluations: Conceptual Considerations." *Bull. Am. Acad. Psychiatry Law* 16, No. 3 (1988) 269–78.

Zola, Emile. *The Dreyfus Affair: 'J'accuse' and Other Writings.* ed. Alain Pagès, New Haven: Yale University Press, 1996.

Other Resources

National Child Abuse Defense & Resource Center
P.O Box 638, Holland, OH 43528-0638
Tel: 419-865-0513 Fax: 419-865-0526

VOCAL (Victims of Child Abuse Laws)
303-770-5096